THE PRACTICE OF ARGUMENTATION

This book uses different perspectives on argumentation to show how we create arguments, test them, attack and defend them, and deploy them effectively to justify beliefs and influence others. David Zarefsky uses a range of contemporary examples to show how arguments work and how they can be put together, beginning with simple individual arguments, and proceeding to the construction and analysis of complex cases incorporating different structures. Special attention is given to evaluating evidence and reasoning, the building blocks of argumentation. Zarefsky provides clear guidelines and tests for different kinds of arguments, as well as exercises that show student readers how to apply theories to arguments in everyday and public life. His comprehensive and integrated approach toward argumentation theory and practice will help readers to become more adept at critically examining everyday arguments as well as constructing arguments that will convince others.

DAVID ZAREFSKY is Owen L. Coon Professor Emeritus in the Department of Communication Studies at Northwestern University, where he has taught for more than forty years. Two of his many books won the Winans-Wichelns Award for Distinguished Scholarship in Rhetoric and Public Address, an award of the National Communication Association: *President Johnson's War on Poverty: Rhetoric and History* (1986) and *Lincoln, Douglas, and Slavery: In the Crucible of Public Debate* (1990).

THE PRACTICE OF ARGUMENTATION

Effective Reasoning in Communication

DAVID ZAREFSKY

Northwestern University

CAMBRIDGE
UNIVERSITY PRESS

CAMBRIDGE
UNIVERSITY PRESS

University Printing House, Cambridge CB2 8BS, United Kingdom

One Liberty Plaza, 20th Floor, New York, NY 10006, USA

477 Williamstown Road, Port Melbourne, VIC 3207, Australia

314-321, 3rd Floor, Plot 3, Splendor Forum, Jasola District Centre, New Delhi - 110025, India

79 Anson Road, #06-04/06, Singapore 079906

Cambridge University Press is part of the University of Cambridge.

It furthers the University's mission by disseminating knowledge in the pursuit of education, learning and research at the highest international levels of excellence.

www.cambridge.org
Information on this title: www.cambridge.org/9781107034716
DOI: 10.1017/9781139540926

© David Zarefsky 2019

First published 2019

A catalogue record for this publication is available from the British Library

Library of Congress Cataloging in Publication data
NAMES: Zarefsky, David, author.
TITLE: The practice of argumentation : effective reasoning in communication / David Zarefsky.
DESCRIPTION: Cambridge, United Kingdom ; New York, NY : Cambridge University Press, 2019. | Includes bibliographical references and index.
IDENTIFIERS: LCCN 2019010669 | ISBN 9781107034716 (hardback : alk. paper) | ISBN 9781107681439 (paperback : alk. paper)
SUBJECTS: LCSH: Debates and debating. | Forensics (Public speaking) | Reasoning. | Rhetoric.
CLASSIFICATION: LCC PN4181 .Z37 2019 | DDC 808.53—DC23
LC record available at https://lccn.loc.gov/2019010669

ISBN 978-1-107-03471-6 Hardback
ISBN 978-1-107-68143-9 Paperback

For my undergraduate students
in "Theories of Argumentation"
Northwestern University
1969–2009

Contents

Preface

Since the late 1950s, there has been an outpouring of scholarly writing on argumentation across a variety of academic disciplines. It has emphasized approaches to reasoning that are neither formal nor deductive but that have a logic of their own and are grounded in the realities of human experience. It both describes and aims to improve the processes by which people seek to justify their acts, beliefs, attitudes, and values, and to influence the thought and action of others. And it recognizes that they do so by engaging in communication with other people. As the title of this book suggests, argumentation is effective reasoning in communication.

Argumentation has emerged as an interdisciplinary field with roots primarily in the traditions of logic, dialectic, and rhetoric. Although scholars recognize and respect the comprehensiveness of their subject, within any given discipline they naturally will be most familiar with their own discipline's insight and perspective. This book, accordingly, reflects my own background and training in rhetoric. It recognizes that beliefs are justified to persons, that arguments are convincing to audiences, and that disagreements are managed by humans. It reflects the ancient assumption that, on matters that are not certain, the exchange of reasons through argumentation is the means by which we reach judgments about what to think, to believe, and to do.

This book attempts to synthesize that rhetorical tradition with the flowering of interdisciplinary scholarship, and to do so in a way that renders the subject accessible to beginners without ignoring or oversimplifying its complexity and subjectivity. It takes the reader from the basic assumptions of an argumentative perspective, to the components of arguments, to the practicalities of case construction, attack and defense, and ultimately back to the question of the personal and social functions of argumentation.

For many years between 1969 and 2009, it was my privilege to teach an undergraduate course called "Theories of Argumentation" at Northwestern

University. I worked with students from the sciences, engineering, history, the social sciences, the humanities, and the performing arts. This book aims to draw together ideas and issues on which we worked in that class. Former students, now scattered in a variety of careers and professions, have indicated that the course was of great value in shaping their approaches to practical reasoning and judgment, not only in their chosen careers but also in their role as citizens. In turn, their willingness to grapple with these ideas has been the greatest stimulus to my own continued commitments to teaching and research. I have benefited immensely from my engagement with students over the years, and it is to them that I dedicate this book.

Professor Hans V. Hansen of the University of Windsor first suggested that I write up my course in a book to make it available to others. He envisioned a series of books on argumentation that would reflect the range of approaches to the subject and could be used by beginning students as well as more advanced readers. I was to represent the rhetorical approach. Regrettably, the series did not develop with the richness that he had anticipated, but it was his insight and vision that inspired the preparation of this work, and I am deeply grateful to him.

Several years ago, I developed an audio and video course for adults called "Argumentation: The Study of Effective Reasoning," produced commercially by The Teaching Company. The notes, comments, and questions I've received from my "students" in that course, as well as from my Northwestern students, have been immensely helpful in refining my thinking and sustaining my interest.

Believing that theories of argumentation should be grounded in actual argumentation practice, I have liberally seeded the text with examples, and have included sets of Exercises at the end of each chapter. Many of the examples, and all of the Exercises, are the work of my editorial consultant, Randall E. Iden. Over the years we have had many conversations about argumentation theory and pedagogy, and he has taught courses in argumentation at Northwestern University and Lake Forest College to audiences of undergraduates and professional master's degree students. The breadth of his interests and the reach of argumentation into virtually every area of personal and public life are evident in the range of subjects addressed in the examples and Exercises. Professor Iden also suggested the "Extensions" feature in several of the chapters, laying a path to more advanced study. I am very grateful for his many contributions to this project.

Throughout the book I make reference to the work of contemporary scholars, whose major relevant works are listed in the Bibliography. One, however, deserves special mention here: Professor Frans van Eemeren of the University of Amsterdam. In addition to his own seminal and prolific work, and his formulation of the pragma-dialectical approach, he has made two remarkable contributions. First, he and a team of coeditors have produced the *Handbook of Argumentation Theory*, an invaluable synthesis and reference work that serves as a guide for scholars around the world. And second, through guest lectures, hosting of conferences, and his own good cheer and unlimited energy, he has assembled an international community of argumentation scholars and encouraged them, in their own ways, to sustain their investigation of this intriguing and rewarding subject.

I am indebted to my daughter-in-law, Emily Zarefsky, for the preparation of the line drawings in Chapters 2–5.

This project was undertaken under somewhat difficult personal circumstances, including especially the serious illness and death of my dear wife Nikki after almost forty-five years of marriage. My preoccupation with these events and my own emotional state undoubtedly delayed the completion of the book. And yet, curiously perhaps, working on this book also served as a form of personal therapy, for it reminded me that scholars, teachers, and students of argumentation are all like an extended family to which I am pleased to belong.

CHAPTER I

The Argumentative Perspective

When students tell their parents or friends that they are about to take a course in argumentation, the response very likely may be amazement. "We have too much argumentation as it is," the parent or friend might reply. "Why would anyone want to study that?"

Such a response reflects the fact that in popular usage in the English language, the word *argument* and its variants *arguing* and *argumentation* often are perceived negatively. If a worker argues repeatedly with his or her supervisor, that is seen as undesirable. A person whose reputation is one of being highly argumentative generally will not be sought after as a friend. And a parent who says to a child, "Don't argue with me about that," is trying to put a stop to unacceptable behavior. These examples associate argumentation with bickering, quarrelsomeness, or petulance – all undesirable personality traits. We usually think that they ought not to be encouraged, much less studied in an academic course such as the one in which you may be enrolled. Rest assured, they are not the focus of this book.

On the other hand, when we need a lawyer to represent us in court, and he or she makes a strong argument in our behalf, we regard that as a good thing. The instructor who assigns students the task of coming up with the strongest arguments for or against the country's foreign policy, for example, anticipates that this will be a serious intellectual exercise. And the parent who, having been asked by a teenager for the use of the family car over the weekend, says, "Let's hear your argument for that," will be favorably impressed by a cogent and persuasive response. Clearly, this set of examples is quite different from the first. It is not about bickering or disputatiousness but about reasoning – supporting claims by giving reasons for them, and convincing others who accept the reasons that they ought therefore to accept the claim. The first set of examples describes undesirable circumstances, but the second refers to outcomes eagerly to be sought.

Argumentation as Reasoning

In several languages, there are distinct words to identify these different kinds of behavior.[1] Unfortunately, in English the same family of terms – arguing, argument, and argumentation – covers them both. And in ordinary usage and popular culture, the first usage tends to predominate. The result is that argumentation is widely seen as something to be avoided, not as a set of theories, habits, and skills in which one seeks to become more proficient.

But the second usage, treating argumentation as a species of reasoning, is the one guiding this book. And fortunately, it has a much older and richer lineage. Its heritage goes back at least 2,500 years, to the establishment of democracy in ancient Greece. Citizens whose property had been seized by the prior tyrannical regime wanted it back. They needed to convince newly established courts that the property in question really belonged to them. This required that they assemble and present strong arguments. Then, if not before, the study of argumentation as we will pursue it here was born. Under various headings – including critical thinking, effective reasoning, logos, analysis, rhetoric, and the most general term, argumentation – it has been studied and taught from then until now as a valuable component of a liberal arts education, offering people essential mental equipment for their professional and civic life. This is the study on which you are embarking now.

Although the terms *arguing*, *arguments*, and *argumentation* sometimes are used interchangeably, we can identify differences among them. *Arguing* is a process, an activity in which people engage when they produce, exchange, and test reasons for or against claims. The units of discourse produced through arguing are *arguments*. Arguments are products, texts containing – at minimum – claims and the reasons offered to support them. And *argumentation* is a point of view, a perspective from which to examine the human activity taking place. The same actions often can be identified from multiple perspectives, one of which is to examine interaction as the invention and exchange of reasons. Argumentation sometimes is also regarded as a genre of discourse, alongside description, narration, and exposition. This view still prevails among some composition teachers, but it is less prevalent than it used to be because in

---

[1] See, for example, Frans H. van Eemeren, "The Language of Argumentation in Dutch," *Argumentation and Advocacy*, 44 (2009), 155–158.

practice the genres are not so sharply defined and the boundaries among them are fuzzy.

A Definition of Argumentation

Argumentation is the practice of justifying claims under conditions of uncertainty. Four of the key terms in this definition require unpacking.

To say that argumentation is a *practice* is to say that it is an activity in which people engage, something that people do. It takes place in specific contexts or situations in which people find themselves, and its meaning and value are determined in relation to those particular settings.

To say that argumentation is about *justifying* claims means that it is about giving reasons for them. We say that a belief or action is justified if we think we have good reason for it. A good reason does not meet the mathematical standard of certainty, but it warrants your belief. It increases your confidence in the truth of the claim. You cannot *know*, for example, that Candidate X will win the next election, but that belief might be justified if someone points out to you that X is ahead in the leading polls by 15 percent and that the opponent is unpopular even among voters in her own party.

To ask whether a claim is justified naturally raises the question, *justified to whom?* This tells you that argumentation is addressed to somebody. The person to whom it is addressed may be the person who decides whether it is justified. If I give reasons that you should invest money in a particular stock, and you subsequently buy that stock, you probably would say that I had justified the claim that you should buy the stock. But sometimes it is a third party who determines whether the claim is justified, as when labor and management present their claims and then submit to an arbitrator the question of whose claim should prevail.

Justifying a claim, then, is different from proving it – in the mathematical or geometric sense of "prove." It is also not exactly the same as persuading another person to agree with the claim. One is persuaded to accept a claim if, by whatever means, he or she is induced to believe it. Justifying a claim involves a specific means of persuasion, namely reasoning. It involves persuading a person to accept a claim by offering what that person will regard as good reasons for believing it. If accepting the reasons increases the likelihood that one will accept the claim, then that person has found the claim to be justified.

We have been speaking about justifying *claims* without having yet defined that term. Simply put, a claim is an assertion to which another person's assent is sought. If you and I are engaged in argumentation and I assert, for example, "The opposition party should be returned to office," I am not only asserting that I believe that statement to be true but that I urge you to do so as well. The term "standpoint" is sometimes used for such assertions to indicate that they are statements that a person is prepared to defend through argumentation. But the term "claim" makes clear that an arguer who utters such statements is making a claim on the belief and action of another person, asking him or her to find the statement justified and therefore to accept it as well.

Finally, argumentation takes place under conditions of *uncertainty*. We do not argue about matters that are certain; there is no reason to. If the question is whether Casper or Cheyenne is the capital of Wyoming, we needn't marshal reasons and engage in argumentation; we can just look at a map or use an Internet search engine that we know is reliable. Likewise, matters that can be settled by observation need not call forth argumentation. Empirical means are more efficient and often more reliable methods to settle a disagreement.

Uncertain matters cannot be made certain through argumentation. No matter how confident we are, for instance, that "wage and price controls are bad for the economy," no matter how carefully we have evaluated the reasons offered for and against that claim, subjecting them to tests of evidence and reasoning to be considered in this book, still we might be wrong. There might be some unknown flaw in our reasoning, or new evidence might change our judgment. Argumentation is always a risky method of justifying claims, so if more certain means are available, we use them.

But this is hardly much of an exclusion, since so much of our lives and our world involves matters that are uncertain. Every question of comparative value, such as whether it is better in a particular situation to promote economic growth or environmental protection, involves uncertainty. So does every question of ultimate value, such as whether affirmative action is a good thing or a bad thing. So too does every question of policy, in which we have to decide whether or not to do something, such as whether to accept and act on the statement, "We should resume the manned space program at the earliest opportunity." And so also are predictions about the future, such as "The Chicago Cubs will win the World Series again this year." On each of these categories of claims, we cannot *know* the conclusion absolutely; we cannot be certain. Yet we often cannot sit on the sidelines or wait to see what the future will disclose; we have to decide now what to believe or to do. This is clearly illustrated by the topic of climate change. Advocates of government action to combat climate change maintain that while the process of change may seem slow, it is irreversible if we pass a point of no return, and we may already be close to that point, so action is urgent. Climate change skeptics may be tempted to respond that the evidence is not clear whether we are witnessing minor short-term variations in climate or the beginning of long-term changes, so we should wait awhile in search of more definite evidence. But the advocates of action warn that by the time we feel more certain about what to do, it may be too late. The question comes down to what we should do in the face of uncertainty – should we act now or should we wait, and if we should act now, what action should we take? Many cases of argumentation are like that, requiring decisions now even in the face of uncertainty. While we should employ more certain methods when we can, we should not hesitate to engage in argumentation in the many areas of our lives in which decisions about what to believe or do must be made in the face of uncertainty.

We have seen, then, how the key terms *practice, justifying, claims,* and *uncertainty* help to shape our understanding of what argumentation is. The goal we seek through argumentation is stated in the subtitle of this book: effective reasoning in communication.

When we speak of *effective* reasoning, we mean reasoning that accomplishes its purpose. In the largest sense, that is the making of sound decisions. But in day-to-day practice, it means justifying to others the claims that we advance. Naturally, we do not make assertions we think are false (except as a rhetorical or literary device, such as irony), and we would like it if others accept our view. This does not mean that *ineffective* reasoning is not argumentation; it just means that such reasoning falls short of our short-term goal. In some cases, it may even promote the larger goal, if it demonstrates to us that some other claim, advanced by someone else, is actually sounder than the one we put forward or leads to a better decision.

When we spoke of justification, we explained that it involves *reasoning*, offering what are thought to be good reasons and linking them to claims that we are asking others to accept. Reason-giving is the fundamental process in argumentation.

And our concern for audience, for justifying claims to others, makes clear that we are focused on reasoning that occurs in *communication*, in the interaction between people. This includes dialogues between people; discourse such as speeches, pamphlets, or editorials that are addressed to a listening or reading audience; visual displays or presentations that imply a message; social practices that function as texts; or even one's private thoughts if they simulate an interpersonal dialogue. The point is that argumentation involves reasoning with an audience in mind.

Logic, Dialectic, and Rhetoric: Three Roots of Argumentation

Argumentation derives from three ancient disciplines, each of which – like argumentation itself – sometimes is misunderstood. *Logic* is concerned with the relationships among the statements in an argument. Sometimes it is equated only with formal or mathematical reasoning, of the sort, "All As are Bs; all Bs are Cs; therefore, all As are Cs." This conclusion is sound no matter what the As, Bs, and Cs are; it is correct purely as a matter of form. If the first two statements (the premises) are true, then the third statement (the conclusion) *must* be true; otherwise the argument would contradict itself. We will learn later that this type of reasoning is called *deduction* and that it characterizes mathematical and purely formal reasoning. But it is not the only approach to logic. In recent years, there has been growing interest in reasoning that *does* depend on what the As, Bs, and Cs are, that is, grounded in specific contexts, and in which the relationships between premises and conclusions are not guaranteed but exist in the world of probability. An entire branch of study known as *informal logic* has developed, especially in Canada, in an attempt to understand and advance such ordinary-language reasoning.[2] For now, we can say that argumentation's concern for form – for the structure of statements and the inferences that link them together – is a reflection of the discipline of logic.

Dialectic, the second disciplinary root of argumentation, is also sometimes misunderstood. It is equated with the broad sweep of historical forces that was imagined by Karl Marx – capitalism vs. communism, liberalism vs. communitarianism, naturalism vs. spiritualism, and so on. This view sees history as the advancing of a position (thesis), its being countered by a contrary position (antithesis), and the clash between them resulting in a new position (synthesis), which over time becomes a thesis itself, beginning the process all over again. Actually, though, the term *dialectic* has an older and simpler meaning. It is the process of discovering and testing knowledge through questions and answers. The model of dialectic is the dialogues of Plato. Plato encounters various characters

---

[2] The "informal logic" movement dates to the 1970s. An early example of its scholarship is J. Anthony Blair and Ralph H. Johnson, eds., *Informal Logic: The First International Symposium* (Inverness, CA: Edgepress, 1980).

who assert claims, and through adroitly asking questions of them, Plato undermines their claims and convinces them that his own are superior. Plato's questioners enter into argumentation thinking that their views are correct, but invariably they come to abandon their prior beliefs and to accept his instead. If logic emphasizes form, dialectic emphasizes the interaction between people. It is the give-and-take between them that propels the argument to its conclusion. In recent decades, the study of dialectic has been invigorated by a number of approaches, particularly that of pragma-dialectics, which is centered in the Netherlands.[3] We will encounter this approach later.

No less misunderstood than logic and dialectic is the third disciplinary root, *rhetoric*. This term has largely unfavorable connotations in everyday use. It is sometimes seen as opposed to reality, when people make charges such as "That's not really true; it is just rhetoric." Sometimes it is equated with ornamentation, figures of speech or stylistic devices that somehow are "added on" to the substance of a discourse. And perhaps worst of all, it is associated sometimes with the usually unpopular course in freshman composition – Rhetoric 101. Each of these views is misguided. Rhetoric is not separate from reality; rhetoric is what creates our understanding of reality. It is not ornamentation; those figures of speech and stylistic devices are part of the substance of discourse. And it is not just the mechanical rules of Rhetoric 101 but a set of theories, practical skills, and orientations to analysis and criticism of discourse.

But enough about what rhetoric is not. A useful contemporary definition is that rhetoric is the study of how symbols influence people. A symbol is anything that stands for something else. Words are symbols, standing for the things or the ideas they designate. Rhetoric regards the desired goal as obtaining the adherence of the audience to a claim, and inquires into how the selection and arrangement of reasons can lead to that end.

Another, equally useful definition of rhetoric was offered centuries ago by Aristotle, who regarded rhetoric as the faculty for discovering, in the given case, the available means of persuasion.[4] Whereas the contemporary definition focuses on the *study* of rhetoric, Aristotle's definition focuses on the *creation* of rhetoric. He emphasizes that it is a faculty – a skill that can be learned. It is grounded in specific cases and contexts, rather than being

---

[3] One of the earliest publications in English reflecting this approach is Frans H. van Eemeren and Rob Grootendorst, *Speech Acts in Argumentative Discussions* (Berlin: de Gruyter, 1984).

[4] Aristotle, *Rhetoric*, 1355b.

based on lawlike generalizations. It is a matter of discovery – of finding out what approaches to influencing another are available. And it recognizes that the facts of the situation constrain what those approaches might be. For example, in an era dominated by the belief that strong government is at odds with the protection of liberty, in most circumstances it is not an available means of persuasion to assert boldly that "big government is your friend."

Whether we focus on the contemporary or the Aristotelian definition of rhetoric, what this field contributes to argumentation is its concern for audience. It regards the approval by an audience – especially by an audience of critical thinkers, as we shall see – as the ultimate test of an argument's soundness and as the goal an arguer wishes to achieve. Aristotle explained this goal by saying that "persuasive" means "persuasive to a person."[5]

Today there are several different approaches to studying argumentation. All the approaches recognize these different disciplinary roots, but they differ in the emphasis among them. This book gives special attention to rhetorical approaches and explanations, but it is hardly insensitive to the crucial roles played by logic and dialectic. Indeed, argumentation might be imagined as the intellectual space in which logic, dialectic, and rhetoric all meet.

Preconditions for Argumentation

Not every decision-making moment rises to the level for which argumentation is appropriate. Indeed, it is unlikely that either individuals or societies have the resources or the energy to subject every decision to argumentation. As we shall see, there are often easier means of deciding whether or not to accept a claim. But when certain preconditions are met, argumentation will be the decision-making method of choice. Five of these preconditions are particularly worthy of note.

First, the arguers must perceive that there is a genuine controversy between them. Their difference in views is not just a misunderstanding, or a case of different uses of the same term or different terms meaning the same thing, or a case of dispute for dispute's sake. Rather, the arguers must maintain what they believe to be incompatible claims. They seek to resolve this incompatibility either by having one of their claims prevail over the other or by coming to agree on a third claim.

[5] Aristotle, *Rhetoric*, 1356b.

Second, the controversy between the arguers must be real and non-trivial. Several years ago, a popular beer commercial featured two people supposedly arguing about the merits of a certain beer. "Tastes great!" insisted one; "less filling!" replied the other. This is obviously not a real controversy because the two claims are not incompatible; the beer could have *both* qualities. All that need be done in such a case is for a third party to explain that the parties really are not in disagreement. For another example, there is the oft-told story of the woman who gave her boyfriend two ties for his birthday – one red and the other blue. The next day, seeing her boyfriend wearing the blue tie, the woman bawled, "You don't like the red one!" Of course, had the boyfriend worn the red tie instead, we could have expected the same scene with the allegation being, "You don't like the blue one!" In the absence of reason to believe otherwise, we must assume that the boyfriend's preference for one color over the other is either a matter of random choice or a matter of personal taste. Either way, the "controversy" between the red tie and the blue tie is probably trivial, not worth arguing about.

Third, agreement of the other party (whether a single individual or a group) is sought. This means that the arguers cannot just avoid controversy by "agreeing to disagree." We often do this when confronted by a position with which we disagree. We decide that resolving the dispute is not worth the hassle and the possible risk of losing a friendship, so we go our separate ways. This makes sense on some matters of taste or of artistic judgment, or on matters on which one arguer is much more strongly invested in the outcome than in the other. If I have a very strong opinion on an issue and the same issue does not matter very much to you, you may be inclined to yield to my point of view. But there are many situations quite unlike this. Suppose I believe firmly that climate change is a hoax. It may be very important to me that I convince you of this statement's truth because I care about you, because it will validate my position to have you agree with it, or because our agreement will signal to both of us that the issue is settled. In this situation I will not be inclined to shrug my shoulders or say, "Whatever," because I cannot just walk away from a claim about which I feel strongly. Because I care about what you think, argumentation is likely to ensue, in which I will try to convince you that my proposal is a better idea than whatever you have in mind.

Fourth, agreement of the other party is desired, but only on the condition that it is freely given. Much as I might want you to agree with my claim, I do not want you to agree in response to a threat, to the use of force, to the exercise of power, or to trickery. These means of assent lead us to question the very value of assent in such a case. I can hardly have great confidence in your coming to agree with me that Social Security benefits should be enhanced if I know that you are saying that in response to force or intimidation, such as my threatening the loss of friendship, not because you genuinely believe it. Besides, if I were content to manipulate your emotions rather than engage in argumentation, I would not show a very high opinion of you as a human being capable of exercising your own critical thinking and good judgment. In contrast, if I know that you have come to agree with my point of view as a result of thinking through my argument, accepting its starting points, and recognizing how they lead to its conclusion, I will have more confidence in the correctness of my position and more regard for you as a person.

To be sure, there are circumstances in which we desire the assent of another person and do not much care how that assent is obtained. Some fundraisers think it important that their audiences donate money to their charitable cause but do not really care why. They may not be likely to have any further contact with the donor and, in any case, they think what really matters is that the fund-raising goal be reached. Or in an emergency, a building manager may need to persuade everyone to evacuate the building, and will not have either time or interest to engage in argumentation with reasons about why. Or a parent needing compliance from a young child who is not yet capable of critical thinking will be more inclined to use whatever approach will work fastest, rather than to engage in argumentation. But in those circumstances in which we do argue, our doing so indicates that we value the other person's agreement only when it is freely given and not the result of coercion.

Finally, we engage in argumentation when there is no simpler means for resolving the disagreement. Sometimes easier means are available. We might follow precedent; we might defer to the judgment of an expert; we might accept the opinion of an authority figure; we might take turns; we might try to split the difference. These are decision-making guides called *heuristics*. Their purpose is to tell us how to resolve the controversy easily. We use them in situations in which we need a "good enough" answer without necessarily settling all points of disagreement to everyone's satisfaction. The psychologist Daniel Kahneman explains that it is necessary for us, in many aspects of our lives, to make decisions in just this way.[6] Otherwise we would get so bogged down in the time and energy required for argumentation that we would be unable to make any good decisions.

---

[6] Daniel Kahneman, *Thinking, Fast and Slow* (New York: Farrar, Straus & Giroux, 2011).

If everyone agrees that "splitting the difference" is an acceptable way to decide how far we should travel each day on a road trip, then it is pointless to engage in argumentation to find the *best* answer to that question. But on some matters that are important to us personally, to others we know, or to the public interest, we are not satisfied with a "quick and dirty" decision. We want one that is more carefully reasoned through because we feel the need for greater confidence in the outcome. Those are the moments when we engage in argumentation.

In sum, then, argumentation is not always the means for managing conflict or making decisions that we will choose. Our mental health and our social survival require that on many of life's more mundane matters, we rely on simplifying devices. But when the parties maintain what they think are incompatible positions, the difference between them is real and significant, they desire the other person's assent, but they want that assent only on condition that it is given freely, and there is no easier way to resolve the dispute, then argumentation will be the method of choice.

Underlying Assumptions of Argumentation

To engage in argumentation takes effort. When people do it, they are revealing several underlying assumptions about themselves, about other people, and about what it is they are doing. These assumptions are seldom voiced explicitly, but they are essential to understanding what is going on. They include assumptions about the influence of the audience, the nature of uncertainty, the process of justification, the fundamentally cooperative nature of what may seem like an adversarial exercise, and the assumption of risk.

The Audience

We already have observed that the assent of the audience is the ultimate test of an argument's strength. It is necessary, therefore, to reason with the audience in mind. Usually, the starting points of argument will be beliefs or viewpoints that are generally held by the members of the audience, and these are drawn upon by the arguers. For example, while we often think of *The Federalist* as a treatise on philosophy, the fact is that it was written for the specific purpose of convincing the people of New York to support the proposed US Constitution. Knowing that there was widespread suspicion of the additional power that the proposed government would assume, and widespread concern that this power would undermine the liberty of the people, the drafters of *The Federalist* addressed themselves to these audience beliefs. They maintained that the additional power to be assumed by the new government was carefully limited, and they suggested paradoxically that the additional power they envisioned would actually enhance liberty by checking the exercise of other powers. Now, these were not the only possible arguments that the authors of *The Federalist* could have advanced. They were selected, most likely, with the beliefs of the New York audience in mind, and with the knowledge that if the New York delegates were to be convinced to accept the new government, those beliefs would need to be addressed. A different audience in different circumstances might have been appealed to by different arguments.

There is a danger in this position, however, which we would do well to recognize. Reasoning with an audience in mind is not the same thing as pandering to an audience, telling the audience whatever it wants to hear regardless of whether one believes it, whether the available evidence supports it, or whether the audience accepts the claim as the outcome of careful reasoning or as a substitute for careful reasoning. Otherwise, one could merely find a particular audience that is known to hold a given belief, assert that belief, and rest in the delusion that the audience's assent had validated the claim. As the literary and rhetorical theorist Wayne Booth wrote, by this perversion of audience-centered reasoning, fanatics are always able to talk their chosen disciples into accepting a predetermined conclusion, but this is not argumentation as we are describing it.[7]

The way to avoid this danger is by critically testing one's claims, seeking agreement not only of the immediately present audience but also of a hypothetical audience of critical thinkers. The twentieth-century Belgian legal philosopher and rhetorical theorist Chaim Perelman referred to this as the "universal audience," which he defines as an audience of all reasonable people.[8] Of course, no such audience actually exists, but it is an audience imagined by the speaker or writer. Pandering would not satisfy such an audience, because not everyone in it would hold specific beliefs and values that make pandering to the specific audience possible. The arguer taking the universal audience into account would exclude reasons and claims he or she knows the universal audience would reject from the set to be used in an attempt to convince the particular audience. In the case of *The*

---

[7] Wayne Booth, *Modern Dogma and the Rhetoric of Assent* (Notre Dame, IN: University of Notre Dame Press, 1974).

[8] Chaim Perelman and Lucie Olbrechts-Tyteca, *The New Rhetoric: A Treatise on Argumentation*, trans. John Wilkinson and Purcell Weaver (1958; rpt. Notre Dame: University of Notre Dame Press, 1969), esp. 31–35.

Federalist, for example, it would not do to advance the claim that the Constitution should be ratified because it would enable New York to dominate Connecticut economically. Even if New Yorkers would beat their breasts with pride, the authors knew that thinking people in Connecticut would not regard that as even a possible benefit of the Constitution, so this position would be excluded from the set that the universal audience would be likely to accept, and hence from the set that the authors could use. On the other hand, it would be sensible to assume that an audience of reasonable people would accept that there should be a division of power between the national and state governments. Arguers could appeal to that belief of the audience and then reason to the claim that the Constitution provided a more effective balance than did the Articles of Confederation.

In other words, reasoning with the audience in mind means that one takes the audience's beliefs and values as the starting point of the argument, and then should reason from those beliefs to the claim the arguer wants to support. Often these beliefs can be left implicit because speaker and listeners share an understanding of what they are. Aristotle used the term *enthymeme* to refer to a structure of reasoning in which one of the premises is drawn from audience beliefs and values and can be left unstated.[9]

Uncertainty

A second underlying assumption of argumentation relates to the nature of uncertainty. We have noted that the *subject matter* of argumentation involves uncertainty. So too does the process of reasoning. The statements we offer are always potentially controversial, which means that the claims we make *could be otherwise*. This recognition justifies a degree of humility on our part. In the controversy between the theory of evolution and the theory of intelligent design, for example, we may have a strongly held belief, we may feel that we are right, but we cannot know *for sure*. When we engage in argumentation, therefore, we implicitly agree that not only are viewpoints at odds with our own, but that *they might be right*.

Controversies have multiple dimensions, and recognizing them should help us to know just what we are dealing with. For example, two political candidates may engage in a debate about approaches to international terrorist threats. Each candidate maintains that the opponent "is not really

---

[9] Aristotle, *Rhetoric*, 1355a.

committed to the destruction of worldwide terrorism." In fact, however, both candidates support that goal. Their real difference turns out to be about what "victory" means and whether either candidate's proposals would achieve it. The controversy, in other words, was about what had been left implicit rather than what was stated explicitly.

Similarly, controversies can be either unmixed or mixed.[10] An unmixed controversy is one in which only one arguer is committed to a position; the other arguer raises doubts or objections to that position but does not commit to any alternative. A mixed controversy, in contrast, is one in which *each* of the arguers commits to a specific claim. In a discussion of health care policy, if one speaker maintains that we should "replace Obamacare" with a single-payer system like that of Great Britain, and the other arguer says, "Well, I am not so sure; I have doubts about whether a single-payer system would work," then we have an unmixed controversy. The question in dispute is "Should we adopt a single-payer system?" and the possible answers are Yes or No. If we choose not to adopt the single-payer system, there is no commitment about what we will do instead. On the other hand, suppose one arguer says, "We should move to a single-payer system of health care," and the other replies, "No, we should retain Obamacare and fix some of the specific problems that have emerged," then we have a mixed controversy. *Each* of the participants supports a position. Now the focus is comparative. The question in dispute is "What health care policy should we adopt?" and the possible answers are "A single-payer system" and "A modified form of Obamacare." Knowing what kind of controversy we are in affects our understanding of what is in dispute, what we will need to establish in order to support our position, and what arguments will be relevant to the question and what will not. Yet whether the controversy is mixed or unmixed is almost never announced explicitly. It is an unstated assumption that has to be inferred from the choices the arguers make about the claims they advance and the questions they raise.

Finally, controversies can be either single or multiple. Single controversies relate to only one subject, whereas multiple controversies involve more than one subject at the same time. Consider the following example:

PARENT:　You mustn't stay out past midnight.
TEENAGER:　You don't trust me!

---

[10] The distinction between mixed and unmixed disputes comes from Frans H. van Eemeren and Rob Grootendorst, *A Systematic Theory of Argumentation* (Cambridge: Cambridge University Press, 2004).

On the face of it, the two statements seem to deal with different topics: how long it is acceptable for the teenager to be out at night, and whether or not the parent trusts the teenager. Obviously, these matters are somehow related. To the teenager, if the two arguers can resolve whether or not the parent trusts him or her, then that determination in turn will resolve the question of how long it is acceptable to be out at night. To the parent, there may be reasons for the curfew that have nothing to do with trust – considerations of health, how much sleep the teenager needs, or the need to be up early in the morning, for example. The parent regards the matter of trust as irrelevant to the issue and a diversion, whereas the teenager regards it as *the* central question. Things will get even more complicated if the next moves in the dispute were the following:

PARENT: No, I'm afraid I really don't trust you on this matter.
TEENAGER: I can't believe it! What do I need to do to earn your trust?

For the parent, the conversation has now digressed to a *third* topic, while for the teenager it has come to the heart of the matter. It is very unlikely that this argument will have a satisfactory result if the nature of the controversy remains unclear. More likely, at some point the parent will say in exasperation, "No! Now don't argue with me," and the teenager will storm off in frustration.

It is easy to see what is amiss when we dissect the argumentation in this way, but very often we get into controversies like this. It seems at times as though everything relates to everything else, because many elements in our lives *are* interrelated. Moreover, we don't stop in the midst of a dispute to map out exactly where the dispute lies. That too is implicit, and whether the controversy is single or multiple has to be figured out from the choices arguers make. Yet doing so may be essential to figuring out whether the controversy can be resolved, and if so, how.

There is one other important observation about the nature of uncertainty in argumentation. Since things could be otherwise and we can't say *for sure* that a claim is correct, there is always an inferential leap. The arguers move from the known to the unknown, and the audience is asked to accept this leap, based on their critical judgment, because a decision is required. For example, suppose we encounter the following argument: "Detroit will require huge amounts of capital to rebuild its inner core, so St. Louis probably will too." We know that Detroit will need a major infusion of funds and we *infer* that St. Louis probably will too. We have made a leap in this inference because we do not *know* anything about St. Louis. That is the leap: jumping from what we know to what we don't.

What makes this inference seem reasonable – what *justifies* it – is a statement called the *warrant*. This is a general statement about similar situations that we are betting will apply to the case at hand. In our example, the warrant might be something like: "Cases that are similar in most respects probably will be similar in the respect under consideration." This warrant is what helps us count the conditions in Detroit as grounds for a statement about St. Louis. Both are aging Midwestern cities that have witnessed an erosion of the central city and corresponding growth in the suburbs. Both have seen a weakening of the economic base and some loss in population. Both are in a weak financial condition and have faced threats of bankruptcy. These and other comparisons might lead us to the conclusion that the cities are basically alike, and therefore to the inference that both will require major infusions of capital if they are going to rebuild their central core. To derail the argument, one will need either to dispute the facts or to undermine the potency of that inference.

As we already have observed, justification is different from proof, although it sometimes is called "rhetorical proof." It states not that something is true for everyone but that a particular audience should believe it. It implies that people are open-minded and willing to be convinced, yet are skeptical enough not to accept assertions unthinkingly. Justification has degrees of strength, ranging from the merely plausible to the highly probable. And it is always provisional and subject to change in light of new information or arguments. Finally, what counts as justification of an inferential leap will vary with such contextual factors as the importance of the issue to the participants, the consequences of being right or wrong, and the possibility of reversing course.

Restrained Partisanship

A third underlying assumption is seemingly counterintuitive: arguers play the part of restrained partisans.[11] It is easy enough to see how they are partisans. They believe that the claim they are advancing is right, and they want to influence their audience to come to the same conclusion. Whatever the disagreement is that has produced the argument, they want for it to be resolved in their favor.

But they want this to happen only if the other party comes to accept their position by having thought about it and having concluded that it was

---

[11] The concept of "restrained partisanship" is advanced by Douglas Ehninger. See "Argument as Method: Its Nature, Its Limitations, and Its Uses," *Communication Monographs*, 37 (1970), 104.

probably right. The second party might have reached that conclusion by realizing that his or her counter-argument was effectively answered by the original arguer and that no other alternatives seemed available. Or the second party may have been convinced that his or her counter-argument was not inconsistent with the original arguer's claim, that it was possible to hold both positions simultaneously and that there was some advantage to doing so. Either way, though, it is the force of the first party's argument and not external factors such as political pressure, desire for approval, economic threats, or the desire for friendship that leads the second party to accept the first party's position.

Why would the first party care why the second party accepts the argument, so long as she or he does so? Indeed, as we have seen, there are some circumstances in which agreement is sought regardless of the process or reasons, and in these situations one is less likely to rely on argumentation as the means to bring about the compliance of the second party. But when a claim really matters to the first party, he or she will prefer argumentation because the outcome will strengthen his or her own commitment to the position. I will be far more confident in my belief if I know you have come to the same conclusion after scrutinizing it carefully and being unable to undermine it.

Cooperativeness

A fourth underlying assumption follows from the third: despite its seem-ingly adversarial nature, argumentation is fundamentally a cooperative enterprise.[12] This may sound strange, because the assumption of partisan-ship suggests that arguers will oppose, challenge, or question one another's arguments – and they do. But these antagonistic elements of argumenta-tion are means toward the end of careful scrutiny and testing. We might imagine argumentation as if the decision-maker or judge had assigned the competing parties the task of producing the strongest mix of claims for their own position and doubts on the opposing position, so that the decision-maker could make a careful and informed judgment. Indeed, one type of argumentation – the debate – does exactly this. But all argumentation shares the feature that the participants are seeking jointly to reach a decision in which they can have the highest degree of confi-dence. Their dispute with one another is the means by which they

---

[12] Douglas Ehninger and Wayne Brockriede, *Decision by Debate* (New York: Dodd, Mead, 1963), 19–22.

cooperate toward that end. They improve the rigor of the procedure, reduce the likelihood that critical considerations will be omitted, and increase confidence in the result.

There are other matters, too, on which the arguers cooperate. They share a common language and a system of meanings. If they are arguing, for example, about whether monetary and fiscal policy should be invoked to combat inflation, they must have the same understanding of what "inflation" is for the argument to be productive, and they also must agree on what set of actions is embraced by the term "monetary and fiscal policy." Otherwise their argument will be unproductive because they will discover that they are not talking about the same thing. This state of affairs is sometimes characterized as "talking past each other."

Furthermore, when people engage in argumentation, they share underlying procedural assumptions and norms. For example, while they may disagree about what the evidence says, they will agree on what counts as evidence. If one accepts the conclusions of astrology and the other insists on empirical observation, they will not get very far. Similarly, if one regards politeness and civility as marks of intelligent discourse, and the other regards these values as masks for the rich and powerful to dominate the discussion, no constructive argumentation is likely to take place.

Finally, arguers share values such as modesty, respect for the audience, willingness to listen and possibly be convinced, and the importance of freely given assent. The competitive elements of argumentation are undergirded by these common values.

Of course, the world is not perfect. Not every situation that we would consider argumentation will partake in all of these values. But to the degree that it does not, it will slide in the direction of sheer persuasion with obtaining consent as the only goal. We cannot claim to be serving the goals of critical thinking, sound judgment, and rational decision-making unless we employ procedures that rely on these various assumptions and values.

Risk

One final assumption is that to engage in argumentation is to accept risks.[13] There are two primary risks we accept when we argue. First is the risk of being shown to be wrong and hence both losing the argument

---

[13] On the risks inherent in argumentation, see Henry W. Johnstone, Jr., "Some Reflections on Argumentation," in *Philosophy, Rhetoric, and Argumentation*, ed. Maurice Natanson and Henry W. Johnstone, Jr. (University Park: Pennsylvania State University Press, 1965), 1–9.

and losing face. Suppose we are convinced that the president is not performing well and we enter into an argument to defend that claim. In the course of the argument we are convinced that the president has made the right decisions on the really important issues. Our earlier belief has been shown to be wrong. But not only that, our credibility to make other judgments about political figures might be called into question as well: if we are wrong about the president, why should we be trusted when we make judgments about the performance of senators or Supreme Court justices? A successful challenge to our beliefs might lower our standing or reputation in the eyes of people we care about.

Beyond that, there is a second risk: we will need to modify our larger system of beliefs or values to take into account the change we have just been convinced to make. Suppose, for example, that we hold the belief that "liberals (or conservatives, if you prefer) make bad presidents." So long as we believed that the current president, being a liberal (or conservative) was not performing well, our belief system was stable and perfectly consistent. But if our adversary were to establish that the current president, though liberal (or conservative), was doing fairly well on the important issues, we would need to rethink our larger position that liberals (or conservatives) make weak presidents. We might conclude that the current president is the exception that proves the rule, or that standards for success have changed, or maybe that we overstated how bad the liberal (or conservative) presidents had been as a whole. But we could not consistently maintain that (1) liberals (or conservatives) make bad presidents, (2) the current president is a liberal (or conservative), (3) the current president is doing fairly well. Having to modify one's system of beliefs can be a major challenge to one's identity and sense of self. It is not a trivial matter.

Why, then, would anyone run the risks that engaging in argumentation entails? As we have seen, when easier methods of decision-making are available we usually will rely on them instead. But sometimes we have no easier alternative. And sometimes, even when we do, we will rely on argumentation despite its inherent risks.

If a person knew, *for sure*, that he or she was in the right about something, there might be no incentive to argue about it. One might merely maintain one's own position and wait for others to come around. To do otherwise might give unwarranted publicity to an erroneous position. This is why, for example, some scholars will not debate against those who deny well-accepted historical facts. Others will refuse to argue with those who deny widely accepted scientific claims such as evolution or climate change. Some will use epithets (calling a claim "repugnant," "racist," or "sexist," for example) as a way to avoid discussing the claim. Still other people will rely on the use or threat of force to squelch disagreement, as seems evident from the rise of press censorship in some countries in Asia and the Middle East.

Why engage in argumentation, and run its risks, instead of using these maneuvers? Because, most of the time, arguers do not know *for sure* that they are in the right to start with. Because, even though they want to win the argument, they value the judgment of the adversary and want his or her assent only on the condition that it is freely given. In holding this view, they bestow personhood on the adversary.[14] He or she is not just an object to be persuaded but a human being whose capacity for thought and independent judgment is to be valued. Moreover, by bestowing personhood on their adversary, they claim it for themselves. A person who values others' capacity for thought and judgment will value it in himself or herself and will expect that others will treat him or her accordingly.

Argumentation and Ethics

Attempts to change other people's minds invariably invite considerations of ethics. To some, any effort to influence other persons by any means seems like manipulating them and doing violence to their individuality as human beings. On this view, argumentation, like any effort at persuasion, should be judged unethical.

The difficulty with this position is that human beings are inherently social creatures. We depend for our mental health on interaction with other people. That is why solitary confinement, even as punishment for the most heinous crimes, is such a controversial procedure. It denies persons something that is as vital to their lives as air and nutrition. And whenever we interact with other people, there is the opportunity to influence them and the possibility that they will influence us. So it cannot be the case that all forms of influence, and hence all uses of argumentation, are unethical.

Furthermore, persuaders cannot imbue people with values and beliefs to which they are opposed. Persuaders can rearrange a person's hierarchy of beliefs, making certain values or emotions seem more important or urgent than they had before. And they can supply new information or put new topics on a person's agenda – but usually by linking them to ideas that he or she already holds. In fact, people typically have strong defense

---

[14] Ehninger, "Argument as Method," esp. 109–110.

mechanisms against being persuaded – the very reason that persuaders often deny that persuasion is their objective! This means that people ultimately cannot be persuaded against their will. And what is true of persuasion in general is even more true of argumentation in particular. So long as one submits his or her arguments to the scrutiny of another, and so long as the other takes his or her responsibilities seriously, one need not worry that argumentation runs afoul of ethics by manipulating the other person.

There is another concern, however, that must be taken more seriously. Does rendering most of our beliefs susceptible to argumentation mean that we have no firm convictions about *anything*, that any value or belief – even something as central to our identity as family solidarity or religious conviction – can be dislodged by argumentation? And if everything is subject to argument, how can we have any standards of ethics or morality at all? This argument is sometimes advanced against the practice of having students debate both sides of a question in school contests. The charge is that educators, even with the best of intentions, are raising generations of amoral relativists. This belief gains support when prominent figures in business and politics who commit ethical transgressions are found to have studied argumentation in school. It also gains support when claims that most people would regard as immoral – such as that nuclear war is good or that the Holocaust was justified – are advanced in the public square.

Although this is a serious concern, it ultimately should be no cause for alarm. Just as it is virtually impossible for a persuader to implant a belief in another person against his or her will, so it is equally difficult to argue a person out of his or her core beliefs by exposure to counter-argument alone. Moreover, people differ far more often in the *hierarchy* of their beliefs than in the content of the beliefs themselves. For example, they believe in both the liberty of the individual and the security of society, and they differ about which is more important than the other. This, in fact, has been at the heart of many disagreements about national security policy since the terrorist attacks of September 11, 2001. No one has argued that individual liberty is a bad thing; nor has anyone argued that protecting the country from attack is unimportant. The question is which value should yield to the other, and this question is raised in the context of specific situations and choices. Sometimes it is answered one way and sometimes the other. These are precisely the circumstances in which it is helpful to argue the comparative merits of the two values in the particular situation. Rather than leading to value relativism, argumentation is more likely to produce a decision tailored to the particular context than one grounded in ideological rigidity.

Even if one's basic beliefs sometimes are called into question by an opposing argument, that is not necessarily a bad thing if it motivates the person to defend those beliefs by marshaling arguments for them. In fact, it is the beliefs that we accept unthinkingly and unquestioningly, that we are never called upon to defend, that are more likely to be undermined by a strong opposing argument, simply because we never have developed the experience of speaking in their behalf. A strong challenge to our values every now and then is more likely to strengthen our adherence to them than it is to lead to a stance of complete relativism. In this as in other matters, the remedy for exposure to messages that challenge our belief is more speech, not enforced silence.

There undoubtedly are people – though probably not many – who have no core beliefs whatsoever. Rather than have their identity defined by core values from which their other beliefs radiate, theirs is defined by pure expediency, chance, or deference to a charismatic leader. When this occurs, it is a serious problem for both the individual and society, but argumentation is neither the cause nor the effect of the problem.

None of this is to deny that otherwise normal people occasionally commit unethical acts while engaged in argumentation. They may assert claims they know to be false, distort evidence, misrepresent the position of their adversaries, or repeat arguments that already have been answered. Most likely, these actions reflect carelessness or nervousness rather than deliberate decision to commit an ethical violation. If it is the latter, an opposing advocate can call it out and thereby question the trustworthiness of the offending arguer. In fact, the knowledge that a counter-arguer might challenge a person committing ethical mistakes is one of the strongest incentives to ethical behavior in the first place. There is a certain self-regulating quality to the practice of argumentation.

Genres of Argumentation

To complete our introduction to argumentation, especially from a rhetorical perspective, it is appropriate to consider the dominant categories, or genres, of argumentation. Although it can be found in any activity in which people engage, argumentation has three dominant genres: deliberation, debate, and public address. They differ in some of their specific practices, though generally not in the basic characteristics discussed in this chapter.

Deliberation is an interaction in which people come together to try jointly to solve problems. It most often occurs among friends or acquaintances or in small groups that exist primarily for some other purpose. During the course of interaction, participants will discover that a controversy exists, because two or more of them maintain what they think are incompatible beliefs. The personal ties among the participants will lead them to try to resolve the dispute. They may or may not succeed, and they themselves will be the judges of their success or failure. Not all disagreements can be resolved, because sometimes incompatible core beliefs really are at issue. But if they fail, at least they will have clarified their difference. They can then "agree to disagree," bracketing the difference and maintaining their relationship (friends who agree not to talk about their political differences, for example). In extreme cases, the disagreement may matter so much that it causes the relationship to collapse.

In deliberation, because the participants are working together, they often can "finish one another's thoughts." Many statements can be left unsaid because they are implicit and everyone understands. Reconstructing the transcript of a deliberation to put all the pieces back in will seem awkward and pedantic. But an argumentation theorist will undertake such a reconstruction in order to be able to analyze what was implied as well as what was said.

Deliberation often will arise by accident. In the course of interaction that probably is not argumentative at all, one participant will assert a claim that another will challenge or doubt. The first party will then need either to abandon the claim or to offer reasons in its defense. The second party might accept the reasons and thus abandon the challenge, resolving the matter. Or the second party might doubt either the truth of the reasons or their standing as support for the claim. Additional supporting reasons and claims are offered; additional doubts and challenges are expressed. Other people may join in the fray. Eventually people may tire of the discussion, start repeating each other, decide there is nothing more to be said, or begin withdrawing from the discussion. Some potential solution may emerge which everyone decides is satisfactory or maybe even the best possible. Or it may be that no solution is proposed or that all the candidate solutions have serious flaws. In that case the participants may decide to bracket the dispute and go on with their lives, to talk some more about it another time, or to "agree to disagree," having come to better understand one another's viewpoints. Both the start and the end of the controversy may be informal and unplanned.

Sometimes, though, deliberation may be planned in order to address a specific issue or concern. For example, to address the topic of race relations in a local community, a neighborhood organization might bring together people of different races to meet together and share experiences and viewpoints. This is an interaction among strangers, and the topic is stipulated in advance. The goal is not to come up with specific proposed policies, although that might happen, but to clarify viewpoints and to understand perspectives to which participants had not been exposed previously. Committees or other small groups that are formed with a specific problem-solving task are yet another occasion for deliberation.

In contrast to deliberation, *debate* is explicitly adversarial, at least on the surface. Two or more advocates present opposing views and a third party chooses between them. The third party is presumed to be disinterested and to make the choice based on the ideas presented in the debate rather than on preconceptions he or she might have. The debaters may be genuinely opposed to each other (competing candidates for political office, for example) or they may be assigned their opposing positions in a kind of role-playing exercise (for example, opposing lawyers who in fact are good friends and may even have similar beliefs about a case on which they are expected to differ). Whether genuine or role-playing opponents, however, their assigned task is to develop and present the strongest arguments they can for their side of the issue, and to raise the strongest challenges or doubts they can about the opposing side of the issue. The purpose for doing this is to enable the decision-maker to make a genuine choice – not one in which one side is advocated strongly and the other weakly if at all, but a choice between the strongest arguments that can be offered for each of the competing positions after challenges have been brought against each.

Typically, the decision-maker will select one side over the other – that is, advocates for one side of the debate will win and advocates for the other side will lose. Occasionally the decision-maker might formulate a third choice that is a compromise between the two opposing positions or that incorporates some elements of each in a choice that splits the difference between them. (This happens, for example, in some court cases when the judge has discretion to formulate an outcome other than those advocated by the parties.) In some cases (legislative or congressional debate, for example), the decision-maker is a larger body including the debaters but not limited to them. In other cases the decision-maker is a third party (such as a judge or jury in a courtroom, a labor or divorce arbitrator, or the voting public in an election campaign).

Negotiation is a setting that combines some elements of deliberation with some elements of debate. It often features dialogue among a small group of negotiators (sometimes only two) and their agreement is in the first instance the test of success. In that sense, they pursue consensus, like participants in deliberation. But the negotiators typically represent larger groups, like debaters, and if they reach agreement, it usually has to be ratified by third parties, especially if the negotiators are hired professionals rather than members of the groups they represent. In this respect, negotiation resembles debate.

The third genre of argumentation is *public address*. Traditionally, public address was associated with a public speaker on the platform, in the courtroom, or in the assembly. In a mediated and highly technological age, public address takes many other forms as well: print, visual representations, nonverbal performances, blogs, and social media, for example. It can encompass any practice of rhetoric that is geared to a specific situation.

Speakers or writers engaged in public address typically will advance one side of an argument. They will present the case for or against an idea or proposal. Usually no one will confront them directly at the time. But other speakers or writers, either concurrently or later, will deliver messages offering other viewpoints and other sides to the controversy. For example, a speaker may oppose proposals to impose a "carbon tax" as a means to control climate change, arguing both that climate change is not a serious problem and that the "carbon tax" is not the best way to deal with it if it is. The speaker's immediate aim is to convince those who are reading or listening to this presentation. Usually, no one will attack the arguments just then. But other speakers and writers, equally committed to the opposite side of the argument, will surely do so at other times and places. They will maintain that the preponderance of evidence supports the reality of climate change, and that one of its biggest causes – the burning of fossil fuels – could be curtailed significantly with a "carbon tax."

Although they do not follow a debate format, public addresses could be imagined as elements in a large debate taking place across a society. The controversy exists across time; eventually the society as a whole will reach a decision. The individual public addresses might be understood as participating in a grand debate, of which ultimately society collectively will act as the judge.

Whether occurring in the genre of deliberation, debate, or public address, or in hybrid combinations of the genres, argumentation is *about something*. The subject can be stated in the form of a question, such as "What, if anything, should be done about climate change?" or in the form of a claim, an assertion that the parties to the argumentation may either support or oppose, such as "Resolved: That the United States government should adopt a carbon tax." This sort of claim, the ultimate focus of the controversy, is sometimes called a *resolution* or a *proposition*. In Chapter 3 we will learn more about the work it does.

Conclusion

This chapter has introduced basic concepts and principles of argumentation when studied from the perspective of rhetoric. Argumentation is the practice of justifying claims under conditions of uncertainty. People argue by constructing and justifying arguments. Justification establishes that a particular audience has a warrant to believe a particular claim. When people engage in argumentation they make basic underlying assumptions about the influence of the audience, the nature of uncertainty, the process of justification, the fundamentally cooperative nature of what may seem like an adversarial exercise, and the assumption of risk.

This understanding of argumentation is far different from popular notions of quarreling and bickering. It is a very important activity with skills that are worth cultivating. It was Aristotle who noted that if it would be a disgrace for a person to be unable to defend himself or herself in a bodily way, it would be at least as much a disgrace to be unable to defend oneself with reason. Argumentation is the means by which people do that.

Beyond self-defense, argumentation is also a constructive activity, involving the creation of claims in an attempt to influence others and the testing of those claims through scrutiny by others. In an uncertain world, it is a means to arrive at convictions with confidence, while realizing that those convictions are always subject to review and possible change.

It is time to move from this abstract perspective to examine the practice of argumentation. And the place to begin is with an understanding of what arguments look like.

Exercises

1. Each of the following statements is a claim; it asserts something that you can accept or reject. For each claim, determine whether your acceptance would require argumentation (reason-giving) or whether there is a more certain way to evaluate the claim.
    a.   The box jellyfish is the most venomous creature on earth.
    b.   Chicago-style pizza is superior to thin crust pizza.

c. "War is the continuation of politics by other means." (Carl von Clausewitz)

d. Vaccinating children is not a cause of autism.

e. William Shakespeare wrote *Romeo and Juliet.*

f. Adopting the metric system in the United States would cost millions of dollars.

g. The Ural Mountains mark the border between Asia and Europe.

h. John F. Kennedy was assassinated on November 22, 1963, by Lee Harvey Oswald.

i. A group of crows is known as a murder.

j. The allosaurus lived during the Jurassic period.

k. The average American household has $5,747.00 in credit card debt.

l. Mariah Carey's song "We Belong Together" was the most popular song of the 2000s decade.

m. A dodecahedron has twelve sides.

n. All species come into being through the natural selection of hereditary variations favoring those that are best suited to survival in a particular environment. (Charles Darwin)

2. We have defined a controversy as the presence of incompatible claims. Choose a controversy from a community with which you identify. This may be your town, university, church, social group, family, etc. Then answer the following questions:

   a. What are the incompatible claims? (There may be more than two.)

   b. Show why the controversy is not trivial. (Why does it matter that the controversy be settled?)

   c. What leads you to think that the parties are interested in seeking agreement?

   d. Is there evidence that the parties are interested in gaining agreement *freely* from others who may have an interest in the controversy?

   e. Is there a simpler way to resolve the controversy, such as an obvious compromise, a higher authority, or a model?

   f. Assuming that the controversy meets the preconditions for argument as mentioned in steps a–e above, list some of the reasons each party may have for their position in the controversy.

   g. How could argumentation be used to resolve this controversy fully or partially?

3. Assume that you are a superhero whose power is the ability to persuade other people to do what you want in any situation simply

by suggesting it. Would you ever suspend this power in order to engage in argumentation with others? Why? In what, if any, situations would the process of arguing be preferable to just having your way?

4. For each of the following, determine whether it represents the deliberation, debate, or public address genre of argumentation.

   a. Three friends are trying to choose a restaurant for dinner.
   b. A jury trial.
   c. Two candidates for the same political office appearing before an audience.
   d. A *Buzzfeed* post claiming to represent the "33 Most Important Animal Selfies in History."
   e. A commencement speaker who tells you that you must learn to fail before you can learn to succeed.
   f. A classroom discussion regarding the future of Social Security.
   g. A rap song that criticizes police violence.
   h. Representatives of the United Auto Workers sitting down to discuss the terms of a new contract with representatives of Ford Motor Company.
   i. A minister's sermon on the importance of religious and racial tolerance.
   j. Discussion at a university board of trustees meeting of a proposal to divest from fossil fuel investments.

5. Read an editorial in a print or online newspaper. Then answer the following questions:

   a. What is the claim of the editorial?
   b. What specific audience is being addressed?
   c. What is the audience being asked to do?
   d. How persuasive is the editorial?

CHAPTER 2

What Arguments Look Like

How would we know an argument when we saw one?

That is a tricky question because we don't actually "see" arguments. They are embedded in conversation, speeches, writings, nonverbal expressions – in the interactions we have when we try to influence other people and to justify the claims we make on their belief or action. In fact, they are what people produce during these interactions. They are sets of statements arranged in the proper relationship to each other. But compared with what is actually said or written, they may need to be reworded, divided or combined, and maybe even made explicit rather than assumed.

In this chapter we will focus on diagramming arguments. We will explore why the model of formal logic is not satisfactory for many arguments. Then we shall consider how to diagram simple arguments, guided by the work of the British logician Stephen Toulmin.[1] After that, we shall examine how to diagram complex arguments, following the suggestion of Dutch communication scholars Frans van Eemeren, Rob Grootendorst, and Francisca Snoeck Henkemans.[2]

The Formal Logic Model

For many years, the accepted model of argument was the *categorical syllogism*, a series of statements about categories and their relationships to one another. Suppose you are engaged in a conversation with a friend who has soured on politics. At one point your friend says:

All politicians should be put in jail.

[1] Stephen Toulmin, *The Uses of Argument* (Cambridge: Cambridge University Press, 1958), esp. 94–145.
[2] Frans H. van Eemeren, Rob Grootendorst, and Francisca Snoeck Henkemans, *Argumentation: Analysis, Evaluation, Presentation* (Mahwah, NJ: Lawrence Erlbaum, 2002), esp. 68–72.

Fig. 2.1

The conversation continues, and when it is your turn, you ask:

Why do you say they should be put in jail?

To which your friend replies:

Well, they're all corrupt, and that's where corrupt people belong.

From this snippet of conversation we can reconstruct the following argument:

All politicians are corrupt.
All corrupt people should be put in jail.
Therefore, all politicians should be put in jail.

We could diagram this argument as a series of concentric circles, as shown in Fig. 2.1.

We can take the circle labeled P (for politicians) and place it inside the circle labeled C (for corrupt people) and, in turn, place that inside the circle labeled J (for people who should be put in jail). We can do this because we know from the statements in the conversation that *all* politicians are corrupt, so they will all be included within the circle representing people who are corrupt, and we also know that *all* such people should be put in jail, which is why the C circle fits entirely within the J circle. Once we have diagrammed both of those statements, we can look and see that the P circle is entirely within the J circle, showing that "all politicians should be put in jail," which is the claim with which your friend began the argument. So not only do we have an argument, we have a *valid* argument. We will explore the concept of validity later.

Notice that we cannot say that the argument is true. We don't know that all politicians really are corrupt, and in fact it's highly unlikely that they are. We also don't know that all corrupt people – regardless of the circumstances – should be put in jail, and that's highly unlikely too. But what we can say is that *if* all politicians are corrupt, and *if* all corrupt people should be put in jail, *then* all politicians should be in jail. We can be

Fig. 2.2a

Fig. 2.2b

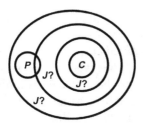

Fig. 2.2c

completely sure of that, because there is no way that the premises could be correct and yet the claim be false. Such an argument would be self-contradictory.

In this example, our statements used the term *all*. Formal logic also can accommodate the terms *none* and *some*. If your friend had said, "No politicians are corrupt," we would diagram that statement like Fig 2.2a and if your friend had said, "Some politicians are corrupt," we would diagram that statement like Fig 2.2b.

For "no politicians are corrupt," we would have two separate circles with no overlap between them, because – according to the statement – there would be no case in which a person would be both a politician and corrupt. For "some politicians are corrupt," we would have overlapping but not concentric circles, because some of the politicians also are corrupt (but presumably some others are not, although we don't know that for sure).

By the way, see what happens to Figs. 2.2a and 2.2b when we try to add the diagram for "all corrupt people should be put in jail" (Figs. 2.2c and 2.2d). We know that the *C* circle will fit entirely within the *J* circle, but we don't know whether the *J* circle should include all, part, or none of the *P* circle. We still have arguments in both of these cases, but they are not good arguments because we don't know whether they are valid or not.

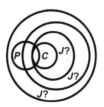

Fig. 2.2d

These examples show us that drawing circles to represent the different statements in the argument, and then positioning the circles to show the relationships among the statements, will enable us both to diagram categorical syllogisms and to decide whether the argument is valid. But how often can we say that we use these syllogisms in the first place?

Our categorical statements had to be about *all*, *some*, or *none*. There were no gradations within "some." But usually we will say something differently depending on the degree of "someness." Consider these examples:

Some people will vote for a third-party candidate.
Very few people will vote for a third-party candidate.
Ten percent of likely voters will vote for a third-party candidate.
Most dissatisfied people will vote for a third-party candidate.

The formal logic model would have us diagram all of these statements in exactly the same way – like Fig. 2.2b. But the meaning and force of the four statements is quite different. If our diagram is to reflect the reality of the argument, we need a diagram that will reflect this difference.

Furthermore, the formal logic model is not very sensitive to the *context* of the argument. Suppose that in reading an article, you find the statement, "there is a 10 percent risk of error." This statement will have different force if the context is medicine, where the risk is death, than it will if the context is a social psychology experiment, where the risk is making inaccurate responses on a questionnaire. The very strength of the formal logic model – that the substance of the argument can be reduced to neutral terms like *P*, *C*, and *J* – is also its weakness, because very few of the things we talk about can be stripped of their context in that fashion.

In addition to these problems, remember that the formal logic model had no concern for whether the statements were true; it was focused only on form – on the relationship among the statements. This is a great strength of the model, because it enabled us to say that, if the premises were true, the claim would follow *with certainty*. But most of the subjects we argue about do not involve certainty but deal with degrees of plausibility, likelihood, significance, or force. We need to represent these nuances in the diagram of the argument.

Other problems can be cited, as well, in the use of the diagramming method for the categorical syllogism. It is not that this method is wrong, but that its usefulness is limited by the fact that the categorical syllogism is an atypical method of reasoning. We are trying to fit round pegs into square holes. Other approaches to diagramming arguments will be more useful for us.

Diagramming Simple Arguments

We begin by considering the structure of a simple argument – one in which only one assertion is advanced with only one instance of support and a single warrant authorizing the assertion on the basis of the evidence. Before we can do that, however, we need to discuss three basic key terms – claims, evidence, and warrant.

Suppose you and a friend are discussing national politics and you assert, "The president's position is weakening." That is your *claim*, your assertion or statement in response to the controversy being discussed. If you and your friend are the only participants in the discussion, this is the statement you want your friend to accept. If others are listening to both of you, it is the statement you want this larger group to accept. It is called a *claim* because you are making a claim on your audience's beliefs. If your audience has not thought about the matter previously, you are asking them to modify their set of beliefs to include this statement among them. If your listeners believe that the president's position really is strong, you want them to abandon that belief and replace it with the one you have asserted, or at least to acknowledge that your assertion is worthy of serious consideration. And if your listeners already believe as you do, you still want them to modify their set of beliefs – by strengthening their conviction or, perhaps, moving beyond holding the belief to doing something about it.

Now consider how your friend might respond to your assertion. She might say, "Yes, I guess you're right," "I think so, too," or some other statement indicating agreement with you. In that case nothing more need be said and no argument takes place. You have discovered that there really is no disagreement between you, so nothing needs to be resolved.

But suppose your friend is not convinced. She might say, "Absolutely not; I don't want to hear another thing about it," and then walk away.

Here too there is nothing more to be said – not because the two of you are in agreement but because there is a strong *dis*agreement that at least one of you does not want to resolve. You conceivably could respond, "Well, then, *I* must be wrong," and abandon your claim. But if you made the claim in the first place, it is not likely that you would abandon it on such a flimsy basis. So if neither of you is willing to yield your position and at least one of you is unwilling to discuss the matter further, there is nothing more to say.

Arguments take place in the middle ground between these two extremes of instant agreement and utter disagreement. This is the area in which people seek to modify another person's beliefs while risking that their own might be modified instead. So imagine when you say, "The president's position is weakening," your friend says something like "That isn't what I think; why do you say so?" Now, having made the claim, you have the obligation to back it up, to provide some support for it. Whatever you offer as support for the claim, your grounds for believing it, is called *evidence*. For example, you might say, "There is a new national poll that shows that the president's approval rating is down by four points." Now you are hoping that your friend will accept that, in fact, the approval rating has declined by four points *and* that this decline is a good reason to believe that the president's political position is weakening. If your friend does indeed accept both of these statements, then the argument is over. You have made a claim and, on request, have offered evidence for it that your friend finds convincing.

But your friend could have questioned either your evidence or your reasoning. She might have said, "I don't think that poll really shows a four-point drop," or "I don't think that poll is reliable," or some other statement disputing the truth of your evidence. In that case your responsibility would become defending that poll or substituting some other evidence for it. The key point is that, ultimately, for the argument to be successful, both parties must accept the truth of the evidence on which it relies.

Alternatively, your friend might agree that the poll shows a four-point drop in approval rating, but question whether that fact counts as evidence for the statement that the president's political position is weakening. In this case your friend is questioning not the evidence but the *inference* you are drawing from it. She is challenging the link you are asserting to exist between your evidence and your claim.

In the case of formal reasoning, as we have seen, the link between the evidence and the claim is automatic. In other words, the evidence *entails* the claim because the inference from evidence to claim is absolute. This does not mean that the evidence is true, but rather that *if* the evidence is true, the claim *must* be true (assuming, of course, that the form is correct). The reason this is so is that the claim merely restates what is already implicit in the evidence statements (the premises); it does not tell us anything new. But when we engage in reasoning with others, we usually want to go beyond what we already know and establish something new in the claim. For this reason, our inference is not guaranteed. It will be correct only to some degree of probability.

In the case at hand, how could it be that a decline in the president's approval rating would *not* count as evidence that the president's political position is weakening? Perhaps the original approval rating was artificially high and was widely expected to fall without impairing the president's political position. Perhaps the next election is far in the future and no one is taking the current approval rating very seriously. Perhaps the president has sufficient leverage over Congress regardless of fluctuations in the approval rating. Or perhaps polls cannot accurately measure approval ratings because the concept of "approval" does not easily reduce itself to a yes or no answer. Any of these possibilities, or others that your friend might imagine, would challenge the link that you drew between measures of approval and the president's political position.

When you made your statement about the polls, you were making an unstated but implicit inference from the poll measures to the president's political position. What authorized you to make that inference was an equally implicit *warrant* for it. The warrant in this case was the statement, "Poll ratings are a sign of one's political position." This statement says that, given evidence of increase or decrease in poll ratings, you can infer strengthening or weakening of political position. Unlike formal reasoning, it does not entail or guarantee the claim. Rather, it is like a train ticket or a driver's license authorizing you to travel from the evidence to the claim. The warrant tells you that, even though the link between evidence and claim is not guaranteed, you are allowed to assert it because it is ordinarily there and is correct with a high degree of probability.

But the warrant is not immune to challenge, and remember we said that your friend might have challenged it. If so, then if you want to sustain your claim, you must back up the warrant by offering support for it. Granted that it holds ordinarily; you still need to show why it holds in this case. You might contend that this is an ordinary case and the exceptional circumstances we imagined above do not apply, or you might explain that historically the warrant has applied the vast majority of the time, so we can

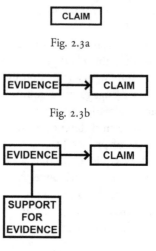

presume that it applies here – unless your friend, rather than just questioning it, can demonstrate that it does not apply in the case at hand. Or you can make some other rejoinder that will defend the applicability of the warrant.

Now we can see how this understanding of a simple argument can be represented in a diagram. These diagrams are suggested by the work of a twentieth-century British philosopher, Stephen Toulmin. They visually represent the links among claim, evidence, and warrant.

Fig. 2.3a represents the simplest case, in which you assert a claim and your friend accepts it immediately. In this case there is nothing to the argument except the initial assertion of the claim. Fig. 2.3b is the case in which your friend asks you how you support the claim, and then, once you provide the evidence, it is immediately accepted as true and as a reason for the claim. Here the statement of evidence and claim are all that is stated explicitly; the link between the evidence and the claim is implicit.

Fig. 2.4 diagrams the situation in which your friend does not accept the truth of your evidence and you must either defend its truth or substitute other evidence that your friend will regard as true. The diagram shows how you back up your evidence. While the diagram shows only one level of support for the evidence, if that level were questioned, you would need to back it up in turn – and so on until you have offered evidence that your friend will accept as true.

Fig. 2.5a

Fig. 2.5b

Finally, Figs. 2.5a and 2.5b represent the case in which your friend questions the link between your evidence and your claim. Fig. 2.5a is a situation in which you make explicit the warrant that was previously left implicit. In our example, you would say to your friend, "Poll ratings are a sign of strength of political position," or words to that effect. This might be enough to convince your friend that the link you have put forward is a reasonable one. But maybe not – in which case you will have to provide support for the warrant, as shown in Fig. 2.5b. You might cite historical evidence – all the years in which poll results were indeed a sign of one's political position – or the testimony of distinguished political scientists saying that poll results do indeed relate to political position. Again, in the diagram only one level of support is indicated, but if the support for the warrant is not accepted, you will need to provide additional levels of support.

Of course, we can imagine a situation in which *both* the evidence and the warrant are challenged. Your friend might not believe the poll results, and also might doubt that poll results are a sign of political strength. In that case you would need to support both, and a diagram of your response would look like a combination of Figs. 2.4 and 2.5b. Now our supposedly simple argument does not look quite so simple!

There is a potential confusion here that we should clear up before proceeding. The statements that you might offer to support the warrant look very much like statements we earlier described as evidence. The difference is not in their intrinsic character but in their function in the argument. The boxes we have labeled "evidence" can be thought of as evidence for the claim. The boxes we have labeled "support for evidence" can be thought of as evidence for the evidence. And the boxes we have labeled "support for warrant" can be thought of as evidence for the warrant. In each case the box is identifying a statement that is support for another statement. But they support different kinds of statements – claim, evidence, and warrant, respectively – and thus contribute differently to advancing the argument.

Diagramming Complex Arguments

We have seen that a simple argument is one containing only one claim, one level of evidence, and one warrant. Now we are ready to consider more complex arguments. Again it will be helpful to begin with an example.

Suppose that in reading a newspaper editorial, you encounter the statement, "Immediate adoption of a carbon tax is the only way to slow the effects of climate change before it is too late." It should strike you immediately that, in order to sustain this claim, several subsidiary claims will have to be established. For example, the claim assumes that climate change is occurring and that it is a significant problem. The claim also assumes that it is an urgent matter requiring action right away. It assumes that no other approach to the problem can work. And it assumes that a carbon tax can. Now, there is nothing wrong with making a claim that assumes other claims – so long as we are prepared to support them, as necessary, along the way to establishing our main claim.

This example illustrates what makes an argument complex. It is not the difficulty of the subject matter, but the fact that establishing the main claim requires establishing one or (usually) more subsidiary claims. To diagram such an argument, one must start by being clear about which is the main claim and which are the subsidiary claims. The main claim (also called the *resolution*) is the statement that you want an audience to accept; it is your answer to the question posed by the controversy. The subsidiary claims can be derived from the main claim. They are the statements that you need to establish along the way to establishing the main claim.

Here is another way to think about this relationship. Each of the subsidiary claims can be thought of as evidence for the main claim. But it can function as evidence only if it is itself supported as a claim. For instance, the statement that climate change is a serious problem is part of the evidence for the statement that an immediate carbon tax is necessary, but only once the statement that climate change is serious is itself established as a claim.

Organizing Complex Arguments

There are different ways in which the subsidiary claims can link to the main claim, just as there are differences in how support for the subsidiary claims can link to those claims. Suppose you are reading an op-ed about the state of the airline industry and you determine that the main claim (the resolution) is "Airline travel is difficult to plan." As you go back through the article, you find that all of the following statements are offered as reasons for this claim:

- The price structure does not make sense.
- Schedules are inconvenient.
- Connecting flights are often missed.
- In order to get a reasonable price, one must buy tickets too far in advance.
- Websites and the online reservation process are confusing.
- Reservation agents don't answer questions clearly.

You can see quickly that each of these statements is evidence for the main claim, but each also is a claim in its own right, requiring additional support. Now ask yourself two questions. First, do these claims depend on one another for their strength as claims? Second, do they depend on one another for their linkage to the main claim?

The answer to the first question clearly is No. The claim that connecting flights are often missed, for example, is entirely independent of the claim that the price structure does not make sense. Whether either of these claims is shown to be true or false has no bearing whatsoever on the truth or falsity of the other claim. The same will be true of any pair of these subsidiary claims, so we can say that they are independent of one another.

Now what about the bearing of each of these subsidiary claims on the main claim? On reflection, you can see that, again, they are independent of one another. The claim that one must buy tickets too early if one is to get a reasonable price is a reason that "airline travel is difficult to plan," whether or not websites and the online reservation process are confusing. Conversely, the confusing nature of these online instruments is a reason that "airline travel is difficult to plan," regardless of whether one must buy tickets too early in order to obtain a reasonable price.

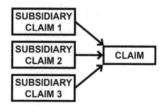

Fig. 2.6

When the subsidiary claims are not dependent on one another and each by itself establishes the main claim, the structure of argument is called *multiple*. This is because there are multiple paths to the main claim, as shown in Fig. 2.6.

The term "multiple" is used by the Dutch argumentation theorists Frans van Eemeren, Rob Grootendorst, and Francisca Snoeck Henkemans, whose work has been cited earlier (see note 2). Other writers may refer to this as an *independent* structure, emphasizing the logical independence of the different claims and links, or a *parallel* structure, suggesting that it resembles a parallel circuit of electricity. Although different terms are sometimes used for this and other argument structures, the same structure is being referred to.

From the standpoint of an advocate advancing the main claim, a multiple structure is especially advantageous, so long as the subsidiary claims are strong. The reason is precisely the fact that there are multiple paths to success. The advocate might have to scuttle one or more of the subsidiary claims (for example, he might be shown to be overgeneralizing in stating that reservation agents at call centers do not answer questions clearly). But he can still sustain the claim that "airline travel is difficult to plan" so long as he can prevail on at least one of the subsidiary claims. Of course, no advocate would be advised to advance weak subsidiary claims with the intent of casting aside all but one of them! Still, it is comforting to know that, when all is said and done, the advocate's burdens will be fulfilled even if he does not sustain all the subsidiary claims he advances.

Now consider what might happen when you discuss the op-ed about airline travel with your friend. In the course of the conversation your friend might be convinced the op-ed is right that travel is hard to plan, but then go on to say, "Not only that, but airline travel is becoming more

---

² Frans H. van Eemeren, Rob Grootendorst, and Francisca Snoeck Henkemans, *Argumentation: Analysis, Evaluation, Presentation* (Mahwah, NJ: Lawrence Erlbaum, 2002), esp. 68–72.

unpleasant." Whether it is unpleasant is a separate question from whether it is hard to plan, so your friend is broadening the indictment of the airline industry by introducing an additional claim. (The two claims could each support the same larger or more general claim, but that is not what is happening in this instance.) Since you do not fly that often, you ask your friend what she is referring to, and she responds with this list of particulars:

- Flights are often delayed.
- Planes are too crowded these days.
- No food is served any more.
- Security after 9/11 is too obtrusive.
- You can't relax in an airport.
- Passengers are really rude.
- You have to overhear people's cell phone conversations all the time.

Consider the same two questions we asked above. It becomes clear that, like our first example, the claims do not depend on one another for their strength as claims. Whether or not you have to overhear cell phone conversations, for example, has nothing to do with whether any food is served on the airlines any more. Likewise, whether planes are crowded or not is unrelated to whether post-9/11 security is too obtrusive. So far this example looks just like the first one.

But now consider how the subsidiary claims bear on the main claim. It might seem at first that they are independent in this respect too, but look carefully. Does each of these claims, by itself, represent a strong enough reason to say that airline travel (taken as a whole) is unpleasant? Some people might think so, but many others would dismiss the complainers as grumpy or as whiners. Even your friend, for example, might be happy to pass up airline food (was it all that good, anyway?) if she could be assured of a comfortable seat on a plane that was not too crowded.

Indeed, what seems to give this claim its strength is the *accumulation* of complaints about airlines. It is the fact that they all come together in a pattern of unpleasantness. It is the pattern, not any one specific problem, that establishes the claim. When subsidiary claims are independent of one another, yet establish the main claim together rather than separately, the structure of the argument is called *coordinative*. (This is the term used by van Eemeren, Grootendorst, and Snoeck Henkemans. Some other writers refer to this as a *convergent* structure.) Fig. 2.7 diagrams a coordinative structure of argument.

In the abstract, a coordinative structure is less attractive to an advocate than is a multiple structure, because one cannot sustain the claim just by

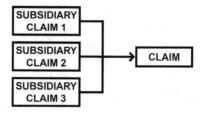

Fig. 2.7

carrying one or a small number of the subsidiary claims. But it's equally true that one does not have to carry each and every subsidiary claim in order to establish that airline travel is becoming more unpleasant. Even if the on-time rate for flights improved, for example, the other factors still would still establish the main claim.

So where to draw the line? This ultimately is not a logical judgment but a rhetorical one. There is a line, somewhere, beyond which the main claim will seem credible and below which it will seem like whining. There is no hard-and-fast way to determine where this line is; it is a judgment call. Since the power of this argument comes from its cumulation, then presumably some degree of cumulation – say, at least three or four of the subsidiary claims – will probably be necessary. Once the cumulative force is established, citing additional subsidiary claims may be piling on more claims than are needed.

This judgment call is also related to the question of what is the advocate's ultimate burden. Suppose that your friend, who advanced the claim in the first place that airline travel is becoming more unpleasant, may not be able to convince listeners that it is impossible to relax in an airport. After all, someone might tell her, there are frequent-flyer lounges, designated quiet spaces, relatively untrafficked areas, priority lines, and so forth. Your friend might concede that yes, it is possible to relax at airports. That concession might *weaken* her main claim, because the remaining bill of particulars is shorter, but it is not likely to weaken it all that much. But if she has to yield similarly on two or three of the other subsidiary claims, the main claim will have been chipped away to an extent that listeners might conclude that it has been defeated. Thinking strategically, then, an advocate will try to imagine the likely fate of individual subsidiary claims before putting them together in a coordinative structure.

Now suppose that yet another person joins this conversation, having been aroused by the direction it is taking, and insists, "It's not just a matter

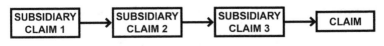

Fig. 2.8

of unpleasantness. Airline mishaps actually cost me my job." "What? How could that be?" others react in surprise. Then the aggrieved participant explained, "My luggage was mis-tagged at the airport. As a result, my bags went to the wrong city. When I got to my destination, I discovered that valuable documents and materials were missing. As a result, I gave a poor sales presentation. And consequently I got fired from my job." Admittedly a bit farfetched, this example illustrates a series of arguments about causality. The main claim, "Airline mishaps cost me my job," is supported by the evidence, "I gave a poor presentation," and the warrant, "A poor presentation was the cause of my being fired." In turn, "I gave a poor presentation" is a subsidiary claim, supported by the evidence that "valuable documents and materials were missing," and the warrant, "Missing important documents and materials caused my presentation to suffer." We can continue the causal chain: each step that is offered as a piece of evidence for one claim is also a claim in its own right, supported by evidence of some other mishap that the warrant asserts was the cause of the alleged failure. Fig. 2.8 diagrams this kind of argument.

This diagram looks significantly different from Figs. 2.6 and 2.7. Each step in the argument connects directly to the next step, and only the step asserting, "I gave a poor presentation" connects to the main claim. What this diagram represents is that the steps in the argument are *not* independent of each other. Rather, each step depends on all the steps that have preceded it. Likewise, the steps are *not* independent in their bearing on the main claim. Rather, all of the previous steps are needed in order to establish the main claim.

Arguments that look like Fig. 2.8 are called *subordinative* structures, because each step is subordinate to the steps that follow it. (As in the previous examples, "subordinative" is the term used by van Eemeren, Grootendorst, and Snoeck Henkemans. Some other writers use the term "series," to suggest that the structure is analogous to a series circuit in electricity, in which if one point of connection is extinguished, the entire circuit will go out.)

With an argument of this form, the burden on its proponent is heavy. She must establish the existence of every step in the chain. Conversely, a critic would need to break only one link in the chain for the entire chain to be broken, because the structure no longer will link everything to the main claim.

To review, then, the three structural patterns for complex arguments are:

Multiple
- Subsidiary claims are independent of each other.
- Subsidiary claims individually establish the main claim.

Coordinative
- Subsidiary claims are independent of each other.
- Subsidiary claims, taken together, establish the main claim.

Subordinative
- Subsidiary claims are not independent of each other.
- Subsidiary claims, taken together, establish the main claim.

From these considerations, we might say in the abstract that the proponent of an argument should always try to cast it in the form of a multiple argument, because that will give the proponent the easiest burden, and that the opponent should always try to cast the argument being refuted in the form of a subordinative argument, because that will place the heaviest burden on the proponent. But in practice this is determined by the context and the particular subject matter of the argument. For example, if the first step in a subordinative argument can be established easily (after all, having one's luggage mis-tagged is hardly a unique experience), and if this creates a sense of momentum so that the links between one step and another are relatively easy to establish, then a subordinative structure might be to the proponent's advantage despite its difficulties in the abstract.

Combining the Argument Structures

What makes a complex argument complex is not just that the evidence for the main claim is also a subsidiary claim. It is also the fact that the same argument can contain different structures. The connection between the subsidiary claims and the main claim may be of one kind, while the connections between the subsidiary claims and the evidence supporting them may be of different kinds. It is not uncommon to find multiple, coordinative, and subordinative structures within the same argument. If we are going to understand exactly what the argument is claiming, to identify the different levels of supporting structure and figure out how to

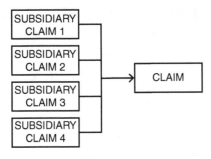

Fig. 2.9

defend or to attack the claim, we have to be able to identify precisely what the argument says.

Let us return to the example earlier in this chapter about a carbon tax. The main claim, remember, was "Immediate adoption of a carbon tax is the only way to slow the effects of climate change before it is too late." We also imagined four subsidiary claims: (1) climate change is a significant problem; (2) climate change requires immediate action; (3) no other approach can work; and (4) a carbon tax can work.

These four subsidiary claims most clearly connect to the main claim via a coordinative structure. The claims are independent of one another. (One might argue that the first and second subsidiary claims are in a subordinative relationship, since the urgency of the problem depends on its significance. But there are matters that present themselves as urgent – we either address them now or lose the opportunity – that are not serious enough to worry about. Seriousness and urgency are two different dimensions; one is not dependent on the other.)

We generated these subsidiary claims, however, by analyzing the main claim and determining what assumptions were built into it. In order to establish the main claim, therefore, we need to establish that *all* the subsidiary claims hold up. If climate change were not shown to be a significant enough problem to worry about, or if addressing it were not urgent, or if there were other solutions that could work, or if a carbon tax would not really work, then we could not conclude that immediate adoption of a carbon tax is the only way to slow the effects of climate change before it is too late. Fig. 2.9 diagrams the relationship between the main claim and the four subsidiary claims.

Remember, though, that each of the subsidiary claims has its own structure of supporting arguments. The first subsidiary claim, "Climate change is a significant problem," might be supported with the following statements:

Fig. 2.10

- Gases trap heat in the atmosphere.
- The result is that average temperatures are increasing.
- Increased temperatures threaten to melt the polar ice caps and to raise sea levels worldwide.
- Rising sea levels threaten worldwide flooding, causing loss of life and major economic catastrophe.

What structure might these supporting statements assume? They seem to resemble the subordinative structure illustrated in Fig. 2.8. There is a series of causal claims, whereby the effect of one cause becomes the cause to another effect. So within an overall coordinative structure we have a subordinative structure in the case of this subsidiary claim, as illustrated by Fig. 2.10.

Now consider the second subsidiary claim, "Climate change requires immediate action." Suppose that the supporting statements here are:

- At an increase of 3.6 degrees Fahrenheit, the effects of melting icecaps are irreversible.
- At our current rate, temperatures will increase 3.6 degrees by the year 2080.
- Reputable scientists overwhelmingly agree that our situation is urgent.

Now look at how these statements relate to one another. The first and second exist in a coordinative structure. In order to establish the claim that immediate action is required, we need to establish *both* what the point of no return is *and* that at the current rate of temperature increase, we will reach that point relatively soon. But the third supporting statement is of a different kind; it relies not on measurement but on the testimony of reputable scientists. It works independently of the statements about measurement to establish the subsidiary statement. So we have two different supports: the coordination of the first and second statements and, independently of that, the third statement. Fig. 2.11 diagrams what the support for this subsidiary claim is like.

Proceed to the third subsidiary claim, "No other approach can work." There are a couple of different ways the advocate might proceed from here. If there are a finite and small number of alternative approaches, the

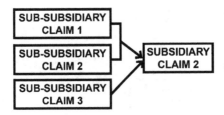

Fig. 2.11

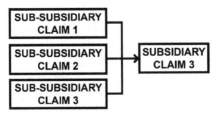

Fig. 2.12

advocate might discuss them one at a time and show why they are deficient. After saying that there are only four approaches, for example, the advocate might claim that approach #1 does not work, approach #2 does not work, and approach #3 does not work, leaving only approach #4, which is the carbon tax. This would be a coordinative structure.

Alternatively, one might claim that only the carbon tax has certain features that are necessary for a solution to work. For example, the advocate might argue that no other approach relies on existing technology, no other approach creates economic incentives to reduce the carbon footprint, no other approach relies on the working of the market, and no other approach internalizes the costs of compliance.

Whichever of these two approaches an advocate might use, the structure for establishing the third subsidiary claim is coordinative. No supporting statement depends on another supporting statement, but all are necessary in order to establish the subsidiary claim. Fig. 2.12 illustrates this structure.

Finally, let us examine the fourth subsidiary claim: a carbon tax can work. One can imagine that the supporter of the carbon tax might offer several reasons that it would work:

- It will create economic incentives to reduce the carbon footprint.
- It solves the "free rider" problem by internalizing costs with polluters.
- It is technologically feasible and easy to administer.

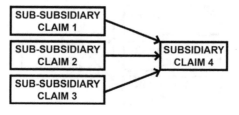

Fig. 2.13

Each of these reasons is independent of the others, and each bears separately on establishment of the subsidiary claim. Fig. 2.13 diagrams the multiple structure of this last argument.

So what we have here is a main claim supported by subsidiary claims in a coordinative structure, with one of the subsidiary claims supported in a subordinative structure, one in a coordinative structure, one in a hybrid of a coordinative and a multiple structure, and one in a multiple structure. And we have gone only to the first level of subsidiary claims! Some of the supporting statements we have used are themselves claims which would require a further level of support, and there might be several steps to go before we are entirely at the level of evidence that does not require additional support. For the sake of clarity, however, we shall not illustrate further levels of support.

How might we diagram this argument about the carbon tax in all its complexity? We need to make a couple of adjustments to our diagramming process. In diagramming simple arguments we have made the warrant explicit, and shown it as supporting the inference from evidence to claim. This means that we have shown the process of arguing as both vertical (from warrant to inference) and horizontal (from evidence to claim). With a complex argument it is hard to draw these relationships in two-dimensional space. So we have left the warrants implicit and have not represented them in the diagram. Of course, in the argument, if a warrant is asked for, it needs to be provided.

Figure 2.14 represents the argument about the carbon tax in all the complexity we have described earlier. As we will see later in the book, not all the steps of a complex argument will be made explicit, and conversely, the argument could proceed for additional levels beyond those shown here. But for purposes of understanding the argument's structure, seeing what it "looks like," this diagram offers a fair representation.

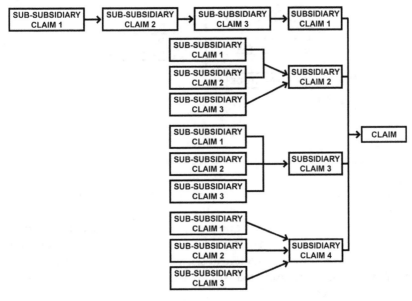

Fig. 2.14

Further Thoughts about Diagrams

We have focused throughout this chapter on diagramming arguments to show their parts and the relationships among them. We have not said much about the assumptions that are built into this activity, and we should do so before leaving the topic.

To begin with, diagrams are *reconstructions* of argument. Put simply, people do not talk in argument diagrams. The diagrams are adapted from conversations, speeches, essays, negotiations, and other forms of discourse. The discourse does not proceed in linear fashion. Steps are omitted; unrelated material is included; there are diversions and digressions; people take things for granted and then circle back and reexamine their assumptions later, and so on. As an example, consider this brief snippet of a conversation:

A: Our baseball team will win the pennant this year!
B: You must be drinking.
A: No, I mean it; this is their year.
B: What are you talking about?
A: Well, they have depth in their pitchers, a strong lineup in every position, and a really good attitude.
B: Give me a break.

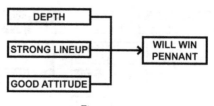

Fig. 2.15

In this example, B's challenges serve as the incentive for A to develop the argument, but aren't themselves part of the argument. A begins with a claim, but A's next turn ("This is their year") adds nothing to the argument and in effect just restates the claim. The evidence is provided only in response to B's further question ("What are you talking about?"). The warrant is left unstated ("Depth in pitching, strength of lineup, and good attitude are strong predictors of success"). Yet when the argument is diagrammed, it is reconstructed to look something like the simple argument in Fig. 2.15.

Not only does the reconstruction omit some of the statements from the conversation and add others, but it neglects entirely the nonverbal aspects of the conversation. For example, imagine different tones of voice in which B might assert, "You must have been drinking." Said with laughter, it will have one connotation. Shouted in anger, it will have another. These connotations are important aspects of the meaning of B's statement and the sort of challenge it is posing to A. Yet the diagrams do not capture these differences. Diagrams represent only the text and hence do not capture all of the argument.

And just as the diagrams do not exactly match the contents of the argument, they also overly systematize the argument. In an actual conversation or essay, for example, it will not always be clear what is the claim, what is the evidence, and what is the warrant. Sometimes there are multiple claims (as in some of the figures above), but the evidence will not be arrayed neatly under the corresponding claim; evidence for one claim may be mixed together with evidence from another. Ordinary discourse is messy, and when arguments are reconstructed by diagramming, the diagrams will impose a degree of order and a system that are not really there.

For these reasons, some instructors believe that diagrams are so misleading that we would be better off not using them as analytical instruments. Yet they are of great value in making clear precisely what is being claimed, what counts as support for it, and where the inferences are. They also prepare us to evaluate whether the argument has met the appropriate standards and hence whether the audience ought to accept the claim. Additionally, diagrams facilitate the use of computer programs to model and test arguments. These are being developed with increasing frequency.

Conclusion

This chapter has focused on the structure of arguments and diagrams to illustrate that structure. In formal logic, the model form of argument is the categorical syllogism, which can be represented using Venn diagrams. But this form of reasoning is limited by the fact that it rearranges what we already know without introducing new information. And it does not enable us to distinguish among degrees of probability and strength; the only qualifiers it recognizes are "all," "none," and "some." For this reason we are well served by a more powerful model of argument.

We can distinguish between simple and complex arguments. Simple arguments are characterized not by their subject matter but by the fact that they put forward a single claim and provide a single level of supporting argumentation. For these arguments we followed suggestions developed by Stephen Toulmin, focusing on the claim that is made on another's belief, the evidence offered in its support, and the warrant that legitimizes making the inference that the evidence *counts as evidence* for the particular claim. If either the evidence or the warrant is contested, then the argumentation continues as additional support is brought forward.

In contrast, the complex argument is characterized by the fact that there will be one or more subsidiary claims, each of which also functions as evidence for the main claim; that these subsidiary claims have supporting statements that also can serve as claims in their own right; and so on. The argument may have a number of supports at each level of analysis. They are connected to the next level in one of three ways: multiple, in which claims are independent of one another and bear independently on the next higher claim; coordinative, in which individual claims are independent of one another but support the next higher claim only when taken together; and subordinative, in which individual claims depend on one another and support the next higher claim only when taken together. There are strategic advantages and drawbacks to each of these possible connections.

There are limitations to diagrams, of course. They are reconstructions of actual arguments rather than exact representations of them. They make explicit factors that often are left implicit; they omit nonverbal elements of the argument that in practice affect its meaning, and they assume a degree of order and system that exceed what is actually present. Although some instructors find these limitations to be reasons to avoid the use of argument diagrams, their analytical value exceeds their limitations.

Now, with an understanding of what arguments look like, we are ready to examine how controversies emerge and develop.

Exercises

1. Place the following statements into the form of a categorical syllogism. Each syllogism will have two premises that together entail a conclusion (that is, if the premises are true, it would be impossible for the conclusion to be false). Remember that the only acceptable quantities associated with any term in the syllogism will be "all," "some," or "none."

   a. My brother says that every single teacher is in it only for the money. He says that since no teachers care whether students get a job, there is no other conclusion if we agree that the only purpose of education is to help students find jobs.

   b. At least a few organisms can survive in the harsh conditions within an active volcano. If there is evidence of life in any place, that place is an ecosystem. Therefore, at least some active volcanoes are ecosystems.

   c. My Uncle Joe is a human being. All human beings have to die someday. I have to come to terms with the fact that someday my Uncle Joe is going to die.

   d. There are no green marbles on the shelf of the toy store, and all of the marbles in the store are on the shelf. This toy store cannot sell me any green marbles.

   e. Some Steven Spielberg movies are kid-friendly. The MPAA certifies that all kid-friendly movies must be rated G or PG. At least some Spielberg movies, it seems, are rated G or PG.

2. In the following examples of short arguments, note the claim, the evidence, and the warrant. In some cases the warrant will be implicit. If so, you should write down what you think would be the strongest warrant (or connection) that would help the evidence to justify the claim.

   a. Bacteria do not necessarily make people sick. Yogurt often contains active bacteria cultures and yet it does not make us sick. If there are examples of bacteria that do not sicken people, then we cannot say that all bacteria cause disease.

  b. Studying the humanities in college should be required. Humanities teach us how to appreciate the beauty of the world. This appreciation is worth more in the long run than any salary or financial benefit.

  c. Some Americans believe that reform of our educational system is the solution to poverty, but if we address only the educational system, we will not be addressing the social issues that are most responsible for creating poverty in the first place. If we do not address the cause of these problems, we cannot solve them.

  d. Increasingly, popular music is more indebted to music producers than to individual players or even composers. Modern music is formed by assembling samples, beats, styles, and instrumental performances into a complex performance. Therefore, we need to find a new way to give credit to producers and assemblers rather than writers and performers.

  e. Since there is strong evidence that the changing climate will have a disastrous effect on the living conditions of Americans over the next fifty years, it is imperative that we begin to elect politicians who are under forty years old and who have children.

3. Diagram each of the arguments in Exercise 2 using the Toulmin model referred to in this chapter. Explain the specific places that will require agreement of the arguing parties if the argument is going to succeed.

4. In each of the following complex arguments, note whether the argument is multiple, coordinative, or subordinative (or some combination). Using the diagramming tools in this chapter, show how the argument can be reconstructed in visual form.

  a. More students should major in history while they are in college. By learning how the structures of society came into being, we can better understand the world we live in. There is no other way to make sense of the contemporary world than to revisit the men and women who shaped our society. Second, history is fascinating. No matter what interests you (peace, war, art, sports, technology, popular culture, etc.), history will allow you to learn more about your interests. There is no need for a historical course of study to be boring to anyone. Third, you will discover that the people of the past are more like you than you might imagine; there are extraordinary people that you discover in history and you will be surprised by how much you can learn from them. Finally, history can be very useful to you in your career, even if you do not work in the field of history itself. As a banker, lawyer, artisan, chef, or psychologist, your knowledge of history will give you the perspective to be better at your job. You may not get rich from studying history but you will be poorer without it.

b.   The "robot revolution" is beginning to transform the way we work. In so doing, it will eventually create a dystopian society with widespread inequality. Therefore, we need immediately to create an international bill of human rights in which we proclaim that the dignity and prosperity of human beings must be maintained or improved by technology. Dignity and equality are the paramount values on which human society must be grounded. If we lose these characteristics, we will lose our humanity to the machines. We are going to see a terrible polarization of people between those who have the education and ability to control or use robots and those who do not. While productivity will rise and the real cost of goods and services may drop, those who are not able to benefit will be far worse off. We must begin today to reimagine a future where robotics and other forms of technology add to human existence.

c.   The rules of American baseball have evolved over the years to take advantage of changing technology, fan interest, fairness, and competition. While there are differences between Major League Baseball and other levels (for example, MLB does not allow metal bats to be used), the rules at the professional level are fairly consistent, with one glaring exception. In the National League, pitchers, like all other players, are entered into the batting order and take their turn at the plate. In the American League, however, the pitcher is not a batter and is replaced by a (presumably) better hitter called the Designated Hitter (DH). The DH rule has been very controversial because it is such a challenge to a game that already carries a fair degree of specialization among players. It puts a premium on developing pitchers who need not bat and gives players who may be defensive liabilities the opportunity to help out with the bat. The original goal of this rule was to allow the teams to generate more offense and score more runs. This higher-scoring baseball would be more entertaining for fans in an era in which baseball seems slow and dowdy compared with high-scoring games such as basketball or football. After many years of watching the American League play with a DH and the National League play without one, it is time that all of baseball should adopt this rule to allow baseball to thrive in the next generation. There are several reasons that this proposal should be adopted. First, pitchers are becoming worse at hitting all the time. This fact makes sense, since pitchers get fewer at-bats than other players since they play only once every five games and are in for only a few innings. In addition, many professional players reach the Majors with only limited experience at hitting. We are seeing increasing specialization and it is unrealistic to imagine that up-and-coming pitchers can be prepared to be effective hitters at the Major League level. The second main reason to bring the DH rule to the National League is that we now have inter-league play. The current system of using the DH in American League parks and not in National League parks is ridiculous. Third, forcing pitchers to bat will lead to unnecessary injuries. Given the value – both strategic and financial – of an ace pitcher, it is reckless to put them at risk for a variety of injuries. Finally, purists have argued that the DH takes one of the most strategic elements of the game away. Managers in the National League often must decide whether to replace a strong pitcher with a pinch hitter, for offensive purposes. The decision-making process has become much less interesting, however. Most of the time the decision is determined by the increasingly statistics-based metrics of the game. If anything, the decisions made by an American League manager can be even more difficult. For all these reasons, it has now become clear that all of Major League Baseball should adopt this rule.

CHAPTER 3

The Emergence of Controversy

In Chapter 2, we examined the structure of simple and complex arguments. But whether the arguments were simple or complex, we treated them in isolation, as if we wanted to show what an argument of one kind or another might look like – as an end in itself. Put another way, we wanted to show how we could express beliefs as different series of related statements.

In "real life," however, arguments do not develop that way. What we argue is related to what others have said or are saying about the matter at hand. This is obviously true when disagreements arise between people. But even when we are formulating arguments without another person present (to write a newspaper editorial or an argumentative essay, for example), we write and speak in a context influenced by our image of what others have said about the subject. Recognizing the interactive nature of argumentation is critical to understanding how it develops and to using the theoretical concepts to be introduced in this chapter.

Argumentation occurs within the context of controversy. So we ought to begin by exploring what controversy is, what sorts of statements cue us that a controversy is present, and how we evaluate controversy.

The Appearance of Controversy

A Definition of Controversy

A *controversy* is a context for communication that is characterized by the following five features:

1. *People recognize that they have a disagreement.* They may have different views about whether a statement is true, what it means, whether it is important, or whether it ought to be discussed. To take a very simple example, imagine that one person believes that interfaith marriages are

likely to fail, whereas another person believes that they are likely to succeed. These two people are in disagreement about the truth of the statements.

2. *The disagreement is not trivial.* Or to state it positively, the outcome of the disagreement matters – at least to the participants, but often to a broader community as well. Imagine that you and your friend disagree about where you should eat dinner tonight. You prefer an Italian restaurant; your friend prefers Chinese. It might make so little difference to you that you could just as well flip a coin, draw straws, or take turns – all outcomes that eliminate controversy. Not every disagreement leads to controversy. But now suppose that you have a strong dislike for Chinese food. Now the disagreement matters to you, and you will be motivated to argue about it. The whole subject still might not matter to anyone other than you and your friend, though. But suppose instead that you are talking about whether the United States should modernize its nuclear weapons. You have different views that reflect your politics and your orientation to national defense. Surely this disagreement is not trivial – not only because it matters to you, but because it matters potentially to everyone in the United States and to those in other countries as well.

3. *Each person desires the assent of the others.* Sometimes when we find ourselves in disagreement, even on important subjects, we really do not care whether others agree with us or not. We very quickly "agree to disagree" and are prepared to go our separate ways. This occurs, for example, when our judgments are based on taste. Our preference for hip-hop music is not affected by another person's preference for soft rock or classical. The adage that "we don't talk about politics or religion" means that we "agree to disagree" about those topics – not because we think they are unimportant but because we place a greater value on maintaining our relationship with the other person and we fear that we might put that at risk by arguing about topics that go to the core of our personal identity. (Other people reject that adage, however, and believe that politics and religion are precisely the topics where we *should* subject our beliefs to argument, lest they harden into prejudice.)

4. *Assent is desired only under the condition that it is freely given.* We don't want to overpower the other person or to bludgeon an audience into submission, because we respect others as human beings and will have more confidence in the outcome of the argumentation if we know

that everyone has reached a conclusion freely, without the application of external force or pressure.

5. *There is no easier way to resolve the dispute.* Arguing is hard. It takes mental and even physical energy and effort; it takes time; it risks generating bad feelings; and it sometimes puts our credibility and respect on the line. Why should we pay these costs if it is not necessary to do so? Sometimes disagreements can be resolved by empirical methods. Or sometimes we can resolve a disagreement by consulting a mutually respected authority and agreeing to accept that person's settlement. The authority might be a document such as the Bible or the US Constitution, or it might be a respected person. Or sometimes we might deduce the outcome from other statements that everyone accepts. The earlier example about where to have dinner might be resolved without arguing if neither party has a great personal stake in the matter. But the example about whether interfaith marriages fail would be harder to resolve without arguing, particularly since there is no universally accepted meaning of "fail" or "succeed"; there probably is no authority who would be respected by all the disputants; and it is unlikely that there are previously made statements that everyone would agree to and from which everyone could deduce the answer.

We explored these characteristics in Chapter 1 as preconditions for argumentation. But it is important also to recognize them as components of controversy, since that is the context in which argumentation occurs. A controversy, in sum, is a significant disagreement that we care about and that is inherently uncertain. We argue about matters that could be otherwise.

Communicative Clues to Controversy

Certain kinds of statements can be taken as clues that a controversy is at least potentially present. Consider the following examples:

1. In October of 2016, Barack Obama was President of the United States.
2. The publisher's price of this textbook is $59.95.
3. The red tie is prettier than the blue one.
4. Our city government is unsatisfactory.
5. Capital punishment is murder.
6. Congress ought to pass the president's budget.

With respect to each of these statements, how would you know whether to accept it if someone asserted it to be true?

Statement 1 is an item of common knowledge; we could imagine ourselves saying, "Well, everyone knows that." If there were any doubt, it could be verified easily. We could look at a newspaper from the month of October 2016 or we could discover in an online encyclopedia that Obama's presidency ran from January 20, 2009, through January 20, 2017. If there were any disagreement, it would exist because someone was wrong – a matter that could be determined quite easily. This statement would not prompt controversy.

Statement 2, while most likely not common knowledge, also is a statement that could be verified easily. The publisher's catalog or website would be accepted by anybody as an authoritative source for the information, and consulting that source would tell us quickly whether the statement is true or false. As with statement 1, there is no need to argue.

Statement 3 is different from the first two in that it presents not a statement of fact but a value judgment. While it can be accepted or rejected, there is no way to verify it empirically. But does this statement matter that much? Most people probably would regard it as an expression of taste, on which we are all entitled to our own judgment. If there is disagreement, it does not have to be resolved. (Of course, we could imagine exceptions. For instance, suppose that the blue tie was a gift from your current romantic partner and the red tie was given to you by someone with whom you recently broke up. Then it would be very important that you and your partner come to an agreement that the blue tie is prettier than the red one, and if you disagreed you most likely would argue about it – maybe vigorously. But this exception does not deny that ordinarily people would regard a preference between colors as a matter on which they could "agree to disagree.")

On the surface, statement 4 appears to resemble statement 3. It too expresses a value judgment, in this case about whether our city government is satisfactory or not. Can it too be considered an expression of taste? Probably not, because the implications of this statement are far greater than the choice of a tie. It would not make sense, for example, to say, "You think the city government is OK; I don't; and so we'll just leave it at that." The very term "unsatisfactory" implies the judgment that something should be done about it. And the reference to "city government" suggests that this is not a private or personal matter; it has effects that spread throughout the population. So statement 4 is one that, if questioned, *would* be worth arguing about. Each party to the conversation would want to justify his or her beliefs and attempt to influence the belief or action of others. In the course of doing so, the participants would address questions such as "What do we mean by 'unsatisfactory'?" "What is it that is wrong?" "How did this defect come about?" "Can we do anything about it?" and so on.

Statement 5 is also deceptively simple on its face. It could be taken as a tautology (a statement that is true by definition) since capital punishment is killing a person, and killing a person is murder. But it will quickly become apparent that, if questioned, this statement is really something of an index of people's beliefs about the justifiability of capital punishment. Supporters of capital punishment will be unlikely to accept the statement that capital punishment is murder, whereas those who favor abolishing capital punishment will be quick to agree with the statement. The term "murder" is being used here for its connotations rather than for its precision. To supporters of capital punishment, "murder" will mean something like "unjustified or unwarranted killing," whereas killing that has the sanction of the state, the society, and the law will fall into another category altogether. There is no point in arguing about which is the "right" definition of "murder," because definitions are matters of usage, not intrinsic rightness. Rather, it should become apparent to the disputants that this statement is really a more intense form of a statement like "Capital punishment is unjustified." On that statement there is very likely to be argument, since people have different judgments about the matter, their judgments are extremely consequential, and there is no way to verify the matter empirically. (There are empirical questions involved, to be sure, but they do not settle the issue.) One advocate might suggest, for example, that empirically capital punishment has been shown not to deter heinous crime, implying that capital punishment is unjustified, only to have another advocate respond that deterring crime is not really capital punishment's purpose. So statement 5, which on the surface is a mere matter of definition, turns out to be a substitute form of a statement that is highly controversial and very much open to argumentation.

Finally, statement 6 is the clearest example of a statement that, if questioned, would open a controversy inviting argumentation. It responds to a disagreement that is important, that needs to be resolved, and that cannot be resolved by easier means. Without congressional action on a budget, the government will grind to a halt, as has happened on several occasions in the United States since the mid-1990s. Essential services will be disrupted and payments delayed. Whether the president's budget is the one that ought to be passed will invite competing claims about the merits of the president's proposals and those of the opposition party. All participants in the discussion will have a stake in answering the question, but they will answer it differently and therefore will need to justify their claims in an attempt to influence others.

These six statements illustrate the circumstances under which controversy develops. A statement is asserted. It may be accepted without question, in which case the discussion ceases. It may be rejected without question, in which the parties indicate that they are not open to considering the matter further. Or it may be questioned or challenged, in the hope that the person making the statement will be motivated to defend or justify it and that the different parties might reach agreement on the matter. This will happen when the parties disagree, when they believe that the disagreement matters, when they desire to convince the other party, when they desire the other party's assent only if it is freely given, and when there is no easier way to resolve the dispute.

Sometimes controversies can be resolved quickly, but sometimes they go on for a very long time. This can happen when previously widely believed assumptions are challenged and eventually overturned. For example, it took more than a century to decide whether earlier beliefs about race relations in the United States should be modified, and while there have been significant changes, this controversy is not over yet. Sometimes, in fact, the same controversial subjects present themselves again and again, even if on different topics and in slightly different form. In the United States, for example, the dividing line between the rights of the states and the duties of the federal government has been controversial since the founding of the government and remains so today with regard to such topics as education, health care, and the direction of the economy. Some philosophical controversies can be regarded as *essentially contested* because, by their nature, they never can be resolved.

Even though some controversies go on for a long time, controversy is not necessarily a bad thing. Controversies open up alternative possibilities and render problematic what we might have thought to be settled conclusions. They remind us that things we thought to be true could be otherwise, and thereby they open up new ways of thinking. They also make clear the implications of taking one choice rather than another. They expose ideas and viewpoints that, even if not immediately acceptable, may ultimately prevail. And, of course, controversies remind us that the world is complex, so that we can be careful not to reach conclusions prematurely and not to hold them so rigidly that we close ourselves off to new information or ideas.

Still, we don't want all controversies to go on all the time. Controversies do end, and a variety of conditions cause them to be settled. Sometimes they end because the participants reach a common understanding or judgment, as in diplomatic negotiations. Sometimes they end because time has run out and a third party renders a judgment that the arguers have agreed to accept, as in an election campaign or in a courtroom. And sometimes a controversy is overtaken by events that make it no longer important; we say that such controversies are *moot*. In the years preceding World War II, for instance, there was a great controversy over whether the United States should be actively involved in world affairs or whether it should take an isolationist position. Pearl Harbor rendered that conflict moot, and isolationism was not seriously discussed thereafter. Similarly, the end of the Cold War in the late 1980s has rendered some argument positions moot. And sometimes there is a conceptual breakthrough that results in looking at the situation in a whole new way, such as whether a tax cut is a good thing or a bad thing as economic conditions change.

Issues, Claims, Resolutions, and *Topoi*

The controversy can be stated in the form of a question: Should we accept the truth of *x*? What do we mean by *x*? Why should we believe *x*? What should we do about *x*? As you may have noticed, each of these questions implies subsidiary questions that must be answered in order to be able to answer the main question of the controversy. For example, in order to answer whether Congress should pass the president's budget, we would need to know such things as: What is the country's current financial situation? Are there needs that cannot be met without approval of the president's budget? Would approval of the president's budget improve our economic picture? and so on. In order to answer whether capital punishment is murder or not, we would need to know what are the conditions that count as murder and whether or not capital punishment satisfies those conditions.

The Issues

These subsidiary questions are called *issues*. Often we use the term "issue" very loosely to mean any sort of dispute. When a supervisor tells a staff member, "Don't make an issue of it," the meaning is roughly the same as "Don't argue about it." But the term *issue* has a more specific meaning in argumentation theory. *Issues are those questions that inhere in the controversy and are vital to an advocate's success.*

There are two key ideas in this definition. The first is that issues inhere in the controversy. This means that they derive naturally from it; as soon as you raise the question in controversy, you are led naturally to the issues it poses. Breaking a large question into its component steps will lead you to identify the issues. They are not some formula that is imposed on the controversy or something completely external to it.

Second, the issues are vital to the advocate's success. This means simply that if you wish to prevail in the controversy, you must respond successfully to the issues. If, for example, you wish to advocate that Congress should pass the president's budget but cannot show that the president's budget will meet our current economic conditions, you are not likely to prevail. Likewise, if you wish to show that our city government is unsatisfactory, you will not be able to do that if you fail to establish and defend some criterion for what counts as satisfactory. Because issues are so important, one of the first steps in analyzing a controversy is to determine what the issues are, so that you will be prepared to speak to them.

Claims and Resolutions

As we saw in Chapter 2, *claims* are statements that the arguer makes and that the audience is asked to accept. They are assertions that, ordinarily, the arguer believes to be true and hopes that the audience will believe them to be true as well. (In some circumstances, such as a lawyer assigned to defend a client or a school debate in which the sides are preassigned, the arguer may role-play a person committed to the truth of the assertion.)

Claims can be understood as proposed answers to the questions that frame the issues. If, for example, the controversy is about whether the president's budget should be adopted and the issues are (a) are the financial needs of the country accurately stated? (b) are the needs met? and (c) are we better off? then claims might include (a) the president's budget correctly assesses the country's financial needs, (b) the budget provides resources to meet the high-priority needs, and (c) by assuring financial stability, the proposed budget will leave us better off.

The main claim in a controversy is sometimes called the *resolution*. Just as the subsidiary claims are answers to questions posed by the issues, the resolution will answer the overarching question posed by the controversy. If the controversy is about "Should the president's budget be adopted?" the resolution might be, "The president's budget should be adopted."

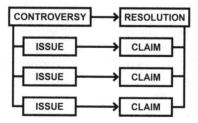

Fig. 3.1

Sometimes the resolution will be a formal statement that can be inspected by all (such as "Resolved: The president's proposed budget for 2022 should be adopted"). But often the resolution is inferred from statements that the arguers make. Even when it is inferred rather than stated explicitly, there should be little trouble to discern what it is.

The relationship among controversy, issues, claims, and the resolution is illustrated in Fig. 3.1. In applying this figure, we can proceed in either direction. The explanation above suggests that we begin with a controversy, derive questions from it, answer the questions by framing claims, and sum those claims into a resolution. But we also could work with the other way, beginning with a statement of the resolution and working our way back to find out what the ultimate controversy is.

Types of Claims

There are four basic types of claims (and, similarly, four types of resolutions): fact, definition, value, and policy. They do different kinds of work. Claims of *fact* involve description of reality. They assert that something is the case. In theory, they can be verified independently of the arguers. If there is a controversy about whether or not something is the case, there presumably is a way to find out that goes beyond the argumentation itself.

But matters are not quite so simple. Claims of fact can be located in the past or the future as well as the present. So they may assert what *was* or what *will be* the case, as well as what *is*. Historical claims can be verified, so long as records are kept. For example, if someone asserts, "All US presidents elected in the twentieth century won both the popular vote and the electoral vote," the claim can be verified by consulting records of vote tabulations. On the other hand, claims about the future – even though they deal with matters of fact – cannot be verified. The statement "The president will be re-elected next time," cannot be determined to be true or false by means other than argument – at least, not until after Election Day. In this respect, claims of future fact are just like claims of definition, value, and policy: it is the strength of the argument, not some independent means of verification, that will determine whether we should accept them as true.

Suppose we are dealing with the claim of past fact, "All US presidents elected in the twentieth century won both the popular vote and the electoral vote." In a discussion of this claim, someone might say, "Wait a minute. In the election of 2000, Al Gore won the popular vote but George W. Bush won the electoral vote." Is this a relevant objection?

The answer depends on what the phrase "the twentieth century" means, and this raises the second type of claim: a claim of *definition*, which concerns meaning or interpretation. In the Bush–Gore case, the question is what the temporal boundaries of the twentieth century are. This may seem like a straightforward matter, but actually it involves a difference of interpretation. Some people believe that the twentieth century ended on December 31, 2000. After all, they reason, there was no "year zero," so the first hundred years were not finished until December 31, 100. Proceeding in the same fashion, they would determine that the twentieth century ended at the end of the year 2000. The reason this matters for our purposes is that by this interpretation, the Bush–Gore election would fall within the twentieth century and this would mean that our claim of past fact was false. For other people, the twentieth century ended on December 31, 1999, when the third digit from the right changed on the calendar (from "9" to "0"). Such people might point out that in fact the world observed not just the turn of the century but the turn of the millennium at the end of 1999, thereby indicating that common usage was in their favor. By this standard, the Bush–Gore election was the first of the twenty-first century rather than the last of the twentieth, and the claim of past fact would be true.

So which is right? There is no way to say, other than by selecting one interpretation over the other. And that is what the argument will seek to do. The dispute is not about a set of facts but about how we should understand or interpret reality. In the election case, we might say that it is "just" a matter of usage, that we might arbitrarily pick one standard or the other and go from there. But definitions are not neutral; often the choice of one definition over another will bring with it a quite different collection of values, priorities, and judgments. Perhaps the most obvious example is the dispute between those who regard abortion as a therapeutic medical

procedure and those who regard it as murder. The choice between interpretations is extremely consequential, and this perhaps is why abortion has
been a subject of such intense controversy since at least the 1970s.

The third type of claim is the claim of *value* involving judgment.
Judgment involves an appraisal or evaluation. Among the objects for
judgment are people, things, activities, and situations, ranging from the
trivial to the highly consequential. The earlier statement, "The red tie is
better than the blue one," is a claim of judgment, but one that most people
would not consider very important. "Our most basic responsibility is the
care of the earth," on the other hand, is a value claim that will have
significant implications for the relative importance of environmental protection and economic development.

Claims of value can be further divided across two main dimensions.
First, they can be either *absolute* or *comparative*. Absolute value claims
assert that something is good or bad in itself. "Racism is deplorable" is a
simple example of an absolute value claim. But often controversies are not
about whether something is good or bad in the abstract, but whether it is
better or worse than something else. Opposing values may both be
desirable and yet we may be forced to choose between them. The statement "It is better to light a candle than to curse the darkness," is an
example of a comparative value claim. So too is a statement such as
"Extracting fossil fuels is a higher priority than protecting endangered
species on public lands."

Moreover, value claims can be *terminal* or *instrumental*. Terminal value
claims are about ends; instrumental value claims are about means to other
ends. "Energy independence is a valuable objective" would be an example
of a terminal value claim, whereas "Energy independence is better than
interdependence as a means to promote world peace" would be an example
of an instrumental value claim. (The fact that the former claim is also
absolute whereas the latter is comparative is coincidental.)

Often, value claims involve considerations that are not just good or bad
in themselves, but also are good or bad in their implications for how we
might act on them. In this respect value claims share some features with
the final category we will discuss, claims of *policy*. These are claims about
action; they are statements about what should or should not be done. They
are characteristic of formal deliberative bodies such as Congress or the state
legislature, but they also emerge in discussions among informal groups of
people trying to reach decisions about what the group should do, or even
an individual deliberating with himself or herself. "We should go to the
Italian restaurant for dinner tonight" is a policy claim, as is "The university

should switch to the semester system," "The federal government should invest more heavily in education," or "The European Union should be dissolved." The differences among these examples involve the stakes in the controversy, not the type of claim that is being advanced. Just as value claims often will raise issues about policy as a consideration in selecting values, so policy claims often will raise issues about values as a consideration in selecting policies. But the two types of claims are different.

Topoi

Why, you might wonder, is it important to distinguish types of claims in the manner we have just described? The answer is that different types of claims give rise to different types or patterns of issues, so that if we know what type of claim we are dealing with, we will have gone a long way toward determining what sorts of statements we must prove in order to establish it.

Types or patterns of issues are called *topoi*, a Greek term which means "places" (the singular is *topos*, place). The places are not literal but metaphorical: they are "places in the mind" to which one might imagine going in order to find the issues for the given claim. They might be thought of as an aid to discovery, in the same way that a mnemonic device is an aid to memory. Also, *topoi* are not the particular issues themselves; they are general categories or patterns of issues.

Perhaps an example will clarify matters. Consider the claim, "The national debt should be increased." An issue that would naturally arise is something like "Is the current level of debt not high enough?" This is a specific example of the category, "Is there a problem?" and that category is a *topos*. The fact that it is one of the *topoi* for claims of policy helps us to know, once we have a policy claim before us, that we should look for one or more examples of that *topos*.

What, then, are *topoi* for different types of claims? For claims of fact, we want to know what the criteria are for determining truth, and whether the criteria have been satisfied by the claim that is being put forward. In the case of claims of definition, the key *topoi* are whether the interpretation put forward is relevant to the situation, whether it is fair, and how we ought to choose among competing interpretations. For claims of value, we will find as *topoi* how we determine good and bad, whether the allegation that something is good or bad is warranted, whether there are competing or offsetting considerations, whether the value has been applied properly to the specific situation, and (sometimes) which among competing values

Table 3.1 *Topoi for each type of claim*

Fact	Definition	Value	Policy
• What are criteria?	• Is the definition relevant?	• How to decide good or bad?	• Is there a problem?
• Are they satisfied?	• Is it fair?	• Is it good or bad?	• What is to blame?
	• How to choose between competing definitions?	• Are there competing considerations?	• Will the proposal work?
		• Applied correctly to situation?	• Are we better off?
		• Which value is better?	

should be preferred. Finally, with respect to policy claims, the key *topoi* are whether there is a problem, whether responsibility for the problem is properly located, whether there is a possible solution to the problem, and whether the solution will leave us better off. (These four policy *topoi* are sometimes abbreviated as ill, blame, cure, and cost.) The *topoi* for each of the types of claims are summarized in Table 3.1.

The concept of *topoi* serves two principal purposes, in sum. First, it is like a shortcut to identifying the issues on a given claim. It is an aid to what the ancients called "invention," by which they meant identifying the available means of persuasion and selecting among them. The knowledge that *topoi* correspond to types of claims is a significant help in this regard. Second, referring to the *topoi* enables us to check whether we have a complete understanding of the relevant issues. If, for example, we know that one of the *topoi* on a policy claim is "Is there a solution?" and we know we are dealing with a policy claim, but we have not yet come up with any issue related to determining a possible solution, that set of circumstances will tell us that we still have more analytical work to do.

Stasis, Presumption, and Burden of Proof

Identifying the issues, claims, resolutions, and *topoi* is crucial to understanding the dynamics of a controversy, but another set of steps is equally important. These terms and concepts will tell us more precisely what the controversy is about and whose responsibility it is to prevail in the end.

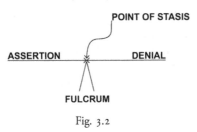

Fig. 3.2

Stasis

Stasis is a Greek term that means "rest" or "equilibrium." That doesn't seem to have anything to do with what we are talking about, but again we need to think metaphorically rather than literally. The center of a storm or the eye of a hurricane is, paradoxically, a space of calm even though there are immense forces swirling around it. When two opposing forces meet, similarly, there is just a moment of calm before the explosive impact is felt. So it is with two opposing arguments, where the imagined moment of calm identifies the fulcrum point on which the ensuing argument will balance. Identifying this point precisely will enable us to know the question that must be settled in order to end the dispute. It will tell us precisely what the controversy is. This explanation is illustrated in Fig 3.2.

This may be clearer if we depart from the world of metaphor and consider a simple example. Suppose two people encounter each other on the street and person A exclaims, "You stole my car!" Person B is taken aback by this flagrant accusation, but after a second recovers his composure and says, "No; I never even had your car." Now this accusation and response frame a controversy around the question, "Did B have possession of the car?" This is a case of *stasis in conjecture.* The central question is "Is it?" or "Did the act occur?"

Now suppose a slightly different case. Person A again accuses, "You stole my car!" But now suppose B replies, "No; I borrowed it." In this case the controversy does not center on whether the act occurred – B does not contest that he had the car – but on what we ought to call the act. This is *stasis in definition,* and the central question is "*What* is it?" or "What should we call the act?" If A follows up with more reasons to believe that B had possession of the car, those reasons will not be relevant to the way in which B's response has focused the controversy, which made it a question of what we should call the act of possession. Obviously, whether we call it theft or borrowing will make a big difference, even though the act of possession is not itself in dispute.

Consider now a third example. Person A asserts, "You stole my car!" Now suppose B says something like "Yes, and it's a good thing too. Person C had fallen on the ice on your sidewalk which you had not cleared, and if I had not gotten her to the hospital right away in your car, she would have suffered serious brain damage for which you would be liable." In this case, B's response focuses the controversy on whether the act was justified, not on whether it occurred or what it should be called. This is called *stasis in quality* and it raises the question of whether the act is justified. In this example, B is maintaining that the act of stealing the car was justified by the extenuating circumstances in the situation, namely the urgent need to get C to the hospital.

Finally, imagine that when A accuses B of stealing the car, B's response is "Look, let's not discuss this matter out on the street. Car theft is a criminal offense. If you think you have a case against me, then prosecute. I'll see you in court." This is a different sort of response entirely. It ignores (neither conceding nor disputing) the questions of whether the act occurred, what it should be called, and whether or not it was justified. Instead the allegation is that A and B are not in the right place to conduct the argument. Here the use of "place" is literal (on the street vs. in the courtroom), but *stasis in place* can involve any kind of jurisdictional question. "This is a matter for the legislature, not the courts," "This is a private matter that does not raise any public issues," "I don't make the policy; I just carry it out," and "Take it to City Hall" are all examples in which stasis deals with place. Unlike the other three stases, place raises jurisdictional questions and asks if we are in the right forum to discuss the substantive issues.

Several characteristics of the concept of stasis are worth noticing:

1. It is the interaction of assertion and denial that determines the stasis, not either alone. It obviously can't be the assertion alone, because the assertion, "You stole my car," was common to all four of the stasis situations. And the statements of denial – such as "No, I borrowed it" – would not mean anything except as responses to an assertion like the one put forward. Because it depends on the interaction of asser-tion and denial, the concept of stasis enables us to eliminate from consideration a large number of potential issues. These are issues that could have been raised but were not. Had they been, they would have been essential to resolving the controversy. But since they were waived

from consideration, they need not be addressed further. So the concept of stasis can be employed to keep the number of issues manageable.

2. We saw that there were three substantive stases (conjecture, definition, and quality) and one procedural stasis (place). Generally, the substantive stases are progressive. In other words, to select a stasis in definition implicitly grants the opponent's claim in conjecture, and to select stasis in quality implicitly grants the opponent's claim in both conjecture and definition. This was very clear in the car theft example. To claim that the car was borrowed rather than stolen implicitly concedes that the car was in the arguer's possession. To claim that the theft of the car was justified implicitly claims both that the arguer had it and that it was stolen. Given a choice among multiple stases, then, the general advice would be to select one as close as possible to the beginning of the chain, provided that it can be sustained. If the respondent can establish that he never had possession of the car, then there is no need to even get into the question of whether it was stolen or borrowed, or the question of whether the action was justified. It is also possible to select multiple stases, using a conditional or "even-if" kind of argument. For example the respondent might say, "First of all, I never had possession of your car, but if I had, it would have been justified." In this case it is clear that the primary stasis is one of conjecture. At the same time the respondent is "covering her bets" by saying that even if she turns out not to carry her claim in response to the conjectural stasis, she still has another possible line of attack – namely, that the act would have been justified. But what one would not want to do is to take advantage of the progressive nature of stasis by moving from one to another. It would severely strain one's credibility if one were to say, for example, "I never had possession of the car," and then, after it had been demonstrated that in fact he did have it, he then said, "Oh, I guess you're right, but I borrowed it rather than stole it," and then he moved to stasis in quality after having lost the definitional argument. One could justly wonder whether the respondent held any of these positions sincerely.

3. Stasis in place generally is preemptive. In other words, if jurisdictional questions are raised, these will need to be resolved before it makes sense to address the substantive ones. Until we are in the proper forum for addressing an issue, there is no point to begin discussing it. Questions of place therefore can play a great role in determining how a controversy will be talked about.

4. The initial assertion also is influential. One can, for example, shape an assertion in order to prompt a particular response, which then will help to identify the stasis.

Presumption and Burden of Proof

Application of stasis theory will enable us to pinpoint precisely what is in dispute. But having done that, we still need to know how the controversy will go forward and whose responsibility it is to resolve it in his or her favor. Will the claim fail unless I predominate with arguments in its favor, or will it succeed unless you predominate with arguments against it? The answer to these questions depends on the interrelated concepts of presumption and burden of proof. Before we proceed to explain and apply these concepts, it's worth noting that they are mirror images of each other: the party bearing the burden of proof is the party without presumption, and the party enjoying presumption is the party without the burden of proof.

Presumption does not mean "presumptuousness" or "arrogance." It refers to what we presume to be correct unless and until we are shown otherwise. It is the position that would prevail if there were no controversy and no argumentation. This does not mean that it truly is correct, but that it will occupy the argumentative ground until good reason is given to the contrary. It could be said that presumption is a statement of the "default" position.[1]

The concept of presumption performs several functions in argumentation theory. First, it determines who must initiate a dispute – the party who does not enjoy presumption. The party with presumption need not start off the argument, because his or her position will prevail in the absence of any argument. Consider as an example an idea that has been floated from time to time, that the President of the United States should be elected by direct popular vote. This idea resurfaced after the 2016 presidential election because the winning candidate did not win the popular vote. In the absence of a concerted effort to change things, the president will not be elected by direct popular vote. That is not the situation that would prevail in the absence of any argument. Rather, the presumption is the continued existence of the Electoral College and the procedures

---

[1] The standard work on presumption is Richard Whately, *Elements of Rhetoric*, originally published in 1828. Various editions exist.

currently used to allocate and select electors. This may be a badly flawed system or it may be a good one, but in the absence of argument that would provide cause for change, it will continue to be the way we elect presidents in the future.

Second, presumption provides a minimal standard of proof that must be met in order for the controversy to proceed. Suppose, for example, that there is a presumption in favor of efforts to limit the risks of climate change. Now suppose an advocate maintains that there are no risks to climate change, and indeed that "climate change" is a hoax. Now the question is: Does the assertion that climate change is a hoax set aside the presumption in favor of efforts to control it? Many would say no, citing the overwhelming judgment of scientists that climate change is a reality, and insisting that a single assertion to the contrary is hardly sufficient to dislodge this presumption. Others might say that, whether the allegation that climate change is a hoax is a strong or weak allegation, it is sufficient to set aside the presumption – at least until it is effectively answered.

Third, presumption provides a decision rule to be invoked when the considerations on each side appear to be approximately equal. We are not talking about precise measurement here, but about a situation in which, after the arguments are presented, attacked, or defended, there is no particular reason to favor one side or another. In such a case, we would conclude that the presumption has not been effectively countered, and so we would side with the party enjoying the presumption. This situation presents itself oftener than we might think. We know that one of the strongest factors influencing a vote in national elections is party identification. Most people who grew up in Republicrat households will think of themselves as Republicrats and will vote for Republicrat candidates. They will consider the merits of the candidates individually, but if they find the candidates to be about equally strong or weak, they will vote for the Republicrat because that is their default position. To such people, Republicrats have the presumption and that is the basis for their vote. (Of course, it is equally true that many people have a presumptive political identity as Demoblicans and will support Demoblican candidates unless the presumption in their favor is overturned.)

Some theorists of argumentation have distinguished between natural and artificial presumptions. Natural presumptions are those existing in nature, whereas artificial presumptions are stipulated by people in order to enhance certain values or beliefs. For instance, especially in Western democracies, many believe that people are by their nature free. If one holds this belief, then one could say that there is a natural presumption in favor of human freedom (or to state the matter negatively, that there is a natural presumption against efforts to restrict human freedom). Of course, there are societies without this commitment to human freedom, and in those societies there would not be a natural presumption in favor of human freedom at all.

Another frequently suggested natural presumption is against paradoxes. In societies influenced by Aristotle's law of non-contradiction (for example, a person cannot be a free man and a slave at the same time), a paradox is a puzzle to be explained and worked out, not an ambiguous condition to be accepted. Presented with a paradox, such a person will presume that there is something wrong with it, something that has to be explained for the seeming inconsistency to resolve itself. A person who holds such a view will accept that the situation really is a paradox only after all attempts to work out the paradox have come to naught. We must remember, however, that individuals in many societies, and some Westerners like the poet Walt Whitman, do not embrace the presumption against paradoxes. Whitman wrote, "Do I contradict myself? / Very well then, I contradict myself. / I am large; I contain multitudes." A person who holds that contradictions are a normal part of nature surely would not agree that there is a natural presumption against paradox.

Possibly the most controversial candidate for the status of natural presumption is the statement by the nineteenth-century archbishop Richard Whately that there is a presumption in favor of existing institutions.[2] His reason was that "since change is not a good in itself, he who favors change must show cause for it." In other words, Whately asserted that people were naturally conservative, not inclined to change unless they were given good reason to do so. Whately's own politics were conservative, and he wished to forestall the efforts toward reform of the British government that were underway during the 1820s and 1830s. Cynics have suggested that Whately may have been developing his theory of argumentation in order to serve his own political goals rather than to advance academic understanding.

After all, one might reply, while change is not a good in itself, neither is stability. Sometimes it is change that must be argued for; sometimes it is refusal to change that must be argued for. In the United States, for example, there is a strong commitment to eliminating vestiges of officially

---

[2] Whately, *Elements of Rhetoric*, part I, chapter III, §2.

sanctioned racial discrimination. So even if such vestiges could be described as part of existing institutions, they would not enjoy presumption.

On reflection, trying to justify a presumption in favor of existing institutions on the basis that there is risk in change is at odds with our initial warning that presumption is not an evaluative concept, just a default position. It might be more accurate to say that, if there is a presumption in favor of existing institutions, it is only because they are existing – and in the absence of contrary argument, they will continue to exist. Inertia, not principle, becomes the basis for locating this presumption.

More generally, this discussion may cast doubt on whether there is any such thing as a natural presumption. Some philosophers have maintained that reality is not a "given." It is out there, but how we perceive it is undoubtedly influenced by our frame of reference, our beliefs, and our values. We may call something a natural presumption because it serves our interests to do so, but in expressing these interests we are stipulating a particular view of the world. For example, in criminal law we stipulate a presumption in favor of innocence, because we want to express the value that it is worse to convict the innocent than to allow the guilty to go free. In retailing we stipulate that "the customer is always right" and we provide for a three-day grace period during which a person who has made a major purchase can change his or her mind, because we want to acknowledge that people may change their view of a prospective purchase once they have paid for it. And we require environmental impact statements before permits are given for new construction projects, because we want to express the judgment that protecting the environment is a primary concern.

In line with this concern, it may make more sense to stipulate that presumption rests against the specific resolution being advanced. This assignment of presumption determines the responsibilities of the advocates but does not impose judgments about any of the substantive questions under discussion. On this view, for example, if the resolution were, "The Second Amendment establishes an individual right to own guns," the presumption would be that it does not, and the existence of such an individual right would need to be justified. But if the resolution were, "The Second Amendment establishes that only members of the militia may own guns," then the presumption would be that the Second Amendment does not restrict gun ownership to the militia and that there is, in fact, an individual right to own guns. As these competing examples should make clear, it is not one's own politics or ideology that determines where presumption should be placed; it is the function of the concept in analyzing the controversy.

One of the hardest questions to answer about presumption is "How strong is it?"

The answer relates to the level of risk involved in being wrong. Suppose, for example, that a medical scientist advocates bringing to the market a new drug that in clinical trials has been shown to be effective 99.9 percent of the time, but in the remaining one case out of a thousand has led to serious injury or death of the patient. Even this 99.9 percent success rate may not be strong enough to overcome the presumption against doing harm. But very few cases of argumentation are like this. Ordinarily, presumption can be overcome by presenting arguments that a reasonable person would find acceptable unless they are countered. In fact, there is a term for such a set of arguments: a prima facie case. The Latin *prima facie* translates as "first appearance" and suggests that the arguments on initial inspection are strong enough to seem convincing unless something were said in response to them. This does not mean that they necessarily are winning arguments, of course. It just means that the other party no longer can rest on the fact that he or she enjoys presumption, but will now need to answer the arguments that have been advanced.

From what we have discussed about presumption, it should not be difficult to understand the concept of burden of proof, because it is the opposite. It is the responsibility ultimately to defend the resolution under discussion, to show that the statement it embodies is true. Like presumption, it is not a substantive matter. It is not that an advocate for human rights would have a burden of proof but that an advocate for economic growth would not – or the reverse. It is not the subject matter or political ideology that determines who holds the burden of proof; it is the advocate's relationship to the resolution. The advocate without presumption holds the burden of proof, and, like presumption, it does not shift back and forth during the course of the dispute.

What we here are calling the burden of proof is analogous to the persuasion burden in law. It is the responsibility ultimately to convince a judge or jury that one's position is sound. In a criminal case, for example, it always rests with the prosecution. Whether the accused is in fact guilty or not, he or she is presumed to be innocent, because of the value judgment stated earlier, that it is better to let the guilty go free than to convict the innocent. If the presumption of innocence is relatively weak because of the circumstances of the given case, the prosecution will have an easier time discharging the persuasion burden. Just so in any argumentative situation: the strength or weakness of the presumption will determine how easy it is for the advocate with the burden of proof to discharge it.

The reason that the concept of burden of proof sometimes seems complicated is that it is often confused with two other closely related and similar-sounding terms. One is the burden of rejoinder, or as it is sometimes called, the burden of going forward with the debate. Once the burden of proof initially has been met, this burden comes into play. The party enjoying presumption now has to respond to the arguments that satisfied the burden of proof. It will not do to say, "Too bad, we have presumption," or anything like that. Moreover, the arguments that this party now puts forward must be truly responsive to the arguments that met the burden of proof; they must answer them. Once these responses are on the table, the burden of rejoinder then shifts back to the person who initially had the burden of proof. In similar fashion, the burden of rejoinder shifts back and forth between advocates until the controversy is resolved, a third party renders a decision, or time runs out.

The burden of rejoinder is analogous to the production burden in law, the responsibility to produce evidence in response to the opposition. The production burden shifts back and forth as the competing lawyers advance their cases. In ordinary argumentation, the party enjoying presumption (the antagonist) meets this responsibility by challenging the justification that has been put forward on at least one of the issues, and the party with the burden of proof (the protagonist) meets this responsibility by offering justification for each of the issues that has been challenged.

The other term related to burden of proof is the burden of proving assertions, which is sometimes expressed in the saying, "He who asserts must prove." During the course of the dispute, each participant is likely to make assertions expressing what he or she believes to be true. If the other party questions the assertion, the person who made it is responsible for providing the evidence that would prove it. Suppose, for example, that the resolution being discussed calls for universal voter registration on Election Day. Opposing that resolution, an advocate asserts that there is widespread voter fraud. The opponent who made that assertion has the responsibility to prove it – even though, in this case, it is the other advocate who ultimately has the burden of proof. Put simply, the fact that you have presumption does not mean that you can make wild assertions and expect your opponent to have to disprove them. Each party in a dispute is responsible for the assertions that he or she makes, regardless of where presumption and the burden of proof may lie.

It may strike you that this discussion of presumption and burden of proof is somewhat theoretical. We have discussed what the terms mean and how they are assigned in the abstract, as an analyst of a particular dispute might assign them. But actual argumentation does not always meet the standards a theorist might impose. Just as parties may not always structure their arguments in the ways we diagrammed in Chapter 2, they may not always understand presumption and burden of proof as we have described them here. Because, other things being equal, it is strategically more valuable to enjoy the presumption than to shoulder the burden of proof, in practice advocates will jockey for presumption or will try to enshrine it in their favor, foisting the burden of proof onto their adversary. There are several ways of doing this. For example, in a discussion on the question, "What should we do about health care?" the advocate who offers a proposal first is likely to dominate the agenda. True, in putting forward a specific resolution, he or she takes on the burden of proof for that resolution. But by offering it first, he or she establishes a presumption that, out of all the possible answers to the question of "what should we do," this is the one that will be the focus of attention.

Another way advocates try to capture presumption is by equating their preferred position with some value that is generally held to be very positive. For instance, advocates for privatizing Social Security in the early 2000s appealed to the value of ownership. Just as it was considered a good thing to own one's home, so it would be good if individuals "owned" the Social Security account that helped to finance their retirement. Even though these advocates were the ones defending the resolution that Social Security should be privatized, they tried to shift the burden of proof by suggesting that it was really "government ownership" of retirement accounts that needed to be justified.

A third example of attempts to capture presumption involves the use of a "question-begging epithet" to characterize the opponent's position – referring to it, for example, as "that sexist proposal." Sexism, like racism, nativism, religious bigotry, and other forms of prejudice, is rightly regarded as an extremely negative value. No one wants to be put in the position of defending sexism or acknowledging that his or her proposal is sexist in nature. Even though the person making the accusation of sexism theoretically has the responsibility to defend it, the value is so negative that the person who is accused of sexism will feel a strong responsibility to disprove the charge – and thereby take on a burden that, in theory, belongs to the person who advanced the charge. In an era that has been called one of "identity politics," where many public issues revolve around matters of personal identity, it is not surprising that charges of racism, sexism, and the like occur frequently – partly because individuals are more sensitive to these conditions and partly because there is strategic value in associating the other person's position with such disfavored terms.

These examples illustrate ways in which the actual practice of argumentation can fall short of theoretical ideals. Gaps between theory and practice are not unique to this subject, of course; we will find them throughout this book. Our twin objectives are to understand the nature of argumentation and to improve its practice. Instances that fall short of what theory calls for can be reconstructed in terms of theoretical requirements, just as we saw with argument diagrams, so that we can understand the dispute from the perspective of argumentation theory.

Exercises

1. For each of the following subjects listed below, apply the five conditions for controversy (disagreement, it is not trivial, each party desires assent, assent must be freely given, no easier way to resolve). Determine whether the issue is a controversy, and give the best one-sentence statement of each of two sides for each issue that you determine is a controversy.
   a. The right to have an abortion in the United States
   b. Climate change caused by human activity since the industrial revolution
   c. The right of private citizens to own guns in the United States
   d. The rights of political refugees to enter the European Union or the United States
   e. The concussion crisis facing tackle football
   f. Cute puppies
   g. Whether toilet paper is dispensed over or under the roll
   h. The legal drinking age
   i. Whether it is healthier to be a vegetarian
   j. Dress codes in public schools
2. Choose a dispute that is covered by local media in your hometown or on your campus. Analyze it to see whether it can be considered a controversy. Can you find the stasis of the argument?
3. For each of the following examples of argumentative claims, (1) determine whether the claim is one of fact, definition, value, or policy, and (2) list the specific *topoi* that would be used to determine the strength of the claim. The first one is done for you as an example.

- New Yorkers get less sleep than Pittsburghers. [Claim of Fact. *Topoi*: Is there an empirical study that shows how many hours people in each place sleep? Is that study adequate to support the claim? Are there other measures or correlations that would support the claim?]

a. While anybody can put a label on some cheese, only cheese made with Greek sheep's milk can be considered feta cheese.
b. We need to build a new dorm next year in order to house the increasing number of students.
c. I love a man in a uniform.
d. Driving is more relaxing than flying.
e. The United States should put a human being on Mars in the next twenty years.
f. Vegans are just better than other people. (Scott Pilgrim)
g. Traphouse music is the most authentic form of hip-hop music.
h. The stock market is an adequate measure of the health of the economy.
i. No one should watch a movie directed by Roman Polanski because he was convicted of a serious and morally offensive act.
j. Cilantro tastes like soap to some people.
k. Using cilantro in a potluck dish is rude.
l. It is morally defensible to earn a lot of money so long as you give some to charity.
m. Vermont is the best place to see the colors of autumn.

4. In the previous section, for each claim that you identified as a value claim, indicate whether it is (1) absolute or comparative, and (2) terminal or instrumental.

5. The following pairs of claims represent the positions of two parties in a dispute. Identify the level of stasis in each situation.
   a. [1] The United States should have a single-payer system of health care. [2] Government control of the health care system is socialism and, therefore, unacceptable.
   b. [1] Setting the speed limit on all interstate highways at 55 miles per hour will save lives. [2] No matter what speed limit you set, people will drive as fast as they can.
   c. [1] A tax on sweetened beverages will help stem the obesity epidemic. [2] Health policy should not be made indirectly by taxation but, rather, directly by the legislature.
   d. [1] You have committed plagiarism on this paper. [2] This paper is all my original work.

e. [1] You never let me have any fun. [2] Let's discuss this at home.

f. [1] You broke into my car. [2] I had to break the window because you had left a dog inside on a hot day.

g. [1] The British Museum should return the Elgin Marbles to Greece. [2] The Elgin Marbles are safer in the British Museum than they would be anywhere else.

h. [1] You are in breach of contract because you did not pay me for the goods I delivered. [2] You were to deliver 1,000 gross of prime-grade gaskets and the parts you delivered were not of prime quality.

6. The Scholastics were a group of medieval philosophers who used argumentation to attempt to reconcile principles of Christian dogma with the classical thought of Aristotle and the Neoplatonists as well as with developing scientific thought. One of the famous (though possibly apocryphal) arguments of the Scholastics is the question of how many angels could dance on the head of a pin. Angels were thought to be both a spiritual concept and beings that existed in the world, so it ought to be possible to determine the mass of an angel by comparing it to something objectively real but very small, like the head of a pin. In time, the idea of computing the number of angels on the pin came to seem ridiculous. The early twentieth-century semanticist Wendell Johnson facetiously proposed to resolve the medieval dispute about how many angels could dance on the head of a pin by saying, "Bring me the pin, and some angels, and we'll soon find out."[3] What does Johnson's comment suggest about certain types of arguments? Can you think of an example of a contemporary argument that confuses philosophical subjects with physical objects to create arguments that are comically impractical?

7. Many of us were taught that it is not polite to discuss politics, religion, and other controversial matters in social situations. Why? Can you make an argument that being able to discuss the most controversial topics is, in fact, necessary for a healthy society? What norms do you think would help people to discuss deeply held beliefs and matters of personal value in the most productive way?

---

[3] Wendell Johnson (1906–1965) was an early adherent of general semantics. The statement widely attributed to him may be apocryphal. For an example of its use, see global.oup.com/us/companion .websites/9780199846313/student/chapter2/quizzes/pre-quiz/2c/.

Extensions: Toward More Advanced Study

The concept of stasis was developed in ancient times for use in addressing legal debates. A legal dispute involves claims of fact and definition; it is about understanding what the law is for a particular situation and then determining whether the case at hand fits that understanding of the situation. Some contemporary theorists have questioned whether the concept is more broadly applicable – to disagreements about policy, for instance. These are more complex arguments than legal disputes, because several different *topoi* are being addressed and they may be addressed in different ways, or there may be multiple points of stasis. At the same time, policy disputes take place in the general public forum, where questions of jurisdiction are usually not pertinent. For these reasons, a contemporary argumentation theorist Lee Hultzén sought to modify the concept of stasis to make it applicable to policy disagreements.[4]

Hultzén proposed two modifications. First, he deleted the stasis in place, for the reasons mentioned above: it did not seem relevant to general policy controversies. Second, he maintained that each of the remaining three stases could be applied to each of the topoi at hand. He summarized the topoi for policy claims as "ill," "blame," "cure," and "cost." He then concluded that stases could include ill-conjecture, ill-definition, ill-quality, blame-conjecture, and so on. For example, under the *topos* of "ill," Hultzén imagined these stases:

(1) Ill-conjecture: Is the state of affairs thus-and-so?
(2) Ill-definition: Is this state of affairs an ill?
(3) Ill-quality: Is it a great enough ill that something should be done about it?

He proceeded in similar fashion for the remaining *topoi* of "blame," "cure," and "cost." We could imagine the result as a 4×3 matrix with twelve cells, each identifying a possible stasis that could apply to one of the stock issues in the policy dispute. In an actual controversy, the participants would determine the particular stases relevant to each of the *topoi* through their patterns of assertion and denial with respect to each. Hultzén's modification made the concept of stasis available as an analytical tool for

---

[4] Lee S. Hultzén, "Status in Deliberative Analysis," in *The Rhetorical Idiom: Essays Presented to Herbert A. Wichelns*, ed. Donald C. Bryant (1958; rpt. New York: Russell & Russell, 1966), 97–123.

use in a much wider range of controversies than those for which it originally had been designed.

Return to Exercise 5 in the Exercises. For problems a, b, c, and g, recast the stasis according to Hultzén's system. Does this more precise identification of the stasis make clearer what the controversy is about? Does it tell you what each advocate needs to argue next?

CHAPTER 4

Evidence in Argumentation

When you advance an assertion in conversation with another person, that person might accept it immediately. Or the person might reject it out of hand, refusing even to listen to any more about it. Most reactions, however, fall somewhere between these two extremes. The other person is not yet satisfied that you are correct in what you assert but is willing to give the matter some more thought. Such a person might respond by asking, "What do you have to go on?" or "What makes you say so?" Questions of this sort are requests for *evidence* that will back up the assertion you have advanced. This chapter is concerned with evidence and its role in argumentation.

Although argumentation is most centrally about claims, evidence is the basic building block advocates use to support their claims. For the argument to be successful, all parties to the dispute must accept the truth of the evidence. They may disagree about why it matters or what it means; they may dispute whether it really functions to support the claim or not; but on the basic question of whether the statement of the evidence is true the disputants need to agree. That is why, when one party does not accept the truth of the evidence, the other must provide additional evidence to back it up. Figure 4.1 shows the structure of an argument in which additional backing is needed for the evidence put forward.

But the agreement of the participants is not the only thing that is needed to make evidence acceptable. A particular audience might have some characteristics not generally shared by audiences exercising critical judgment. For example, a particular audience might believe in astrology, but evidence grounded in astrology will not usually pass muster with critical audiences and therefore ought not be used. Likewise, a specific audience might be susceptible to allegations that a conspiracy is afoot, plotting evil designs. But most people, thinking critically most of the time, do not accept conspiracy allegations, so they should be used quite sparingly as evidence.

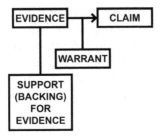

Fig. 4.1

Furthermore, the advent of social media has been accompanied by a vast increase in "fake news," assertions that are alleged to be statements of fact but that are made up. During the 2016 US presidential campaign, there was great concern about the frequency of false statements made by candidates or campaigners as if they were true. With both social media and campaign inaccuracies, the fact that many people agreed that the statements were true did not make them acceptable evidence. They did not square with what we could have known about the nature of reality, and they did not satisfy the tests of good evidence. These tests determine whether the evidence has characteristics that have been found through experience to make it likely that it is true and of high quality. These are tests that people impose when they are exercising their critical judgment. Of course, people in fact do not always subject evidence to these critical tests. When they fail to do so, they are more likely to go astray and to accept claims they later wish they had rejected (or to reject claims they later wish they had accepted).

The question an arguer should ask is whether an audience, reading or hearing a piece of evidence and exercising its critical judgment, would be more likely to accept the claim on the basis of that piece of evidence. Will the claim be more likely, given the evidence, than it was in the absence of the evidence? If so, then it is a piece of evidence that the arguer will want to cite. The goal of evidence, after all, is to increase the acceptability of the claim.

Objective Data as Evidence

There are many different ways to categorize evidence. We will discuss three major types of evidence – objective data, social consensus, and source credibility – and will consider varieties and tests of each.

Objective data are statements that can be independently verified and are widely agreed to. They do not require the arguers' intervention. Anyone, using widely established procedures or measurements, could investigate them and reach the same conclusion. This does not mean that they are not subject to interpretation. An unemployment rate of 5.0 percent, for example, is an objective datum, but it will be subject to very different meanings depending on the trend line, the expected unemployment rate, and the political dispositions of the persons who are examining the claim. But the disagreement is about what the data *mean*, not about what they *say*.

Examples

Examples are one common type of objective data. They are objective because they are occurrences independent of the arguers that can be cited as specific instances of more general claims.

Some examples are briefly alluded to without being developed. During political campaigns, candidates will often refer to "the people I saw in X town who were suffering from ..." The brief allusion serves mainly to assure audiences that the example is there and could be fleshed out, and the example would serve to make an abstract reality concrete.

Other examples are more fully developed, with details, and are sometimes referred to as *illustrations*. Establishing the claim that there has been serious suffering in recent natural disasters, an arguer might tell the story of one family whose house was destroyed, possessions lost, and savings wiped out. The provision of details makes the point that here is a realistic case of what had been described as a more general process.

It is sometimes confusing to talk about examples, because – as we will see in Chapter 5 – they are a kind of argument scheme as well as a kind of evidence. The argument scheme will reveal how people reason from examples to claims and what tests they should impose in understanding the example. Here we identify the example as a form of evidence and merely note that the truth of the example itself must be agreed to before argumentation on the basis of the example can proceed.

Statistics

Another form of objective data is statistics. These are quantitative statements of enumeration or measurement and take several forms.

1. *Raw numbers.* You might read that, as of 2010, 4,500 US soldiers had died in the Iraq war, or that as of 2020, there had been exactly two

father–son presidential pairs in the United States. These are measurements that are simply the result of enumeration (although the enumeration itself may not be simple, of course).

2. *Percentages, ratios, and index numbers.* These are different ways of comparing numbers. A simple example of a *percentage* is a statement such as "55 percent of baby boomers state that they plan to continue working at least until they reach age seventy." This statement indicates, in summary form, what baby boomers state they will do (not necessarily what they actually do) with regard to a decision to retire. "The ratio of women to men in nursing school is 8 to 1" is an example of a *ratio* statement. It indicates how many in one category correspond to one instance in another category, and hence serves as a measure of relative strength. In this case, it tells us that there are vastly more women than men in the nursing profession. But it goes beyond that to quantify the relationship. Finally, the statement, "If gas prices in 1995 were 100, they are 280 now," is an example of an *index* statement. It posits a certain number or time period as the base number and sets its value at 100, then calculates other time periods or other categories in relation to the number 100. In this case it is a way of making plain that the price of gasoline at the pump has nearly tripled since the base year of 1995.

3. Measures of *central tendency* (that is, the tendency of data points to cluster around a central point) also constitute statistical evidence. The three most common measures of central tendency (as students most likely have encountered earlier in their education) are the mean, the median, and the mode. These are different ways of determining the "average." The mean is the number you will get by adding up all the individual values and dividing by the number of items you measured. The median is the middle number if you arrange all the values from highest to lowest. If, for example, you have 100 scores, half of which are higher than 65 and half of which are lower, then 65 is your median number. Finally, the mode is the most frequently cited number. In your previous list of 100 scores, if ten scores were 90 and there were no more than six scores of any other number, then 90 would be the modal score in the group. Of course, it is important that the appropriate measure of central tendency be used, especially since each could give misleading results. A mean could be influenced unduly by a single very high or very low score. A median can be misleading if the individual scores vary widely and do not seem to cohere around any central number. And the mode can be misleading if the number of people selecting any option is small.

4. *Rates of change* sometimes are important statistical measures if you want to know how fast or slowly a condition is changing. For example, "Prior to the bursting of the real estate bubble in 2008, Las Vegas was adding 20,000 people per day." The important message conveyed by this statistic is not just that change is taking place, but that it is doing so quickly.

5. *Probability statements* are a final kind of statistical evidence. If you read the results of a psychological experiment and encounter the statement, "These results are significant at the 0.05 level of confidence," that means that if you were to repeat the same experiment 100 times, then 95 times you would get the same results as a result of the experimental design, whereas on average 5 times out of 100 you would get results by chance or accident.

To be sure, it's important to use the right kind of statistical measure for purposes of your argument, and it's important to be sure you have calculated it properly. But then the key question is whether the accuracy of the statistical statement will be accepted by all participants so that it could serve as the base of an argument.

Tangible Objects and Documents

A third kind of objective data consists of tangible objects and documents – the actual things that figure into a controversy. Tangible objects can play a very important role in criminal trials, as is illustrated by the importance of finding the murder weapon in order to establish the claim that a murder has taken place. During the trial of O. J. Simpson in the mid-1990s, a crucial question was whether the defendant fit into a particular glove or not. Fifty years earlier, the espionage case against Alger Hiss, which dominated the news in the late 1940s and contributed to the national reputation of Richard Nixon, turned on the existence of microfilmed papers stored in a hollowed-out pumpkin on a farm in Maryland. The home movies taken by Abraham Zapruder in Dallas in 1963, capturing on film the assassination of President Kennedy, became important parts of the documentary record of the case, and were widely examined to try to determine whether it was likely that there was a second gunman in addition to Lee Harvey Oswald. And in 2003, the presentation by US Secretary of State Colin Powell to the United Nations Security Council, to justify the war in Iraq, relied on videos, photos, and objects.

The power of tangible objects is captured in the adage, "A picture is worth a thousand words." But sometimes words themselves will be tangible objects, as in the case of historical documents that are drawn on to establish a record. Advocates for expanding human rights will seek to ground their case in the wording of one or more of the amendments in the Bill of Rights of the US Constitution, or perhaps the International Declaration of Human Rights adopted in 1948 by the United Nations. Advocates in a legal case will cite the text of the decision in an earlier case that they contend is analogous to the one at hand. In a labor–management dispute, both sides will have recourse to the language of the current contract in order to establish arguments that it is or is not being followed.

Tangible objects and historical documents bring to the fore "the thing itself" to ground their arguments. Of course, the claims may go in diametrically opposed directions, and there may be competing notions of what the tangible objects mean. But these disputes proceed from a common recognition of the evidence itself.

Direct Observation

The final kind of objective data to be discussed is the most empirical of all: a person observes something and reports it. A traffic study determines how many cars make left turns at a given intersection over the course of a week; this observation becomes evidence for the claim that a protected left-turn signal is needed at that spot. A student group places recycling bins on the campus and observes that less material that could be recycled is thrown into the garbage afterward. A bird-watcher sees a rare bird in an unusual place and reports on the findings.

These examples all rely on the premise that "seeing is believing" or that our eyes do not deceive us. Yet we know that observations can be distorted by color-blindness, light, distance, and related factors, and also that there is a strong disposition to see what one wishes to see. This is why, for example, eyewitness testimony in court is sometimes questioned, although in theory having an eyewitness is quite desirable. In relying on direct observation, one should make all possible effort to determine that the data are, indeed, objective.

Social Consensus as Evidence

Although we say that objective data are statements that could be verified independently, it is also true that they are statements that command extremely widespread – almost unanimous – assent from critical listeners. A second category of evidence involves statements that, while they cannot be verified independently, also depend on widespread, if not unanimous, assent.

Commonplaces are beliefs that are so widespread that they are taken as facts by most people and evaluated accordingly. "Politicians manipulate budget numbers," "The United States is an exceptional nation," "You can't trust people in Washington to solve our problems," and "If you want something to get done, do it yourself" are all examples of commonplaces widely believed in the United States in the mid-2010s. They show up frequently in campaign advocacy but also in legislative debates, budget hearings, and presidential statements. Typically no further proof or support is needed for these statements because they are treated as if they were self-evident truths. They function in public discourse as strong presumptions, and an advocate wishing to challenge them would have to meet a strong burden of proof.

Shared value judgments also can function as evidence. For example, around the world there is a nearly universal preference for what is best for one's children. Likewise, in the modern era, war, though frequent, is generally regarded as so horrible that it is believed that everything reasonably possible should be done to avoid it. And, while expressed in various ways, there is a widespread belief that older people deserve respect. In each of these cases, the value judgment could serve as evidence for a claim, without the requirement for further proof to establish the value judgment itself.

Shared historical understandings are another example of social consensus that serves as evidence. Even though the meanings of historical events can be ambiguous, there are widely shared "lessons of history" that can serve as evidence. Most people, at least in the West, believe that the United States "won" the Cold War, for example. And while problems remain, most people in the United States believe that the civil rights movement made real gains as a result of protests during the 1950s and 1960s, that the Civil War was about slavery at least as much as about states' rights, that sexual expression is much freer than it used to be, and that the role of world leader and policeman largely passed to the United States at the end of World War II. These common understandings seldom will require further proof and can represent grounds for claims.

Previously established claims also become the basis for new claims. Once sufficient proof has been provided for a claim, that claim can serve as evidence for other claims without the requirement of further proof.

Stipulations are yet another example of a social consensus. These are agreements by the parties to a particular dispute to accept certain statements as true or to waive them from consideration. These are frequent in law; for example, in a trial opposing attorneys may stipulate to the competence of a witness, so that his or her credentials will not need to be laboriously established; or they may stipulate that the defendant was at a specific place at a certain time because the independent evidence for that claim is very strong and the lawyer who tried to deny it would look silly. In ordinary interactions, stipulations may be made to reduce a complex issue to its core elements and prevent confusion from trying to argue multiple claims at once.

Testimony as Evidence

The final kind of evidence to be discussed is testimony, of either fact or opinion. Testimony is the statement by a qualified source that such-and-such is the case. We rely on testimony about things we cannot know directly or on which we ourselves are not qualified to have an expert opinion. We accept the testimony because of the credibility of the person providing it.

Credibility is often a function of expertise in the subject matter being discussed. This is not the same thing as celebrity. Sports figures who endorse pain remedies or articles of clothing are not particularly credible for those purposes; they are trading on the fact that they are particularly well known for their athletic achievements. The same would apply to any individual who is speaking or writing outside his or her field of expertise.

Credibility is also a function of one's track record. A person can be expert in a field and yet repeatedly offer testimony that turns out not to be reliable. Everyone errs in predictions occasionally, but a stock market analyst who consistently recommends purchasing stocks that subsequently decline in value will lose a good deal of his or her credibility. So too will the public opinion pollster who consistently is off in predictions about how an election will go. There are always multiple experts to choose from, and the one whose track record of successful judgment is stronger will ordinarily be the more credible.

Self-interest also is a factor affecting credibility. A person who stands to gain from the testimony he or she offers will be less credible than a neutral party, and considerably less credible than a person who is testifying against his or her own self-interest. Other things being equal, the person of wealth who testifies in favor of tax increases on the wealthy, knowing that he or she will have to pay the higher taxes, will be more credible than the person of wealth who calls for tax *cuts* for the rich in the belief that the benefits will trickle down to the rest of the population. So will the department head who advocates increasing workload expectations, knowing that he or she will have to meet the higher standards, be more credible than the department head who argues for reduced expectations that will make his or her job easier.

Testimony that favors one's self-interest is called *eager*; testimony that goes against one's interest is called *reluctant*. In general, reluctant testimony is favored over eager testimony. It is not that people who advocate their self-interest are always wrong; far from it. But we can never be sure how much of their judgment is the result of their training and experience, and how much is the result of their desire to benefit their self-interest. In contrast, when a person is speaking against his or her self-interest, we can be reasonably certain that the testimony is based entirely on the merits of the subject. After all, why else would a person voluntarily make statements that could harm him or her?

Credibility is not always a matter of expertise, strictly speaking; it involves who is in a position to know. In the case of an auto accident, for example, the eyewitness on the scene may have more credible testimony than the professional insurance adjuster or road design specialist who arrives later. Offering testimony about how inflation affects household budgets, ordinary homemakers may be in a better position to know than are analysts of the economy who do not personally suffer from inflation. (Of course, the person in the best position to know may also be the person more likely to be motivated by self-interest, so there are competing considerations.)

Finding Evidence

In the pre-Internet era, finding evidence – unless it was readily available through one's own experience or through sources such as the daily newspaper – was a time-consuming and laborious experience. It required going to the library and locating books, periodicals, newspapers, government documents, and sometimes unpublished reports. These sources are still valuable, especially when the subject matter is obscure or the evidence is older. Textbooks on argumentation published before the Internet age will often include extensive discussion of these types of sources and the finding aids and indexes for locating them. This information remains valuable.

Today, however, the principal means for obtaining evidence is by an Internet search. There are more than 870 million active websites containing information. To navigate this mass of data, most researchers use a *search engine* such as Google, Bing, or Yahoo! Search engines use different procedures, called *algorithms*, to determine what websites to feature in response to a search term and how to prioritize them. For this reason you may not want to confine yourself to a single search engine. There also are specialized search engines that will focus on particular types of material. For example, Google Scholar limits its searches to academic journals, whereas Google Books searches the text of books, and Google Images can help you find visual resources.

The search engine will list and briefly describe websites containing the terms you entered, usually arranged according to their perceived relevance or to the frequency with which they have been consulted (or "hit") by others. The sites that are consulted most often are not necessarily the most credible, however, particularly if they are sponsored by an organization with a particular agenda. Also, advertisements may "pop up" in the midst of the listed websites.

Search engines respond to the directions you give them, so you should be as precise as possible in what you ask. Moreover, there are standard search commands (such as quotation marks around a phrase if you are looking for the phrase rather than for the words separately); in some cases different search engines will have different commands.

The search engine will direct you to publicly available websites. These will often be a good source of information, but sometimes you can find better evidence in subject-specific electronic databases. These provide abstracts and full-text entries from a variety of popular and academic sources. Some are free, but others require subscriptions that are so costly that ordinarily they can be obtained only by libraries. Fortunately, if you have access to any college or university library, it probably will subscribe to many electronic databases in different fields of study, and these will be important sources of evidence that should not be overlooked. Some common electronic databases are EBSCOhost, JSTOR, Proquest, Project MUSE, and Lexis-Nexis.

Also online, you can find the catalogs of many library collections. These are the equivalent of the older card catalog that was maintained on index cards filed in drawers. You can search the online catalog according to subject, author, or title, just like the older card catalogs. In addition to the resources in your own library, you can use WorldCat (www.WorldCat .org) to check the holdings of more than 10,000 libraries worldwide.

Even in this Internet age, sometimes it will be desirable for you to leave your computer screen and actually go to a physical library. First, hard as it may be to believe, many sources are still not available electronically. Second, at the library you can browse other materials that are shelved near the item you are looking for but that you had not known about previously. Third, you can access electronic materials that are available only by subscription and not accessible on your home computer. Finally, you will be able to consult with professional librarians who may be able to give you valuable advice or to direct you to materials you didn't know anything about.

You might be wondering whether all this detail about finding evidence is really necessary just to engage in an argument, especially when you think you already know what position you want to take. It all depends on the stakes of the argument. If you and a friend are arguing about where to go to dinner, you will not need electronic databases requiring subscription – but you might want to consult restaurant reviews on Yelp or in a few key newspapers. If you are arguing about allocations of your university budget, you will want to have access to basic budget and financial data, as well as information about the state of the general economy that affects funding for higher education. If you are part of a citizens' group deliberating about which health care policy you should support, you will want access to a much wider range of evidence about health care policy, the effects of different financial plans on the economy, and a host of other subjects. Sometimes you will need to do very little research; other times you will need to do quite a lot. It is always better to err on the side of having more evidence than you can use than to err on the side of not having enough. With a surplus of evidence, you will be able to pick and choose the strongest grounds for the claims you want to support. With not enough, you will be forced to make your evidence do more work for you, and you will run the risk of overstating the facts and overclaiming the evidence.

Evaluating Evidence

The Problem

Unfortunately, many people are far too quick to accept questionable evidence. Research shows that people's judgments are skewed by whether or not they agree with what the evidence says, even if the evidence itself is of poor quality. They are swayed to accept evidence that "sounds good" or is delivered by a speaker in a tone of voice that suggests reassurance. In fact, delivery can outweigh the content of the evidence in people's judgment of its reliability.[1] Recently it has become clear that many people are willing to accept "fake news" – news that is fabricated – if it is presented in a format that appears authoritative. (It is also easy to label true evidence as "fake news" if one does not like the conclusion.) Precisely when the Internet has so democratized the presentation of evidence and more is available than ever before, we have become less rather than more vigilant in the evaluation of evidence.

The consequences of taking weak evidence too seriously can be vast. On February 5, 2003, US Secretary of State Colin Powell presented to the United Nations Security Council the case for the United States (and selected allies) to take military action against the regime in Iraq. This was the major statement of the US government's position and it appears to have had significant effect in swaying votes on the Security Council. Powell's presentation included significant amounts of evidence of different types. There were intercepted telephone conversations involving the plotters. There were historical facts about previous terrorist activities supported by the regime of Saddam Hussein. There was overheard testimony from the leaders of al-Qaeda, captured on tape. And there was the fact that Iraq had not publicly demonstrated that it had destroyed its weapons of mass destruction, a "negative example" that was used to support the claim that the stockpiles of such weapons were still there.

It was an impressive presentation on Powell's part. The links in the chain of reasoning connected the various steps in the argument, the inferences were sound, and the speech made a solid case for war – that is, if the evidence was reliable. But virtually each of the types of evidence on which Powell relied was subsequently shown to be false.

- The intercepted conversations had to be translated, and words in one language often do not translate exactly to words in another; translation requires interpretation and is subject to context. In this case, keepers of the evidence allowed translations to be skewed to come out in favor of the policy outcome that they preferred.
- The historical facts fit into a pattern largely because those assembling the speech wanted to find one. Secretary Powell did not want to be put in the position of saying that there was no clear pattern in the evidence but that we would go to war anyway.

---

[1] A review of some of the research findings on use of evidence is Kathy Kellermann, "The Concept of Evidence: A Critical Review," *Argumentation and Advocacy, 16* (Winter, 1980), 159–172.

- The sources whose testimony was intercepted were of unknown credibility.
- Contrary to common assumptions, the "message" of a photograph is not transparent. Pictures do not speak; they must be spoken for. Attempts to interpret the photographs led to mistaken judgments about the meaning of different gestures and facial response across cultural divides.
- The argument that weapons of mass destruction were still there because there was no evidence that they had been destroyed fell victim to an old cliché: "Absence of evidence is not evidence of absence." The fact that there was no public demolition of the weapons did not prove that they were still around. To cite an obvious possibility, they could have been removed from Iraq or destroyed privately so as not to tip off Iraq's neighbors in the region that they were gone.

In short, the evidence on which Secretary Powell relied was consistently flawed, consistently interpreted to match the desired results rather than subjected to critical inspection. When a distinguished Secretary of State is found in this predicament, it is all the more important that ordinary arguers, working without a team of researchers and information gatherers, carefully evaluate the evidence they use.

General Standards for Evaluation

Contemporary argumentation theorist James A. Herrick has proposed seven general tests for the evaluation of evidence.[2] These are critical questions which can be asked of evidence of virtually any type.

1. *Accessibility*. Is the evidence open and available for inspection by others? If evidence is kept in secret, it is impossible to know what it might say, whether it has been used in context, whether it can be replicated, and so on. Evidence that cannot be checked out should be automatically suspect.
2. *Credibility*. Is the source of the evidence reliable? We have discussed the importance of credibility above with respect to testimony. But the tests apply to other kinds of evidence as well. For example, can the accuracy of statistics be trusted? Was there bias in the selection of examples to be used?

---

[2] See James A. Herrick, *Argumentation: Understanding and Shaping Arguments*, 4th ed. (State College, PA: Strata, 2011), 80–88.

3. *Internal consistency.* Does the evidence contradict itself? The quality of evidence will be seriously weakened if it appears to undermine the claim it is intended to support. Even Abraham Lincoln fell victim to this problem early in his career when he finished a speech about reason by passionately calling out, "Glorious consummation! Hail fall of Fury! Reign of reason, all hail." These and similar statements were not calm or reasonable; his tone and message were at odds.[3]

4. *External consistency.* Does the evidence contradict the best available evidence from other sources? We will have less confidence in a piece of evidence if it seems to work at cross-purposes from other things we know to be true. Evidence of massive voter fraud in a particular state, for example, will seem strange in the face of much other evidence that nationwide the problem of voter fraud is statistically insignificant.

5. Recency. Has the evidence been superseded by more timely evidence? During the 2012 US presidential election, a major concern was that the unemployment rate had remained above 8 percent for more than forty months. Citing this evidence would not be likely to do an advocate much good when the unemployment rate almost immediately after dropped below 8 percent and continued a steady decline until Election Day and even after. Of course, recency is not always a relevant consideration. There are timeless questions that do not change and that may have been stated just as effectively by Aristotle 2,500 years ago as by one of his descendants today. But when timeliness of evidence does matter, than recency is an important consideration when evaluating the quality of the evidence.

6. Relevance. Does the evidence bear on the conclusion? This might seem to be self-evident, but it is not uncommon for tangential or irrelevant evidence to be drawn on because, in its own context, it is evidence of high quality. But evidence is not valued for its own sake. Its value comes from its ability to help in establishing a claim. If the evidence really does not speak directly to the question at hand, it will not do that. Evidence about President Trump's business dealings with Russia, in the aftermath of the 2016 US election, may have called into question the new president's ability to be impartial, but it did not relate to the question of what US foreign policy with regard to Russia ought to be.

---

[3] The reference is to the conclusion of Lincoln's "Temperance Address" delivered on February 22, 1842. See *Collected Works of Abraham Lincoln*, ed. Roy P. Basler (New Brunswick, NJ: Rutgers University Press, 1953), *1*, 279.

7.   Adequacy. This last test asks whether the evidence, if satisfactory in other respects, is enough to support the claim in whose behalf it is put forward, or whether still other evidence is required to do the job. Proving that there are major needs for infrastructure programs, for example, is necessary to establish that infrastructure spending would stimulate the economy, but it is not sufficient. Among other things, one would need also to establish that laborers with the necessary skills are available and ready to work in the places where they would be needed.

Herrick's tests represent a "first cut" of questions to ask to assess whether evidence is satisfactory. In addition, a few additional criteria should be noted:

8.   Accuracy. Does the evidence say what it purports to? In introducing the evidence, the arguer will characterize it a certain way. For example, she might say that it establishes that in 2018 the gross domestic product grew in all the major industrial nations of the world. Is that what the evidence actually says? Does it in fact refer to *all* the major industrial nations? Does it mean the same thing as the arguer does by such terms as "grew" and "major"? Were all of the supporting data really from 2018?

9.   Context. Evidence does not exist in a vacuum; it gets its meaning from the context in which it is embedded. But if we are not careful, we can ignore or – worse – misrepresent that context by stating accurately what it is in the evidence but changing its intended meaning. This is even more likely if we paraphrase the evidence rather than quote it directly. Creative additions and deletions can worsen the problem. In advertisements for movies, for example, a few key words from critics' reviews are taken as if they were reliable guides to the overall context. Thus "the most interesting movie to cure insomnia that has ever been made" can become "the most interesting movie . . . ever made."

10.   Appropriateness to the purpose. Some types of evidence are more appropriate than others for certain purposes. If the number of cases of a communicable disease can be counted, for example, then measurement is probably better for the purpose than the statement of a politician who says, "I believe it is a disaster for the current administration." Factual evidence is more appropriate for a factual claim than is testimonial evidence. Conversely, a statement like "The health care system is a patchwork that is coming apart," is more

appropriate as an expression of a judgment than would be, say, a chart showing rising medical costs over time. To say that something abstract like "the health care system" is "coming apart" is a judgment, not an empirical statement, so the important consideration would be the credentials of the source, not the fact that testimony rather than empirical measurement is being employed.

These are general tests that can be applied to all types of evidence. In addition, some special considerations are appropriate for evaluating evidence from the Internet.

Evaluating Internet Evidence

Compared with the Internet, traditional hard-copy print publication utilizes scarce resources. Everything from paper to ink is relatively expensive. Consequently, access to publication depends on judgments about the use of resources. This is the basis for an editorial structure that includes peer review and editorial judgment. These "gatekeeping" mechanisms also provide an important element of quality control. In contrast, almost anyone can post almost anything on the Web. There is no editorial or quality control except for what the producer of a given site may choose to exercise. The Internet is the most democratic means of publication there is. That is its strength, in that it is likelier to offer a wider range of viewpoints than more traditional publication. But it is also its weakness, in that you are less able to be sure of the strength of any given piece of evidence, and hence you will need to be more careful.

At one extreme, an online version of a printed publication, such as an electronic copy of an article from a scholarly journal, will reflect exactly the same editorial judgment as the printed publication, since it is just a copy of the same thing published by other means. But at the other extreme, an individual's personal website may have no editorial control at all. And further to complicate matters, organizations that exist to promote a particular viewpoint may have websites that are somewhat deceptive, presenting passionate advocacy disguised as if it were dispassionate scholarship. Search engines may attempt to distinguish between websites that are reliable and those that are not, but they cannot do the job perfectly.

You may be tempted to give weight to a website that "looks professional," but that is not a sure indicator of quality either. It is easier to design a sophisticated-looking website than to produce an unimpressive-looking book. In fact, websites that look like those of easily recognized reputable organizations have been created for the specific purpose of inducing individuals to reveal their Social Security numbers or other personal identification in order to facilitate identity theft. This practice is known as phishing and constitutes fraud. The point is that just inspecting the appearance of the website will not be enough to tell you whether it is reliable.

Since the Web is largely unregulated, the responsibility to evaluate Internet evidence rests with you, the user. For this reason, you should consider the following additional precautions about evidence taken from Internet sources.

1. *Basic standards.* Does the site meet the basic standards of credibility? A credible website, at a minimum, will indicate the name of the sponsor, identification of expert and believable contributors, and current information that is appropriate and that can be checked for its accuracy.

2. *Creator.* Who set up the website? If you cannot tell who sponsors the site, approach its contents with suspicion. People or organizations dedicated to a particular cause can disguise their motivation or even their identity, leading you to assume that they are nonpartisan or that biased information is actually neutral. A site's *domain name* is one clue to its reliability. Generally, URLs ending in .edu (an educational institution) or .gov (a government agency) may be considered more reliable than those ending in .org (a voluntary organization) or .com (a commercial source).

3. *Credentials.* What are the source's credentials? Does the author have expertise on the subject? To find out, you may need to check a credentials page. This may require tracing back in the URL (the Internet address) to find such a page. If the author has a specific ideology or agenda, take that into consideration. That does not automatically disqualify the evidence, but keep in mind the distinction noted earlier in the chapter between eager and reluctant evidence.

4. *Purpose.* Is the goal of the website to sell a product or service by electronic means? If so, you should examine the content more skeptically than you would if the goal is only to provide information. Of course, as we have noted, the goal of the site may be obscured or misleading. The title of the website and the name of the source may not be sufficient to reveal its purpose. Sometimes you will need to read through the material on the site in order to form a judgment about whether it is appropriate for you to use as evidence.

5. *Scholarship.* Does the content appear to reflect scholarship? Look for characteristics of scholarly writing such as documentation for claims, sources for information, mention of the limits of the data and claims, discussion of alternative viewpoints and fair characterization of those viewpoints, and evidence of critical thinking skills. The site is more likely to be propaganda or biased advocacy if it contains excessive claims of certainty, suppresses alternative views, and presents ideas out of context.

6. *Confirmability.* Can you confirm the information (or, alternatively, can you determine under what conditions the information is falsifiable)? If you find what seems to be airtight confirmation of your case or conclusive refutation of someone else's ideas, be careful. These might be "self-sealing" arguments – circular reasoning in which the claim merely restates the evidence – or they might be tautologies or statements that are rendered true or false by definition rather than by analysis or proof. A good general procedure is to check what you find against other sources. You may not be able to find the exact same facts or ideas, but what you find on the Web should be compatible with what you find on other websites or in print.

7. *Recency.* When was the site last updated? A chief virtue of the Web is that it can provide you with very timely information. But often sites are not updated regularly and the information can become obsolete without your realizing it. If you cannot tell when a site was last updated, that may be a reason to be skeptical of its content. Of course, this is not an issue with regard to matters that are "timeless" or do not depend on recency of the content, as noted earlier in the chapter.

Whether concerned with print or Internet evidence, these evaluation factors affect whether the evidence, taken on its own, will or should be acceptable to the audience. If it is not, then arguments based on that evidence will not get very far.

In addition, of course, we want to know whether the evidence *counts as* support for the claim. This is primarily a matter of the inference and the warrant for it, and that subject will be the concern of Chapter 5.

Exercises

1. In the following examples, find the claim and the evidence being offered in its support. Is the evidence best classified as objective data, social consensus, or source credibility?

a.   My cousin Phil told me that eating seeds can cause diverticulitis, so it's best never to eat a sesame seed bun.

b.   The weatherperson on Channel 3 said that it is going to rain later today, so I'm going to take an umbrella.

c.   The same weatherperson said that it is only 31° Fahrenheit (0° Celsius) in the city this morning, which is why I am wearing my warm coat.

d.   Everyone should support Delia Smith, the candidate for the open Senate seat, because she's the only candidate who supports the interests of working people.

e.   We need to remove statues of Confederate generals, because there is now agreement that these statues are a vestige of white Southern resistance to civil rights.

f.   Milton Friedman was a Nobel Prize–winning economist who argued that "inflation is always and everywhere a monetary phenomenon." The current low rate of inflation therefore can be traced to the success of the administration's monetary policies.

g.   You should change the oil in your car every three months because an ounce of prevention is worth a pound of cure.

h.   The security camera footage showed that the burglar was no taller than 5'7". Since Charles is 6'2", he cannot have been involved.

i.   The patient's blood pressure is dangerously low, so we need to prescribe medication to raise it.

j.   The patient reported that she has had severe pain in her abdomen for thirty-six hours, so I think she has appendicitis.

k.   No team has ever won three Super Bowls in a row; therefore, I cannot bet on the Patriots to win this year.

l.   Because I have traveled extensively, I suggest never putting your passport into checked luggage.

m.   The government never should have begun the project before it had the funding; it put the cart before the horse.

n.   I am getting a size 11 shoe this time. The salesman just measured my foot and told me I needed a size 10, but everybody knows you should buy your shoes one size larger so we can grow into them.

o.   The jury found the defendant guilty because his best friend testified that he saw the defendant with the gun, even though the forensic tests did not show the defendant's fingerprints on the gun.

2. Examine the evidence in each of the examples in Exercise 1. Identify a potential problem with the evidence. How confident would you be in supporting or opposing the claim based on the evidence given?

3. Bill Gates, one of the wealthiest men in the world, walks into a bar in which there are nine other people, none of whom has a net worth in excess of $50,000. Which method (mean, median, or mode) will best represent the average of the net worth of all of the patrons at the bar? Why?

4. Choose a controversial issue from the news. Enter a claim associated with this issue into a web browser (for example, "Climate change is caused by human activity; therefore, we must take significant steps to control its effects"). Look at the first ten or so "hits" and evaluate each as a credible source, using the precautions for Internet sources in this chapter. Which sources do you find to be the most credible? Which are the least credible?

5. Choose an editorial from an online or print newspaper. Determine the main claim or thesis of the editorial. What evidence is offered to support this claim? What type(s) of evidence are used? How credible is it? Does it stand up to the general tests for evidence developed in this chapter? Newspaper editorials are usually brief and evidence often is not clearly developed. Is there any implied evidence in the editorial?

6. Go to the website for TED talks (www.ted.com/talks). Choose any examples that interest you. What are the claims that the speaker makes? What evidence does he or she use? Write down each piece of evidence and evaluate it using the general tests for evidence developed in this chapter.

CHAPTER 5

Argument Schemes

In this chapter, we will be concerned with the *relationship* between the evidence and the claim. Together with the truth and quality of the evidence, discussed in Chapter 4, this is the major consideration affecting the strength of an argument. The question is what enables the evidence to *count as* evidence *for the particular claim*.

The Concept of Validity

The answer to that question is bound up with the concept of *validity*, which designates a test for the quality of an argument that is independent of the content of the evidence or claim. It does not ask whether the evidence is true, but rather *if* the evidence is true, whether the claim would be true. Before we can understand how this concept applies to ordinary argumentation, we need briefly to review its roots in formal deductive logic.

Validity in Formal Deductive Logic

In Chapter 2 we reviewed the difference between formal deductive logic and ordinary argumentation, which is inductive. Contrary to common belief, the difference between deduction and induction is *not* that one makes an inference from the general to the specific, whereas the other makes an inference from the specific to the general. In fact, either one can infer in either direction. Rather, the difference is that in formal deductive logic, the claim is *entailed* (or guaranteed) by the evidence. Another way to say this is that if the evidence is true, the claim *must* be true: to have true evidence but a false claim would be contradictory. What determines validity, then, is entirely a matter of form, and validity is understood as correctness of form.

Consider the simple argument, "All heavenly bodies are made of green cheese and the moon is a heavenly body, so the moon is made of green cheese." We can say without a doubt that at least one statement offered as evidence is false. We know conclusively that not all heavenly bodies are made of green cheese (in fact, so far as we know, none is). But that is not the point. *If* all heavenly bodies were made of green cheese and the moon was a heavenly body, then it would *have to be* the case that the moon is made of green cheese. To say otherwise would be to utter a contradiction. This is what is meant by saying that the evidence *entails* the claim.

Why is it that formal deductive logic can insist on such a seemingly rigorous standard? The answer is that the claim is already present, at least implicitly, in the premises themselves. If we know, for example, that *all* heavenly bodies share a certain characteristic, then a *particular* heavenly body (which is included in the category of *all* heavenly bodies) would have that same characteristic. This is just rearranging what we already know from the statement about all heavenly bodies. It is not adding any new information. So the seemingly rigorous character of formal deductive logic turns out not to be a source of profound claims.

Formal deduction has the characteristic of entailment – a guarantee of the claim, given the truth of the evidence – as a result of one or the other features of the statements it contains. First, the claim may simply repeat what the evidence says. Suppose on reading a map, someone tells you, "The map says that it is 100 miles to Grandmother's house, so the map says that it is 100 miles to Grandmother's house." The claim absolutely must be true if the evidence is true, but we have not advanced our knowledge at all by this insight. Of course, it is extremely rare to find such a blatant example of repetition, but sometimes the two identical statements will be separated by other narrative or descriptive material. When people encounter the statement a second time, they are less likely to remember that it is a direct repetition of what already has been said.

The other circumstance that could lead to perfectly valid but trivial deductions involves the invocation of norms or rules of language. Take as an example the argument that says, "Joe's Restaurant is a good downtown restaurant, so some downtown restaurants are good." Now this argument does not literally repeat itself as the previous one does, but it might as well have done so, because it relies on a convention of language that says that the general category subsumes the particular member. If we know that something is true of Joe's Restaurant, then we know it is true of *at least one* restaurant (Joe's being at least one), and "at least one" is the understood

Fig. 5.1

definition of "some." So we can conclude that the argument is formally valid – the evidence entails the conclusion. But it has not taken us very far.

For years, most theorists of argumentation regarded formal deductive logic as the "gold standard" they would try to emulate. But far fewer theorists hold that view today, because they recognize that formally valid arguments are, as a consequence of that very feature, not robust. They merely rearrange what we already know. In everyday argumentation, though, we want to go *beyond* what we already know. We want to use evidence to support a claim that *does* tell us something new. We use reasoning, in other words, as a tool to move from the known to the unknown while justifying our move.

Applying Validity to Ordinary Argumentation

In Chapter 2 we looked at a simple diagram of an argument, reproduced here as Fig. 5.1. Notice first that we have connected the evidence to the claim with an arrow pointing from the evidence to the claim. The arrow indicates an *inference* from the former to the latter. This suggests that the strength of the evidence is expected to strengthen the claim. Another way to say this is that the claim is stronger on the basis of the evidence than it is as an assertion alone. Notice, too, that we have drawn a box labeled "Warrant" whose function is to license the inference, since (except in the case of formal deduction) it will not be self-evident.

The arrow representing the inference could be understood as saying "Therefore," as in, "This evidence is true, therefore the claim deserves your agreement." The warrant will be a more generalizable statement authorizing inferences of the type being discussed here. For example, a warrant for an analogical inference would say something like "Things that are alike in most respects are probably alike in the respect under discussion."

If there is disagreement about the meaning or applicability of the warrant, you may need to provide additional support to back it up. Similarly, your opponent may argue that there are exceptions to the warrant, or that there is a contrary warrant that is stronger than yours

and sets yours aside. These challenges would need to be met with additional argument in defense of your warrant, or – if necessary – the
substitution of a different warrant.

The claim will not be entailed by the evidence in the sense described
above. Because the claim goes beyond the evidence, involving a mental
leap symbolized by the arrow, it is always possible that the claim could be
false even if all the supporting evidence were true. So in ordinary argumentation, we say that an argument will be valid if the evidence *supports* it.
This means that the claim has *more probative force* when supported by the
evidence than when left standing alone.

The determination that the evidence adds to the force of the claim is
provided not by formula or linguistic rule but by the exercise of human
judgment. That judgment is known to be fallible, and yet to make it is
reasonable if over time similar judgments have been borne out by subsequent experience to be reasonable and not to lead people astray. That is
what the warrant licenses us to assume.

The Concept of Argument Schemes

Just as we saw that there are several types of evidence, it is also true that
there are several types of inferences and warrants. (For purposes of cat-
egorization, we can use the terms "inferences" and "warrants" interchangeably at the moment, since an inference of type X will be authorized by a
warrant of type X.) For any given type of inference, there will be patterns
within that type, there will be critical questions to ask in order to decide
whether the inference is reasonable in the given case, and there will be
situations in which one should be extremely cautious about making the
inference. What counts as *valid* will vary with the pattern of inference.
These different patterns of inference are called *argument schemes*.

Just how many such patterns are there? Here scholars differ considerably. Some organize inductive arguments into a very large number of
argument schemes with different model forms of each.[1] Others employ
so few categories that it may seem like there is too much variation within
each category.[2] This is a matter of taste and judgment; there are no
standard methods of characterization. In this chapter, we will consider

---

[1] For example, see Douglas N. Walton, *Argumentation Schemes for Presumptive Reasoning* (Mahwah, NJ: Lawrence Erlbaum, 1996), which describes approximately thirty argument schemes.
[2] For example, Frans H. van Eemeren, Rob Grootendorst, and Francisca Snoeck Henkemans, *Argumentation: Analysis, Evaluation, Presentation* (Mahwah, NJ: Lawrence Erlbaum, 2002), 95–96, reduces the number of argument schemes to three.

six reasoning patterns, some of which have subsidiary patterns: argument from example, argument from analogy, argument from sign, argument from cause, argument from authority, and argument from form. The term "argument from" suggests that categories of arguments are built from the pattern of inference and warrant identified in each of the six categories.

Argument from Example

Arguments based on example are arguments that relate parts to wholes. The underlying warrant is that the whole is basically like the part, or the part is basically like the whole – depending on the direction in which we are proceeding.

Types of Example-Based Warrants

There are two types of example-based warrants: *generalization* and *illustration*. Generalization is used when the evidence relates to a part and the claim relates to a whole. The warrant asserts that what is true of the part is true of the whole. Illustration is just the reverse. It begins with evidence that relates to the whole and the claim relates to a part. Generalization proceeds from specific to general; illustration, from general to specific.

As noted above, the difference between generalization and illustration is sometimes taken to be the difference between induction and deduction. But either pattern could be either induction or deduction. It depends on whether the enumeration of the parts is complete. Suppose, for example, there are exactly five students in a class and we know that each of the students individually had a passing score on the most recent examination. If we were setting this up as an argument, our evidence would be "Student A passed the exam," "Student B passed the exam," "Student C passed the exam," "Student D passed the exam," and "Student E passed the exam." The (probably unstated) warrant would be "What is true of the part is true of the whole," and the claim would be, "Students in this class passed the examination." Now, this example proceeds from specific to general, and yet it is deductive. Why? The conclusion is entailed by the evidence and provides no new information – the two standards we established for deduction. The key fact that made the warrant deductive was that we conducted a *complete* enumeration, including *all* the students and leaving nothing uncertain. As a result, the claim refers to exactly the same set of cases as the cumulation of the evidence. This would be true, by the way, whether we began with the specific examples or with the generalization. If the generalization is based on a complete enumeration, then the argument is deductive. Also, if the generalization were understood to be deductive, then a single counter-example would defeat the generalization (since it no longer would be based on a complete enumeration).

But it is highly unlikely that generalizations will be based on a complete enumeration, whether they start with the general or with the specific. Especially if the category is large, we are unlikely to have data about *all* the members of the category. Besides, we usually *want* for the enumeration to be incomplete, because we want to say something about a potentially wider range of cases than we know about to start with.

When we have an incomplete enumeration and a warrant that says "what is true of the part will be true of the whole," we are asserting in the warrant that the examples are *representative* of the whole. In other words, we are saying that the examples are typical manifestations of the whole. They are not unusual or exceptional cases. We cannot know this for sure; we can only assert it with some degree of probability.

There are two major patterns of inductive generalization: *statistical* and *anecdotal* generalizations. Statistical generalizations are the result of drawing a sample at random from a larger population, determining what is true of that sample, and then inferring that what is true of the sample is also true of that larger population. This is the approach to argument used by surveys and polls. For example, a random sample of 1,000 inhabitants of Center City is asked how they will vote in the upcoming election, and two-thirds of the sample say that they plan to vote for the Republicrat candidate. The survey designers forecast that two-thirds of Center City voters will support the Republicrat, just as two-thirds of the sample have done.

Anecdotal generalizations are less rigorous. They occur when an arguer cites several specific instances from a category, infers that they are representative of the category as a whole (although this can be known only with less precision than in the case of the statistical generalization), and then asserts a claim about the entire category from which the examples were taken.

Everything that has been said about generalization also applies to illustration, since they are two sides of the same coin. The effect of illustration is to increase the power of an abstract or more general claim by applying it to a specific instance, translating the large claim into terms that could be understood easily because they are more concrete and specific. Again, the assumption is that the particular case that has been selected is representative of the whole.

Tests for Example-Based Warrants

Knowing that your evidence does not entail your claim (unless your enumeration was complete), the following are some important tests that can be applied to inferences based on example.

1. *Are there enough examples?* If the number of examples is very small (especially if you are considering a statistical generalization), you may not be able to infer anything about the category as a whole. The reason is that you very well may have left out significant features of the population as a whole. If your university is doing an outstanding job of teaching argumentation, you still probably want to refrain from saying, "Today's colleges are doing an outstanding job of teaching argumentation." Your university may be an atypical case and you do not have enough examples to know.

2. *Do the examples represent all the important dimensions of the category?* A famous example from the 1930s involved a poll that sampled only owners of telephones. Remember that this was during the Depression, when telephone ownership was not divided equally among the population. The poll confidently predicted that President Franklin D. Roosevelt would be defeated for reelection. Imagine the pollsters' surprise when they realized that they had not considered a representative sample of the population.

3. *Are the examples ambiguous?* Sometimes the same example could support different, even conflicting, interpretations. Suppose that 70 percent of a company's employees indicate that they are dissatisfied with new computer systems that have been adopted recently. Does that mean that a significant majority of the employees want to get rid of the new system, or does it mean that they are eager for more training so that they can use it effectively? The example by itself will not tell you.

4. *(for generalization) Does the argument commit the fallacy of composition?* Fallacies, as we will see in Chapter 6, are defined by some scholars as inferences that appear to be valid but actually contain some significant flaw. The fallacy of composition results from assuming that what is true of the part is automatically true of the whole, when in fact the part and the whole are two different levels of analysis. Sometimes the whole is more or less than the sum of the parts. For example, each individual athletic fan can improve his or her chances of getting a good seat by trying to buy a ticket as soon as they go on sale. But if

everyone followed that practice, no one would be better off, because the supply of good seats is fixed.

5. *(for classification) Does the argument commit the fallacy of division?* The fallacy of division is just the opposite of the fallacy of composition: assuming that what is true of the whole will automatically be true of each part. A real estate investor is trying to buy a plot of land for $2 million in order to build a shopping center. The owner of one-quarter of that land cannot necessarily assume that his land is worth $500,000 (one-quarter of the total). The land may be worth $2 million *only* if the investor can get the whole plot.

In selecting examples, figure out how many you need in order to show a pattern that supports your inference but does not bore the audience by essentially repeating what you already have said. Avoid obvious or overused examples that just tell listeners what they already know. And make sure that each example is believable. A single example that casts doubt on your credulity will taint all examples you present, even if you've never said anything else that seems implausible.

Argument from Analogy

A second pattern of inferences and warrants is *analogy*. If example-based warrants are about the relationship between parts and wholes, analogical warrants are about similarities. The model analogical warrant is that things that are alike in most respects are probably alike in the respect at hand.

Types of Analogy-Based Warrants

As with warrants from example, there are two key subtypes of analogy-based warrants: the literal analogy and the figurative analogy. The difference between them involves the items being compared.

A *literal analogy* is a direct comparison of persons, places, things, or events of the same basic type. The evidence is that these items are similar in many essential respects, and the warrant is that they are probably similar in the respect under discussion. Consider a simple example. A speaker asserts that Los Angeles, Houston, and Miami all are Sun Belt cities that experienced rapid economic development after 1950. Each of these cities is heavily dependent on the automobile rather than mass transit. The speaker notes that Phoenix is also a Sun Belt city with similar development patterns. Therefore, she asserts, Phoenix also is probably heavily dependent on automobile transportation as well.

Literal analogies are used to establish parallel cases, as in the example above. The comparison is between cases with which we are more familiar and cases with which we are less familiar. The inference is that the less familiar case, being basically like the more familiar cases, is probably also like them in the specific respect that we are considering.

Sometimes the parallel cases are different in magnitude, and the inference is that what is true of the relatively familiar case is even more (or less) likely to be true of the unfamiliar case. Suppose, for example, that the speaker said, "Tucson, a moderate-size Sun Belt city with steady but modest economic growth, is dependent mainly on the automobile for its transportation needs. All the more so, then, is San Diego, a much larger city with rapid economic growth, likely to depend on the automobile." This pattern is called the argument a fortiori, and it is concerned with more and less. The standard form of this specific inference is that what is true (or false) of the lesser (or greater) case is all the more likely to be true (or false) of the greater (or lesser) case.

A specific use of literal analogies is to establish precedents for the situation at hand. This use is common in legal argumentation. In establishing, for example, that the US Supreme Court case of *Griswold v. Connecticut*, which established a right to privacy, was a precedent for the case of *Roe v. Wade*,[3] which established a woman's right to abortion under certain circumstances, the courts ruled that the privacy considerations involved in a decision to terminate a pregnancy were essentially similar to the privacy considerations involved in the decision by a couple to use contraception (the issue in *Griswold*). Similarly, the equal-protection considerations invoked in the marriage equality cases of 2015 were claimed to be the same as in the case in the 1960s that struck down prohibitions on interracial marriage. The value of arguing from precedent is that, if a current case can be shown to be essentially similar to one that already has been decided, then it is easy to infer that a similar decision should be reached in the current case. This is especially the case in the light of *stare decisis* (meaning "the decision stands"), the principle that there is strong presumption against repealing a decision that established the precedent.

Besides literal analogies, the other main type of analogy is *figurative*. Here the items being compared – whether objects, people, events, or

---

[3] *Griswold v. Connecticut*, 381 US 479 (1965); *Roe v. Wade*, 410 US 113 (1973).

things – are *not* of the same basic type. In fact, they usually are of quite different basic types. What is being compared is not the items themselves but the *relationships* among them. Consider this example: "Appointing industry leaders to head commissions regulating their own industries is like putting an arsonist in charge of the fire department." Now the arguer is not suggesting that industry leaders are like arsonists, nor that regulatory agencies are like the fire department, but rather that the relationship between the two is similar, so that the appointment in one case is likely to be as unwise, even counterproductive, as in the other.

The way figurative analogies work is that one of the two relationships is presumably better known to the audience. In the example above, what it would mean to have an arsonist head the fire department is something that audiences easily could understand, but they might not have thought as carefully about what it would mean to have industry leaders head regulatory agencies. So an arguer will seek to convince the audience of the less familiar relationship by showing that it is essentially similar to the more familiar relationship that audience members are already prepared to evaluate. In this comparison, the relationship of which the arguer is trying to convince the audience is called the *theme* and the more familiar relationship is called the *phoros*, and the argument works by transferring the key characteristics of the *phoros* to the theme.

Figurative analogies sometimes are dismissed as literary devices, and indeed we often find them in literature. But they also have significant argumentative content in that they seek to make audience members more aware of an unfamiliar relationship by establishing that it is basically like a familiar one. Accordingly, figurative analogies are used to make abstract or unfamiliar concepts more concrete and easier to grasp, by showing that they are essentially like other concepts that already are accepted.

Tests for Analogy-Based Warrants

An analogy tries to show that two different things (or two different relationships) are essentially alike. But they are not the same; they are merely brought together for consideration in the argument. Since we are concerned with similarity and not identity, it is always possible that the items being compared differ in the point of comparison, *even though* they are basically alike. This means that analogies are always inductive inferences. For this reason, logicians sometimes regard them as the weakest kind of inference. Generalizations could be deductive if the enumeration were complete, but analogies cannot because the items being compared are never identical; in fact, we posit that they are different. This realization should suggest the following basic tests for analogy-based warrants.

1. Have all the relevant characteristics of the items been considered? If we look at a very narrow range of characteristics, or omit some that obviously are relevant, we are more likely to go astray in concluding that the items are alike in the respect under discussion. Suppose, for example, that for geographic reasons Los Angeles suffers from smog and the other Sun Belt cities do not. (Like the other examples, this one is hypothetical.) The desire to control smog may give Los Angeles an incentive to develop mass transit that the other Sun Belt cities do not possess, even though all of them are sprawling cities that experienced massive growth and development after 1950. It is never possible to enumerate all the characteristics of the items being compared, and not all will be relevant to the comparison. The Latino population of Miami may be larger than of the other cities, there may be more immigrants in Houston, and people in Phoenix may be more likely to have been born in the area, but these considerations may have no relevance to the matter of dependence on the automobile. Of course, determining whether or not characteristics are relevant is a judgment call and may itself be the subject of argument.

2. Among the relevant characteristics, do the essential points of similarity outweigh the essential points of difference? Again, since the items being compared are not identical, they will have significant differences as well as significant similarities. The fact that there are some significant differences is not by itself reason to discredit the analogy. The question is which are greater or more important, similarities or differences. This, too, is not an open-and-shut matter but is subject to interpretation and argument. The outcome of such an argument will determine whether the analogy-based warrant is valid in the given case.

As with example-based warrants, there are general guidelines for the use of analogies. First, they should not be trite or far-fetched. An overused analogy will seem stale to an audience, whose members may be likely to discount its significance. And an analogy with no obvious basis in common sense will focus so much attention on itself that it will distract from the argument that the analogy is being used to advance. Second, analogies that are too complex or nuanced likewise should be avoided; they probably will require more attention and intellectual energy of the audience than they are worth. Third, analogies should be used sensitively. If the arguer is not careful, the analogy may have unintended implications that demean an individual or group. Attempting to poke fun at his poor performance at bowling, President Obama once compared his score to that of a contestant in the Special Olympics. He meant to be humble about his own ability, but his analogy was interpreted by some as belittling the Special Olympics and its athletes. Finally, analogies should be used sparingly in an argument. Although they contribute to the content, they also are like ornaments, and too many ornaments may obscure the main point at hand.

Argument from Sign

A third argument scheme is based on inferences (or warrants) about signs. Sometimes this is referred to as argument from symptom or symptomatic argument, but these terms all are referring to the same thing. The basic pattern of this inference is that the presence of the sign enables us to infer the presence of the thing signified. The key relationship is coexistence of the two. If two events or things habitually occur together, and we notice one of them, it is a reasonable inference that the other is present as well – not a guaranteed inference, but a reasonable one. It is important to be clear at the outset that a sign inference does not establish any influence of one thing on the other, but merely that they coexist. Perhaps the simplest example of a sign relationship is the barnyard adage that the crowing of the rooster in the morning is a sign of the rising of the sun.

Types of Sign-Based Warrants

One type of sign-based warrant is *physical observation*. We notice the presence of a sign and we infer the presence of the thing signified. Suppose that your neighborhood has experienced a series of tear-downs of small older houses followed by the construction of large new homes on the lots that the small houses once occupied. If, when driving down a street in the neighborhood, you noticed another old house being demolished, you reasonably could infer that a large mansion was about to be built on that site. You couldn't be positive, of course, because there are other reasons that a house might be torn down. But because demolition is associated with impending construction, you could reasonably infer that a new house would soon be built on the site. And while the two events typically occur together, you cannot say that either influenced the other. It is not that demolition *caused* the new house to be built, but rather that demolition and construction coexist in a predictable pattern.

A second sign-based warrant is the *measurable index*. A good example is the measurement of a person's IQ. It is necessary that we have a sign of intelligence, because "intelligence" itself is an abstract concept that there is no way to measure. By common consent, the measurable IQ score is taken as a sign of the unmeasurable concept of intelligence. In a similar way, the Dow Jones Industrial Average and the NASDAQ are compilations of the prices of selected stocks in the market. They are widely understood to be signs of the overall health of the stock market and, indeed, of the economy in general. Like "intelligence," "economic health" is an abstraction that there is no way to know directly, much less to measure. So by common consent we take these often-used indexes as signs of the health of the economy. Steady increases in the price of the stocks in the index, unless it is the result of artificial speculation producing a temporary "bubble" in the market, can be taken as a sign of economic health. Rapid declines in the stock index, conversely, can be taken as a sign of a weakening economy. As a final example, the Consumer Price Index is widely understood as a sign of inflation. "Inflation" is also an economic abstraction that is understood by inference from the index score.

A final example of a common type of sign-based warrant is *institutional regularity*, a predictable pattern of norms or behavior within the framework of a given organization, culture, or society. To take a simple example, in some universities the academic year begins with a formal assembly at which the faculty appear in caps and gowns, the traditional academic costume. Since wearing academic regalia is something we can associate with the start of the academic year, if we were to look at the calendar and notice that the new school year is starting up next week, we could safely predict that an assembly in academic costume is coming within the next several days. Another example of institutional regularity is the practice of leaving a tip after finishing a restaurant meal and paying the check. This is a common practice in the United States, so that, on having been presented with a check, we could safely assume that the diner is about to leave a tip. We would not go up to the unsuspecting diner and point out that he or she had left money on the table. Knowing the institutional regularity that tipping follows presentation of the check, we would understand that that was exactly the diner's purpose.

From this discussion of the types of sign-based warrants, we should be able to understand how they are used in actual argument. Two uses are especially prominent. First, we use sign-based warrants to infer the existence of the unknown from the presence of the known. We saw this in the discussion of statistical inferences. We cannot know directly something that we're concerned with, since it is an abstraction rather than a concrete reality, so we infer its existence from something we can see. In technical terms, we could say that we are making an inference about the *essence* of something from our knowledge of its *properties*. The properties are external characteristics of what we are trying to know about. The essence is its "true" or "deep" nature, to which we do not have direct access. From the known quantity, we infer the unknown thing of which it is believed to be a sign.

The other prominent use of sign-based warrants is to make predictions. Knowing of the relationship and finding the sign, we predict that we are about to see the thing that was signified by the sign. This is a straightforward inference so long as we remember that we are not in a position to say anything about *why* the relationship is about to reveal itself.

Tests for Sign-Based Warrants

Long ago, Aristotle distinguished between *fallible* and *infallible* signs. An infallible sign is one that always and necessarily coexists with the thing signified. Such a sign would be a deductive warrant because the presence of the sign would guarantee the presence of whatever the sign stood for. The claim would repeat what already was present, at least implicitly, in the subsidiary claims, and there would be no new information.

But it is hard to imagine how such a thing could be possible. The rooster's crowing does not assure us that the sun is about to rise; it could be a rainy or cloudy day. In like manner, the economy could be in bad shape despite good numbers from the stock market. The university faculty at the start of the school year might be responding to a sudden heat wave by leaving caps and gowns off, even though they normally wear them. To increase the likelihood that a sign-based warrant will turn out to be valid, the following are some tests that can easily be employed.

1. Can the alleged sign be found without the presence of the thing it signifies? Suppose we know that a man named Jenkins habitually watches a certain television program at a certain time and day. We think we can predict confidently that the television set is about to come on when we see the right time on the clock. But what if at that same time, Mr. Jenkins also frequently opens the newspaper, returns phone calls, and shuffles a deck of cards, rather than watching television? Then we would not have a strong sign-based warrant. Since the sign is a sign of more than one thing, we are not confident making *any* inference about what it might stand for.

2. Is the sign part of a pattern, or is it likely to be a single, unusual case? In inspecting the warrant of a sign-based inference, we want to be sure that it establishes a strong pattern; otherwise we will not be justified in applying the pattern to the case at hand. Suppose someone asserts, "A woman is paid less than a man in this industry; that is a clear case of gender discrimination." Now, if the meaning of that statement is that women generally are paid less than men generally, taking into account all other considerations, then the warrant that gender differences are a sign of discrimination would seem fairly strong. But if the statement meant literally that one particular woman was paid less than one particular man, it would be more of a stretch to assume that differentials in pay could be taken as a sign of gender discrimination.

3. Can a sign actually signify two or more different, or even opposite, things? Nowhere is it written that a sign can stand for only one thing. If multiple sign relationships are possible, we should be cautious in assuming that the sign relationship points clearly in any one direction. For example, the 2003 Iraq War was launched in the belief that Iraq possessed weapons of mass destruction. The United Nations inspectors, however, had failed to find such weapons. Some said that was a sign that Iraq did not have any weapons of mass destruction and concluded that the war was fought under false pretenses. But others responded that the failure by the UN to find weapons of mass destruction was a sign that the Iraqis had hid the weapons prior to the inspection, and made the war subsequently launched by the United States all the more clearly justified. In principle, there is no way to establish one sign relationship as stronger than the other. (In the Iraq case, as time went by and inspections became more rigorous, still without any evidence turning up of weapons of mass destruction, it became easier to argue that the Iraqis did not have them.)

4. Is an alternative account of the relationship more credible? There are many cases of unusual sign relationships. Even though there is a pattern of coexistence, there might be other, nonobvious explanations for it than the one at hand. Sometimes the explanation is that there is a simple coincidence. For example, from 1840 through 1960 every President of the United States elected in a year ending in "o" died in office – and there was an attempt on the life of President Reagan, elected in 1980 and thus presumably extending the cycle. But there was no sensible explanation for this pattern; it was widely regarded as just a coincidence. Certainly, few if any people accepted the statement, "Being elected in a year ending in zero is a sign that the

president will die in office," and this pattern did not deter anyone from running for the office in a "zero year." George W. Bush, elected in 2000, may have "broken the curse," but it appears that neither he nor his opponent gave a thought to this spurious sign relationship as a reason not to run for the office in that year.

Another term that sometimes is used to describe a sign relationship is *correlation*, although strictly speaking, this term is about covariance rather than coexistence. But covariance is also a way to establish a sign relationship. It suggests that two things vary in a predictable way. Suppose that whenever a stock index goes up by 100 points, the president's popularity goes up by half a percentage point. Then an increase in the stock index is a sign of an increase in the president's popularity, and the same analyses discussed above apply in that situation.

This is also true in reverse. Two things may covary in opposite directions. For example, for many years economists believed that inflation and unemployment were inversely related. If inflation went up, unemployment could be predicted to go down, and vice versa. So the fact that unemployment varied in one direction could be taken as a sign that inflation would vary in the opposite direction. (This belief was confounded by the experience of the United States during the 1970s, when inflation and unemployment both went up at the same time.)

There are statistical procedures to measure correlations, ranging from +1.0 to −1.0. A correlation of +1.0 would mean that every time one factor moves in one direction, the other factor would move in the same direction. (There still would be no guarantee that this would continue to happen.) A correlation of −1.0 would suggest that the factors always move in opposite directions, again without a guarantee. A correlation of 0.0 means that the relationship between the two factors is purely random so that neither is predictable from knowledge of the other. Correlations gain in strength as they move from 0.0 toward either +1.0 or −1.0. While these measurements can be very useful for certain arguments, they cannot be used when the relationships between factors are simply conceptual rather than measurable, or when they refer to simple coexistence rather than covariance.

Argument from Cause

So far we have considered three argument schemes: example, where the inference is about the relationship between parts and wholes; analogy, where it is about similarities; and sign, where it is about coexistence. One of the frequently used but complex schemes is argument from cause, where the inference is about *influence* of one factor on another. It is complex because influence usually is unobservable and is inferred by residues – by the failure of any other factor to substitute for the influence that is asserted. Some examples may make this clear.

During the nineteenth century, the philosopher John Stuart Mill identified several approaches to establishing causality.[4] One was called the *method of difference*. Take two things that are different, Mill proposed. Hypothesize what causes the difference. Then systematically hold the two things constant with respect to every other factor. If the only factor in which they are different is the one that you hypothesized, and they are nonetheless different in the end, then the cause of that difference must be the factor that you hypothesized – for the simple reason that the things are alike in every other respect. By residues, the cause of the difference must be the factor that you identified.

Mill's second approach, the *method of similarity*, is just the reverse. Take two things that are similar to each other. Hypothesize what causes them to be similar. Then isolate every factor that you can, other than the one you hypothesized, and make sure that the two things are different with regard to every one of those other factors. Then, since the items are similar in the end, the cause of the similarity must be the one factor that you held constant – because none of the other factors, being different, could have produced similarity.

Mill proposed other methods as well, but these two should be able to explain his approach. And while he had the scientific laboratory in mind, it is not difficult to see the limitations of his procedures if intended as tools for everyday argument. First, it usually is not possible to "hold everything else constant." Argumentation is part of the world in which everything is in flux. And second, it never is possible to assure that we have isolated "all other factors." In a complex world, there is a theoretically infinite number of factors making up anything, so there always can be alternative causes, other than the ones we are hypothesizing, that we did not isolate or hold constant because we were not aware of them.

In everyday argumentation, then, we must be prepared to establish causal warrants by supporting arguments that justify them. Such

---

[4] John Stuart Mill, *A System of Logic* (London: Longmans Green, 1843), Book 3, chapter 5, and Book 6, chapter 2. For a brief description of Mill's concept of causation as sufficient condition, see John Hospers, *An Introduction to Philosophical Analysis* (Englewood Cliffs, NJ: Prentice-Hall, 1967), 291–297.

arguments would explain how it is possible that our alleged factor could be the cause (opportunity) and why it is more likely than are other possible causes (motive and means). These supporting arguments for the causal warrant often are not made explicitly, but the advocate must be prepared to offer them if the causal warrant is challenged.

Types of Cause-Based Warrants

Two basic types of inferences from cause are *explanations* and *predictions*. The former attempts to account for given effects by making inferences about their causes, while the latter attempts to predict effects from knowledge of given causes.

One subtype of explanations is the *retrospective hypothesis*, which seeks to answer the question, "Why did x happen?" These arguments take place after x has happened and try to identify one or more causes for x. The effects are known and the task is to account for the cause(s). This is an exercise in assigning responsibility. For example, given the fact that average temperatures in the world are increasing, most scientists argue that the cause is human action, such as the use of products that trap heat-containing gases in the atmosphere. A minority of scientists and some politicians, however, maintain that the rising temperatures are caused by cyclical rather than long-term factors and that the causes are natural rather than human in origin.

What we have labeled the retrospective hypothesis is called by some theorists *abduction*, by which they mean inference to the best explanation. Given a set of conditions, the goal is to identify the simplest, most plausible, most likely, or most coherent account for them. Abduction is sometimes discussed as if it were different from deduction and induction, but that view assumes a very narrow definition of induction – sometimes limited just to generalization. In contrast, we have defined induction broadly, to include all forms of reasoning in which the claim is not entailed by the premises. By this standard, retrospective hypotheses clearly involve inductive inference.

A second subtype of explanations is the *resolution of paradox*. Paradoxes are situations that are at cross-purposes with what they seemingly ought to be. For example, widespread adoption of computers has made electronic communication a fact of life, making the use of paper less necessary and even giving rise to the expression, "the paperless society." Yet the paperless society uses even more paper than was used before the advent of computers! How can this be? Again, the effect is known and we are trying to determine the cause – an especially puzzling task because the effect is the opposite of what we would be led to expect. An advocate might argue, for example, that computers make possible more extensive and complex systems and processes, and that because many people suspect that computers will fail, they needlessly print everything, keeping duplicate paper records of files and documents that could be stored electronically alone. Other explanations might be offered to compete with this one, but the idea is that the exchange of arguments will seek to explain this seeming paradox.

A final subtype of causal explanations is the *causal generalization*. These statements are sometimes called "covering laws." They are general statements about what causes what, which can be used to make causal statements in a particular case. A famous example is the possibly tongue-in-cheek statement known as Parkinson's Law: Work expands to fill the time available for its completion.[5] This causal generalization could be used, for instance, to explain why automating one step in a production process need not speed up the overall production. The explanation would be that the time "freed up" gets used to check other steps in the process more thoroughly or to add new steps, so that the time available for the project's completion is still taken up by all the work involved. The framework for this argument is (1) E (the effect) occurs; (2) C ➔ E (the causal generalization); therefore (3) C is the cause.

Causal generalizations can also be used to make predictions, so this is a suitable transition to the second major category of subtypes of cause-based warrants. Continuing with the Parkinson's Law example, imagine now that management is considering the automation of part of the production process and is attempting to predict what will happen. One manager suggests that automation will speed the overall process so that products can be finished faster. Another interrupts to say, "Oh, no, you must remember Parkinson's Law: Work expands to fill the time available for its completion." The second manager is using this framework: (1) C (the cause, in this case automation) occurs; (2) C ➔ E (the causal generalization, in this case Parkinson's Law); therefore (3) E (the effect) will occur, in this case no saving of time.

In addition to the causal generalization, there are two other major patterns of cause-based warrants used for predictions. One is the *means–end* prediction. The basic pattern is: (1) doing X will bring about Y (that is, X ➔ Y); (2) we want (or do not want) to achieve Y; therefore (3) we

---

[5] C. Northcote Parkinson, *Parkinson's Law* (Boston: Houghton Mifflin, 1957).

should (or should not) do X. For example, an advocate might suggest that developing solar power is the best way to avoid a future energy shortage. The (probably unstated) statement of ends is that "we wish to avoid a future energy shortage." From the means–ends statement and the statement of the desired end, the advocate would conclude that "we should develop solar power now" (the means to be pursued toward the end). This form of cause-based inference is sometimes called the *pragmatic argument*, because it suggests that we should choose actions based on their consequences. In the solar power example, it is not some inherent good of solar power that recommends its adoption, but rather the consequence of averting a future energy shortage.

The final example of predictive cause-based inferences to be discussed here is the *slippery slope*. Unlike other patterns of causal argument, which can be used either to support or to discredit a claim, this pattern is used exclusively as a way to undermine the claim. It consists of a (sometimes long) series of means–end predictions resulting finally in a claim that something disastrous will occur. Perhaps the most significant example of a slippery slope with major implications for foreign policy was the "domino theory" developed during the 1950s by President Eisenhower to explain why it was important for the United States to defend South Vietnam. The domino theory suggested that if South Vietnam fell to communism, Laos would be likely to do so as well; if Laos fell, so would Thailand; if Thailand fell, then India would be threatened; and so on in a series that ended in a claim that was caricatured as "we will have to fight the communists in San Francisco." The point of President Eisenhower's argument (which got its name from his analogy to a row of dominoes that would all fall if the first one was knocked over) was to discredit the claim that the United States lacked vital interests in South Vietnam.[6]

Tests for Cause-Based Warrants

Whether employed for explanation or prediction, uses of cause-based inferences should be checked using the following tests:

1. Has a sign relationship been mistaken for a causal relationship? Sometimes what is really a correlation can be wrongly claimed to be a cause. For example, the early studies on smoking and health

---

[6] President Eisenhower used the metaphor of "falling dominoes" in a press conference on April 7, 1954, to illustrate why keeping Indochina noncommunist was important to the United States.

suggested that cigarette smoking was correlated with higher rates of lung cancer. Those opposed to regulating tobacco responded that there was no reason to believe that there was a causal relationship. (Subsequent research weakened this response by effectively eliminating other possible causes and furnishing an explanation of how tobacco use led to lung cancer.)

2. Is there a post hoc fallacy? The Latin phrase *post hoc* means "after this." While it is true that a cause must precede its effect, the fact that something comes after something else does not necessarily mean that what came later is an effect of what came before. Republicans note that the Cold War ended while President Reagan was in office and maintain that he was the cause; Democrats note that the economy enjoyed sustained growth while President Clinton was in office and maintain that he was the cause. Both claims are dubious. In the absence of good reason to believe the causal link, they are likely both self-serving cases of the post hoc fallacy.

3. Is there a common cause? Sometimes one thing may be asserted to be the cause of another, when in reality both are effects of a third factor that is the cause of both. For example, some advocates suggest that widespread alcohol use on college campuses, compared with earlier years, leads to an increase in suicides among college students. There may indeed be a causal influence of alcohol after holding other factors constant. But there is also a strong argument that an increase in various personality disorders among students entering college is what leads both to increased alcohol use and to increased rates of suicide, without either alcohol use or suicides directly affecting the other.

4. Is there a plausible alternative cause? Sometimes what appears to be the cause really is not. For several years beginning in 2014 there were prominent cases of unarmed African Americans who were killed by police in the course of their investigations. Some suggested that the cause was that African Americans were more likely to live in high-crime areas and thus to encounter the police in ambiguous situations, but others suggested that the more plausible causal explanation was racial discrimination on the part of many police officers.

5. Are there significant multiple causes or effects? These questions come into play especially when cause-based inferences are used to justify policy positions. The world is complex; causes have both intended and unintended consequences; and effects seldom have only one cause. Suppose that a problem – differences in educational achievement

between urban and suburban schools, for example – has many causes, including differences in budgets, teachers' preference to work in suburban schools, differences in transiency of the school populations, difference in parental commitments to education, and so on. In such a case, addressing one of the causes – spending more on urban schools, for example – may not make a huge contribution to solving the problem unless it is part of a coordinated strategy that addresses the whole complex of causes. Likewise, a single cause may have multiple effects. Some may be undesirable, while others are desirable. Getting rid of the cause could diminish or eliminate the desirable as well as the harmful effects; the popular expression for this is "throwing the baby out with the bath water." Attempts to limit global trade in order to protect domestic jobs, for example, might also harm the telecommunications and shipping industries, raise domestic prices, and invite retaliation by other nations – effects that could be argued to be far more substantial than the protection of domestic jobs.

Because causal arguments are so frequently used, it is important that they be able to satisfy these tests.

Argument from Testimony

In Chapter 4 we considered testimony as a form of evidence. But there is also an inference pattern in which we reason from the testimony to a claim. This is how the testimony comes to count as reason for a claim. The basic pattern is: (1) X asserts a claim; (2) X is a reliable authority concerning that claim; (3) therefore, the claim is probably true. Our willingness to act on the basis of testimony reflects the fact that none of us can claim authority over every subject affecting our lives, so we have to rely on the judgment of those who can be considered authoritative in any given case. The inference, then, is about the *credibility* of the source.

Types of Testimony-Based Warrants

There are two basic dimensions to testimony, whether fact or opinion: (1) expert vs. lay testimony and (2) quoted vs. paraphrased testimony.

In most cases, we seek expert testimony – the statement by a person widely regarded as an authority on a particular subject, whose knowledge of and concern for the topic far exceed the average person's. We are willing to accept the person's judgment on the basis of his or her expertise.

But sometimes we deliberately use *lay* testimony – testimony from people who are not experts. We do so when they are in the best position to know what is at issue (such as eyewitnesses to a crime), when the audience is more likely to identify with laypeople whom they imagine are basically like them, or when the very point of the argument is to establish what ordinary people think about a subject.

Quoted testimony represents the exact words used by the person quoted, whereas paraphrased testimony approximates the substance of what the person said, though not in the person's own words. Quoted testimony is generally preferred, because it is more likely to represent the source accurately. But sometimes the quotation may be too long, too technical, or too confusing for an audience to follow. In these cases, a paraphrase will allow you to represent what the source said without losing the attention of the audience.

Tests for Testimony-Based Warrants

It is sometimes tempting to think that any testimony about a claim will strengthen the case for that claim. This position may reflect the naïve belief that only authorities make public statements or that all people quoted in print are equally trustworthy. But, in fact, usually someone can be found to make just about any statement on any subject. Therefore, using testimony-based inferences should be subjected to the following tests, in addition to those suggested in Chapter 4 to be sure that the testimony is accurate.

1. Is the source an authority on the particular topic? It is not enough that the source be generally well qualified; he or she should be an expert on the particular subject. Celebrities are usually not expert on the merits of different consumer products, just as a nuclear physicist is probably not an expert on popular culture.
2. Is there a basis for the source's statements? If the source is offering judgments, it should be clear that he or she has a basis for them. Without such a basis, the source is *pontificating* – making statements with no support other than the source's say-so. One clue that a source may be pontificating is the use of hyperbolic statements such as "Governor Smith is the worst governor our state has ever had." Such statements deserve little weight. When we accept a claim on the basis of what an authority has said, we assume that the authority has some reason for the statements made.

3. Is the source reasonably unbiased? No one is completely free from bias or susceptibility to a particular viewpoint. An inference from testimony is more likely to be suspect if the source has a personal self-interest in the testimony or stands to gain financially from it. For example, a real estate developer is probably not the most impartial person to testify about whether a development in which he or she is involved is likely to be environmentally safe. The fact that an expert stands to gain from testimony does not necessarily make the testimony wrong, but it does suggest that healthy skepticism should be in order. This is the same reason that, as noted in Chapter 4, reluctant testimony generally is preferred over eager testimony.

4. Is the testimony up-to-date? Some subjects are timeless: moral principles stated centuries ago are usually just as valuable now as they were then. But on most matters, especially when statistics or empirical data are involved, recent testimony may be of greater value than older testimony.

One way to hedge one's bets against these tests is to offer testimony from multiple sources. If a claim depends on the testimony of a single source, it can be weakened if that source cannot satisfy all of these tests. But if you can establish a strong consensus among multiple sources with different backgrounds and interests, it is less likely (though still possible) that they all will suffer from these problems.

Argument from Form

The last type of argument scheme we will discuss involves inferences based on the *form* the argument takes. The central idea was stated more than eighty years ago by the literary and rhetorical critic Kenneth Burke, who wrote that form is an arousal and fulfillment of appetites.[7] In other words, the basic pattern of a form creates expectations about what will complete the form, and when those expectations are satisfied, the listener or reader is more likely to be convinced of the conclusion because it satisfied the form – it was what the audience expected.

As we saw earlier, in formal deductive reasoning the validity of an argument depends entirely on the correctness of its form. There are also inductive arguments that seem to mimic deductive forms, and their

---

[7] Kenneth Burke, *Counter-Statement* (1931; rpt. Berkeley: University of California Press, 1968), esp. 124.

strength depends on the audience's acceptance that the form is correct in the particular case.

Types of Form-Based Warrants

Three basic types of warrants licensing inference from form are quasi-mathematical arguments, quasi-logical arguments, and narrative arguments.

Quasi-mathematical arguments rely on the application of mathematical properties to nonmathematical subjects. For example, if A is greater than B and B is greater than C, then A is greater than C. This characteristic is sometimes applied to determine which is the "best" sports team. If team A defeated team B, it is presumably better than B; likewise if B defeated C, it is presumably better than C. Does it follow, then, that A is better than C? Not *necessarily*, especially if it is also the case that C defeated A! Whether the argument is valid or not depends on how the arguers are using the concept of "best" in a specific situation. The same is true of other mathematical features, such as reciprocity, equivalence, and transitivity.

Quasi-logical arguments apply seemingly logical rules to nonformal situations. Imagine, for example, the scientist testing a hypothesis in the laboratory. The scientist might reason that if the hypothesis is true, the test will yield results of a certain kind. The scientist might then conduct the experiment and get the anticipated results. Does this mean that the hypothesis has been confirmed? Again, not *necessarily*, because the results could have come about for reasons other than those hypothesized. (In fact, the scientist may have committed the fallacy of "affirming the consequent.") The reason many scientific studies are considered valid is that they are carefully controlled. That is, the procedure is designed to rule out as many alternative explanations for the results as possible, giving the scientist more confidence that the hypothesized explanation is correct. Validity of the inference depends on audience agreement that the controls are adequate.

Narrative arguments use storytelling to support a claim. They depend on a different kind of form – the narrative structure with characters, plot, some sort of conflict, and an ending.

Narratives are used to build to a climax, to lead to the "moral" or point of the story, to fit together seemingly isolated ideas into a pattern, and to arouse or calm apprehension about the advance of opposing ideas or forces. Sometimes they are used for no purpose other than to make the central ideas of the story more interesting or to make an abstract subject more concrete. Narratives can be personal, relating an episode in which the arguer is a main character, or they may be about other people. They may describe real events and people, or they may be about hypothetical situations. Fables, children's stories, biographies, and historical accounts all furnish material for narratives.

Tests for Form-Based Warrants

Arguments from form rely on familiar patterns to make a claim easier for audience members to understand and to accept. A quasi-mathematical or quasi-logical argument allows the audience to reason along from premises to conclusion, provided that the use of the form is accepted as appropriate. Telling a story likewise can be more powerful than other ways of developing an argument. It is personalized, converting general or abstract ideas into the experience of particular people in a particular situation. Listeners become involved in the plot and begin to think about what will be coming next, so that there is often an element of suspense.

As with the other argument schemes, there are tests that should be satisfied for arguments from form:

1. Is the use of the particular form in the specific context appropriate?
2. Has the form been employed correctly?
3. Is the resulting argument coherent? Does it hang together and make sense, or are there unexplained elements and loose ends?
4. Does the argument have resonance? *Resonance* is the characteristic of striking a responsive chord in the audience, so that audience members can identify personally with the argument.

Conclusion

Warrants, and the argument schemes built from them, are especially important in understanding everyday argumentation. While they are not absolutely certain, they are not arbitrary or capricious either. They furnish licenses for making claims on the basis of the evidence that has been advanced. In this chapter we have examined six basic argument schemes and their underlying warrants: example, based on the warrant of representativeness; analogy, based on the warrant of similarity; sign, based on the warrant of predictiveness; cause, based on the warrant of influence;

testimony, based on the warrant of credibility; and form, based on the warrant of expectation.

We have suggested that properly warranted arguments can be considered valid: if their evidence is correct, their claims should be acceptable. This is the everyday equivalent of validity in formal deductive logic. Everyday arguments do not assert that the claims follow absolutely from the evidence, but rather that the claims are justified – sufficient reason has been given for reasonable people to accept them. Conversely, unwarranted or improperly warranted arguments can be said to be fallacious: the claim is not justified even if the evidence is true. The factors making for fallacious arguments are the subject of Chapter 6.

Exercises

1. Which of the following examples represent(s) a formal deductive argument in which the premises (if true) entail or guarantee that the conclusion will be true? Which are nondeductive because we move from the known (premises) to the unknown (conclusion) with probability, not certainty?

   a. All turtles are reptiles; all reptiles are cold-blooded; therefore all turtles are cold-blooded.

   b. Bill has worked for the *Washington Post* for twenty-five years, so he must be a great writer.

   c. The number of new home starts in Phoenix rose to 13,000 in 2015. Therefore, I conclude that the population of Phoenix also rose during 2015.

   d. If the doorbell rings, then my brother has arrived. The doorbell just rang, so my brother has arrived.

   e. My professor told me that when somebody starts to sweat, it means she is lying. The witness looks like she is sweating, so she must be lying.

   f. That rash has only three possible causes: eczema, an allergy, or chemical burn. You do not have eczema or a chemical burn, so the rash must be caused by an allergy.

   g. Ninety-five percent of students who read the material carefully will pass the examination. Camila has read the material very carefully, so she surely has passed the examination.

   h. We all know that a rolling stone gathers no moss. Jill has been up since 4:30 this morning and hasn't stopped for a moment. She has had a very productive day.

i. Some of the large copper pots are leaky and all the large copper pots are on the shelf, which means that there is at least one leaky pot on the shelf.

j. Buying in bulk generally is cheaper than buying smaller quantities. I got this rice at the warehouse club so it is cheaper than the rice you bought at the convenience store.

2. In the following examples, determine whether the argument pattern most closely represents an example (either generalization or illustration) or an analogy (either literal or figurative). Apply the appropriate tests to each argument and determine the overall strength of each argument.

   a. In a recent poll, 78 percent of likely voters in Kentucky supported spending taxpayer money on new infrastructure improvements in the state. Some 787 people were randomly selected to take the poll and the margin of error is calculated to be ±3 percent. Based on this survey, I have concluded that a bill that allocates $200,000,000 in state funds for bridge repair will be popular with voters.

   b. Jabril asked me to recommend an engineering school for him. I told him I had heard good things from several students about their experiences at Purdue University.

   c. I never like to discuss why I love Justin Bieber so much. As someone once said, "Talking about music is like dancing about architecture."

   d. I am very concerned about the future of the European Union. The experiences of the former Yugoslavia and Iraq show how difficult it is for alliances of different ethnic and religious groups to thrive.

   e. I will never go to the Fulton Market Trattoria again in my life! The first time I was there, they were out of calamari, and the second time, the service was terrible.

   f. There is no reason you cannot finish college while also working full time. My neighbor Svetlana was able to graduate from college even though she was working full-time and raising a family of three children.

3. In the following examples, determine whether the argument pattern more closely represents a sign warrant or a causal warrant. Apply the appropriate tests and determine the overall strength of each argument.

   a. Financial analysts have identified a phenomenon they call the January effect, in which stock prices tend to rise during the month of January in most years. This is caused, analysts believe, by the fact that small investors tend to sell stocks in December for tax reasons and then reinvest in January.

b. Studies have shown that people who eat a good breakfast do better on standardized tests. Therefore, if we give everyone a good breakfast, they will all do better on standardized tests.

c. We have seen that people who grew up before the Internet was widespread were in better shape than those who are growing up today. Therefore, we should reduce Internet screen time if we want people to be happier.

d. Last night I left the milk on the kitchen counter instead of returning it to the refrigerator. Today the milk was sour. I have determined that heat causes milk to spoil because bacteria thrive in warmer temperatures.

e. I was on the bus the other day when I noticed the girl sitting across from me taking picture after picture of herself sitting on the bus. I was puzzled until I realized that it must be Snapchat.

f. After the accident, the investigators were able to recreate the wet roads and limited visibility. They determined that the driver of the car could not have seen the truck stalled on the road. They were able to conclude, therefore, that the driver of the car was not at fault for causing the accident.

g. We have noticed that most of the successful managers in our company had significant work experience in manufacturing and did not hold degrees from four-year universities. We have concluded that the skills that make one successful as a manager tend to be more practical than theoretical. We have determined that no manager will be hired unless he or she has more than five years of manufacturing experience.

h. The most highly watched television shows in the fall season all were dramas set in large cities. Our production company has now dropped all projects except for urban dramas so that we can produce higher rated programs.

i. I have noticed that when I stay up too late reading mysteries, I tend to fail my examinations the next day. I have decided that the mysteries must be making me fail the exams, so I have decided to stop reading them.

j. Children who are exposed to violence in video games and on television have been found to have anxiety disorders and criminal records. From this fact we can conclude that children are heavily influenced by the environment they grow up in.

k. Every night I can see that my neighbors' light is still on when I go to bed. I have decided that they are true night-owls.

4. The following examples represent arguments from testimony and arguments from form. Apply the appropriate tests to determine whether the arguments are sound.

a. When my brother was seventeen, he was allowed to stay out until midnight. I am now seventeen and my curfew is 10:30. The only difference is that I am a girl. Since my parents have a duty to follow the rule of justice (people in equivalent situations should be treated the same way), I should have my curfew extended until midnight.

b. In 1996, Oprah Winfrey had a show that examined certain practices in the US beef industry. At one point, Winfrey said that the story "stopped me cold from eating another hamburger." Winfrey's statement caused many of her viewers to swear off beef as well.

c. Last spring, I got a great job offer from this software company downtown. My neighbor Joe the plumber told me that his nephew had worked at the company and thought that it was a terrible place to work. Therefore, I reluctantly turned down the job.

d. Xena would like to walk to the beach, which is quite some distance away. Before she can get to the beach, she must get halfway there and before she can get halfway there, she must get one-quarter of the way and before she can do that, she will need to get one-eighth of the way, and so forth. Therefore, she will never reach the beach. (Zeno's paradoxes)

e. During the hearings on building the new subdivision, a world-renowned expert on monarch butterflies testified regarding the recent decline in local butterfly populations. He argued that no one needed the ugly McMansions the developers were proposing.

f. During the trial, the star witness described seeing the defendant leave his house in a hurry sometime after 11:00 p.m. The witness stated, "It reminded me of that Liam Neeson movie where he goes after his son's killer. He seemed like the kind of guy who would want to get revenge."

g. When I moved into this apartment, the landlord told me that I would have use of the backyard for gardening. I think the lease said that the tenant would have full rights to use the grounds for any allowed purpose, or something like that.

h.   My nephew Bandar is one of those Horatio Alger types. He is always thinking of new business ideas and he works all the time. If you have a chance to invest in one of his ventures, you definitely should.

Extensions: Toward More Advanced Study

Each of the types of warrants we have explored in this chapter is somewhat abstract, but several of them are not difficult to imagine – similarity or representativeness, for example. Causal warrants may be more difficult to grasp, because the concept of *influence* itself is abstract and has to be inferred from what can be observed.

Possibly for this reason, there has been dispute among philosophers for centuries about just what a cause is. What is its essential nature, or what counts as a cause? Here we will survey some of the leading answers to that question, as a gateway for more advanced study of causal warrants.

The skeptical philosopher David Hume proposed that causation was nothing more than a name we give to *constant conjunction*, meaning a sign relationship that is so strong that it is not known to have any exceptions.[8] Such a relationship, Hume suggested, is different from an ordinary sign relationship, so we give it the name of cause. The primary criticism of this approach is the observation that there are various constant conjunctions that, in actual usage, nobody regards as causes or effects. The most basic example is the regularity with which day follows night and night follows day, and yet nobody believes that the day causes the night or the night causes the day.

John Stuart Mill discussed the concepts of *necessary condition* and *sufficient condition* as possible answers to the question, "What is a cause?"[9] A is a necessary condition for B if, without A, B cannot exist. The presence of A does not assure B but the absence of A assures B's absence. The problem with this view is that there is an infinite number of necessary conditions for anything – the existence of the universe, the existence of life, and so on – which people will regard as unstated background conditions but no one speaks about as causes.

[8]   David Hume, *An Enquiry Concerning Human Understanding*, sections 7 and 8. Many editions exist.
[9]   See Hospers, *An Introduction to Philosophical Analysis*, 297.

The concept of sufficient condition is a bit stronger for our purposes. A is a sufficient condition for B if the presence of A will assure the presence of B. Presenting a boarding pass, for example, is a sufficient condition for being allowed to board a plane. This is not to say that you would be unable to board unless you had a boarding pass, but rather that if you *did* have a boarding pass, that would be enough to assure that you could board the plane. Sometimes if there are many causes operating together, the sufficient condition is the one that acts last, followed by the appearance of the effect. Sufficient condition is sometimes called the "proximate cause." This seems like a stronger explanation of causality than constant conjunction or necessary condition. Yet the two are not always distinct. A sufficient condition often can act only in the presence of the necessary conditions, for example. Besides, there might be a situation with several sufficient conditions for a given result, yet none considered its cause.

The twentieth-century philosopher R. G. Collingwood proposed that only human actions could be considered causes.[10] Natural events just happen, he surmised, and causes are confined to the actions of human beings intervening in the natural world. The strength of Collingwood's position is that it regards causation as motivated action and assumes that only human beings can have motives that impel action. A consequence of Collingwood's view is that we would not ask about such things as the causes of tornadoes because they cannot have causes; they are just natural events. And yet almost everyone would regard "What caused the tornado?" as a perfectly reasonable question, and indeed one whose answer would influence how we might choose to combat the tornado.

As a final example, the twentieth-century legal theorist H. L. A. Hart suggested that causation requires deviation from a norm.[11] Regularities in the world are not causes of anything; rather, it is an interruption from the normal that might be a cause of something. Much like Collingwood's position that we do not inquire about the causes of natural events, Hart suggests that we do not inquire about processes or events that are ordinary or repetitive. Only when something comes up to disrupt the pattern do we imagine it as the cause of some new or different result. His view would suggest, to invoke a cliché, that there is no such thing as a cause for a dog biting a man – it is an ordinary event – but that one might well inquire about the cause of a man biting a dog.

[10] R. G. Collingwood, *The Idea of History* (Oxford: Clarendon Press, 1946).
[11] H. L. A. Hart and A. M. Honore, *Causation in the Law* (Oxford: Clarendon Press, 1959).

These views of the nature of causation have different implications for what, in an actual argument, counts as establishing a cause. We have not tried to adjudicate among these philosophical positions, first, because there is no way ultimately to resolve them, and, second, because the difference does not matter. Whatever one's view on the nature of causality, a cause-based inference will need to establish both that it is possible and reasonable for a causal relationship between two things to exist and also that it is more likely that there is a causal relationship than any other kind of linkage between the two things, or than no linkage at all.

CHAPTER 6

Fallacies

We saw in Chapter 5 that valid arguments are those in which the inference from evidence to claim is properly warranted. Now we will continue our analysis of inferences by examining the nature of fallacies and considering some common types.[1]

Understanding Fallacies

Fallacies are invalid arguments. Even if the statements they offer as evidence were all true, those statements would not warrant an inference to the claim. Another way to say this is to say that the relationship among the statements and the claim is not right.

In deductive reasoning, fallacies are errors in the *form* of the argument. The content of the argument is irrelevant to fallaciousness; substantive content could be replaced by symbols or letters of the alphabet and judgments of validity or fallaciousness would be the same. In ordinary argumentation, however, content, context, and form are all intertwined. Still, fallaciousness means something more specific than "anything that is wrong with an argument," the meaning it sometimes receives in common usage. Specifically, it refers to a deficiency in the relationship among the statements in an argument, leaving aside the truth or falsity of those statements. The term sometimes is also used to refer to violations of procedural rules by the participants in a dispute, but it seems preferable to keep the two usages separate, referring to the latter as *procedural error*.

Some definitions consider a fallacy as "an argument that seems valid but is not." Until about fifty years ago, in fact, this was the most common definition of the term, but it was largely discredited as a result of the work

---

[1] A fuller examination of fallacies is available in Christopher W. Tindale, *Fallacies and Argument Appraisal* (Cambridge: Cambridge University Press, 2007).

of the philosopher C. L. Hamblin.[2] It is true that many fallacies have a superficial resemblance to valid arguments and it may be necessary to think critically in order to spot the deficiency. But that is not the defining condition. In fact, many of the examples commonly used to teach fallacies have deficiencies that are quite obvious even to the untrained observer; that is why they make such good illustrations for teaching. Besides, such a definition fails to answer *to whom* the argument "seems valid" and, furthermore, how any person to whom it truly seems valid would recognize it as fallacious. Training in argumentation can make a person better able to identify fallacies, but a person so trained will also be less likely to think that fallacious arguments "seem valid" in the first place. It is better to avoid all these confusions by ignoring any question about how an argument *seems*, focusing instead on what a fallacy *is*: a deficiency in the relationship among the statements in an argument, setting aside their truth or falsity.

What makes the relationship deficient is that the warrant, if properly understood, does not authorize the inference from evidence to claim. It may authorize some other inference entirely, or – even more often – we cannot know from the argument *what*, if anything, it will authorize or where it will lead. It might lead to the claim, but it might just as likely lead to one or more alternative claims; there is no way to know.

Common fallacies are grouped under four general headings: fallacies of specific warrants, fallacies of clarity, fallacies of relevance, and fallacies of vacuity. But it must be emphasized that, unlike in deductive reasoning, none of these patterns is *inherently* fallacious. At least for most of them, one can imagine situations in which they are perfectly reasonable arguments. Take a specific example. Argumentum ad personam (a species of ad hominem) is usually thought to be a fallacy because it attacks the person's character instead of the person's argument. Name-calling is an obvious example. The warrant does not lead to a denial of the argument but to an irrelevant (and unsupported) claim about the arguer. But sometimes the person's character is directly relevant to the argument. If a person testifying as a character witness in a criminal trial can be shown to be a habitual liar, then the testimony on behalf of the defendant's truth-telling will be called into question. A known liar cannot be counted on to tell the truth.

For another example, equivocation – using the same word in two different senses in the same argument – is usually a fallacy. But if equivocation is used in order to show that a certain statement has no clear meaning, because

---

[2] C. L. Hamblin, *Fallacies* (London: Methuen, 1970).

it could take on either of the two possible meanings that have been used in the case, then it not only is not a fallacy; it is a constructive argument.

But if faulty relationships among statements in an argument are not always fallacies, who decides whether or not they are fallacious in a given case? The answer was suggested earlier in the book: the arguer (or the critic, as the case may be) invokes a notion of an ideal audience. We have defined that ideal as *the reasonable person, acting reasonably*, and have expanded that definition by suggesting that it is a person to whom you might go for advice about an important matter, knowing that the person's judgment will be impartial, carefully considered, and relevant to your specific situation. If you have good reason to believe that such a person would use a specific pattern of argument, then you can presume that the pattern is valid. If not – or, even better, if when such a pattern has been employed, it usually has led the arguers astray – then you will be better off to treat the argument pattern as fallacious, avoid its use, and evaluate it adversely when you find it in the argumentation of others. Fallaciousness, then, is governed both by your sense of what the ideal audience would do and by your knowledge of how a given pattern of reasoning has fared in the light of experience.

Fallacies of Specific Warrants

Chapter 5 presented several different patterns of inferences and the warrants that authorize them. For each, there are common fallacies that result from making inferences that are not warranted because the relationship among the statements is wrong.

Example

Warrants from *example*, you will recall, justify inferences that relate parts to wholes, by showing either that a specific instance is an example of a generalization or that a generalization applies to a specific instance. Three principal fallacies associated with this warrant are hasty generalization (sometimes called by the Latin term *secundum quid*), the fallacy of composition, and the fallacy of division. Hasty generalization results when a generalization is made from too few or from unrepresentative examples. The fallacy of composition assumes that what is true of the part is true of the whole, in a situation in which the whole is more or less than just the sum of the parts. And the fallacy of division is just the reverse, assuming that what is true of the whole is necessarily true of the part. These fallacies were all illustrated in Chapter 5 and you may want to review the cases offered there.

Analogy

Warrants from *analogy* justify inferences about comparison, suggesting that items alike in most respects probably are alike in the respect being discussed. The major fallacy of this warrant is false analogy. The two items being compared may be similar, but remember that they are not identical. They might differ in some essential feature directly relevant to the comparison. It is always necessary to ask whether the essential points of similarity outweigh the essential points of difference. If the answer is No but you proceed as if the answer were Yes, there is greater risk of invoking a false analogy – wrongly assuming a similarity in one respect merely because there are other respects in which the two items are alike.

Sign

Warrants from *sign* are used in arguments about representations, justifying inferences that relate unknowable essences to their observable properties. They enable us to make predictions about the underlying condition or abstraction from the presence of the tangible representation. If we accept that one thing is a sign of another, then the presence of the first thing should enable us to infer the presence of the second. But the relationship between the sign and the thing signified could turn out to be nothing more than coincidence, or the same sign could herald more than one underlying condition – even underlying conditions that are inconsistent and work at cross-purposes. And another difficulty with sign inferences is that they tell us nothing about *why* the essential feature and the external property go together. In particular, we do not know that either condition exerts any influence on the other, so making judgments about what we should do in the future based on a sign relationship can be fallacious. Suppose we know that inflation tends to be low when presidents of the Republicrat party are in office. Since we don't know why this relationship exists, it does not follow that if we elect the Republicrat candidate in the next election, low inflation would ensue. We need to remember that sign warrants justify inferences based on correlation, not causal links.

Cause

Warrants from *cause*, in contrast, go beyond correlations. They not only assert that one thing represents another; they *account for* the relationship by maintaining that one thing exerts influence over another. They are used to justify inferences that predict the consequences of our actions, to explain the reasons for a given condition or circumstance, or to relate means to ends ("if you want to bring about X, you should do Y"). The difficulty is that causal influence is not observable, and, as we saw in the "Extensions" section of Chapter 5, there are differences among philosophers about what it means. Whichever view of the nature of causality one accepts, other inferences that may even resemble causal inferences will turn out to be fallacious.

For example, a cause must precede its effect, but just because one event comes first does not mean that it causes the one that comes second. To assume otherwise is to commit the fallacy known by the Latin term *post hoc ergo propter hoc* (after this, therefore because of this). It is the wrongful attribution of causality to what is merely a temporal sequence. Or the causal relationship might be the reverse of what it looks like: the alleged cause is really the effect, and vice versa. Or the factors that look like cause and effect may actually both be effects of a common cause. Violence on the border between two nations, for example, may be thought to cause political disruptions when in fact it is political disruptions that lead to the border violence.

It is also possible, of course, for effects to have multiple causes and for causes to have multiple effects. This can be especially problematic when we employ causal arguments to justify taking action to solve a problem by removing its alleged cause. If there are multiple causes, removing one might not improve the situation; it might just result in another cause's now becoming more prominent. And if there are multiple effects, disrupting the cause might also disrupt other effects as well. On balance, the situation might be made worse.

Testimony

Warrants from *testimony* justify inferences on the basis of assertions by a credible source. We are led to accept a claim ("p is true") because of trust in X ("X is a reliable authority concerning p"). Trust in X is what enables us to get from "X says p" to "p is true." But these arguments can go astray if the connection is unwarranted. This can happen if X is not really a reliable authority, if X is not really speaking about p, if X has no possible way to know about p, or if X has not thought about p and is merely pontificating.

Form

Warrants from *form* justify inferences from the sense of anticipation or completion that characterizes formal systems such as mathematics or deductive logic. There are various patterns of inference, illustrated in

Chapter 5, in which arguments may resemble formal systems but actually depend on a nonformal element that could turn out to be fallacious. And some of the fallacies in formal logic also apply to everyday argumentation. A good example is hypothetical reasoning (if X, then Y; X; therefore Y). The two fallacies associated with this pattern are affirming the consequent and denying the antecedent. Affirming the consequent (Y in the example above) tells us nothing about the presence or absence of X, because even though X would bring about Y, Y could also occur for reasons entirely independent of X. In the same way, denying the antecedent (asserting "not-X") tells us nothing about the presence or absence of the consequent, because Y could have occurred for reasons unrelated to X. These two fallacies can be found not only in formal deduction but also in everyday argumentation.

Another example of a fallacy of form occurs in categorical reasoning, which is reasoning about the relationship between categories. A classic example of categorical reasoning is: all dogs are mammals; all mammals are living beings; so all dogs are living beings. This all happens to be true, but that is not the point. It is a valid argument because the members of the first category are placed within a second category which in turn fits entirely within a third; so necessarily all the members of the first category will fit within the third. (Equally valid would be a similar structure composed of statements that are false.) But now consider the following example: all dogs are mammals; all cats are mammals; so all dogs are cats. The first two statements happen to be true, but something clearly is wrong with the argument because the claim does not follow from those two statements. The technical term for this error is an *undistributed middle term*. The term appearing in both premises but not in the claim ("mammals" in this case) is undistributed, meaning that in neither appearance of the term does it refer to *all* mammals. There may be, and in fact are, mammals that are neither dogs nor cats. An easier way to remember this fallacy is to say that two things can both be related to a third thing without necessarily being related to each other at all. This fallacy also occurs in everyday argumentation as well as in formal reasoning. Consider, for example: all liberals favor big government; all Communists favor big government; so all liberals are Communists. It is a fallacy to conclude anything about the relationship between liberals and Communists from the fact that they both relate to a third category (supporters of big government).

A third example of a fallacy of form is the confusion between the exclusive and the nonexclusive sense of the term "either/or." This may sound complicated but it really is quite simple. The phrase "either A or B" has two possible meanings: "either A or B or both" and "either A or B but not both." The first is nonexclusive; it means "at least one of A or B." The second is exclusive; it means "only one of A or B." Which meaning is intended in a given case depends on whether the options A and B are mutually exclusive. If we say, "either the victim is alive or he is dead," the choices are mutually exclusive. Whatever definition of "death" we may use, a person cannot be both alive and dead at the same time. So if we determine that the person is alive, we can claim validly that he is not dead; just as we can claim that he is dead if we determine that he is not alive. Compare that example to the statement, "Either we will study at the library tonight or we will go out to eat." These options are not mutually exclusive because we could do both. So if we decide to study at the library, we have not ruled out the possibility of going out to eat. (The options could become mutually exclusive only with additional information – for example, we can meet only at 6:00 p.m., and the library closes at 5:00.) In the case of the exclusive either/or, affirming one option rules out the other and denying one option commits us to the other. But in the case of the nonexclusive either/or, while denying one option commits to the other, affirming one option does not permit claiming anything about the other. The fallacy consists of treating one use of either/or as if it were the other – claiming too much from the nonexclusive sense or too little from the exclusive sense. Like the other fallacies of form, it occurs in everyday argumentation as well as in formal deductive reasoning.

The final example of a fallacy of form involves narrative reasoning. Because we find a coherent story satisfying, we do not always notice when story elements are missing, and we may assume their existence without a foundation for doing so. When we do that, we are more likely to make fallacious inferences, such as imaginary plots and conspiracies, where none exist. Or we may assume that people's motivations are so strong and all-consuming that they overwhelm contrary tendencies and lead to unbalances and unrealistic accounts of actions. We also are more prepared to believe that good things happen to us because of our own actions and that bad things happen to us because of events beyond our control than we are to believe the opposites of those claims.[3] Consequently, we are more likely to see our successes and failures as motivated than to ascribe them to luck or chance. This bias sometimes will lead to fallacious reasoning in those

---

[3] These tendencies illustrate applications of attribution theory. See Robert S. Wyer, *Social Cognition, Inference, and Attribution* (Hillsdale, NJ: Lawrence Erlbaum, 1979).

situations in which we assume the existence of a plan where in reality there is none.

Fallacies of Clarity

A second group of fallacies results from the inherent inexactness of language. We sometimes think we are being very clear and precise, only to discover that there is more than one way to understand what we have said. When that happens, we may not know what the relationship among our statements really is, and thus we will have no more basis to make one claim than another.

Vagueness

An obvious example of such a fallacy is *vagueness*. This is a situation in which a term could have many possible referents and we have no way to determine which is meant. Consider the term "middle-aged." To a boy of age 15, the term might mean something like "anyone between the ages of 30 and 50," while a man of 40 might believe that "middle age" begins at 50, and a man of 70 who still feels youthful might say that "middle age" starts at 85. None of these answers is "right" in any objective sense; they reflect different orientations and patterns of usage. But imagine an argument in which one person says, "Middle-aged people are just as athletic as those who are young," thinking of middle age as 30, and the other replies, "That is just clearly not so," thinking of middle age as 70. There is no way to reach any valid conclusion because the key term has an unlimited number of possible meanings.

Ambiguity

Closely related is the fallacy of *ambiguity*. In this case a term has multiple, but finite, meanings, and it is not clear which meaning is intended in the argument. A simple example is "The downtown area is crowded because the Cardinals are coming to town." Is the speaker referring to birds? To a baseball team? Or to officials of the Roman Catholic Church? The problem with ambiguity is similar to that with vagueness: participants in an argument may have different meanings in mind, without acknowledging that such is the case. They may appear to be testing each other's statements through attack and defense when in reality they are talking about different things and do not realize it.

Although advocates generally are advised to avoid ambiguity, there are some times when it is called for. The positive use of strategic ambiguity will be discussed in Chapter 9.

Amphiboly

While ambiguity refers to a *term* with multiple meanings, the same condition applied to a phrase or sentence as a whole is called *amphiboly*. In this case, the meaning of each term individually may be quite clear, and yet the statement as a whole may be unclear. Here are some examples. Does the statement, "Visiting professors can be boring," mean that it is a boring experience to go out and visit one's professors, or does it mean that those who hold the title of "visiting professor" are bores? Does the statement, "The president sent her congratulations," mean that the president, who is a woman, sent congratulations to someone whose gender is unknown, or does it mean that the president, whose gender is unknown, sent congratulations to a woman? Does the statement, "Only sons marry only daughters," mean that persons who are only children marry each other, or is it a proclamation against same-sex marriage? Finally, does the statement, "I cannot say enough good things about this person," appearing in a letter of recommendation, mean that the person in question is a superb candidate or that the person is so demonstrably bad as to fall short of even a minimum standard of acceptability? You can imagine in each of these cases how an argument could go astray if the participants had different meanings in mind. The relationships between the parties' different versions of the statement would not permit them to make any valid inference or to advance any claim with confidence.

Equivocation

Another closely related fallacy is *equivocation*. This fallacy is committed when a word can be used in multiple senses and the sense in which it is used changes during the course of the argument. Instead of two arguers using the same term but with different meanings, the same arguer uses the same term differently during the same argument. A simple example is "Six is an odd number of legs for a horse to have; an odd number cannot be divided by two; so six cannot be divided by two." The fallacy is not that the claim is false, although it is. The fallacy is that the term "odd number" changes its meaning between the first and second statements. In the first statement it means "strange" but in the second statement "odd" is used in contrast to "even" as a category of numbers. Examples like this, especially in which the statements are adjacent to each other, are easy to spot and may provoke a laugh. Examples that occur in different places of a lengthy argument are more elusive and more dangerous.

Heaps and Slippery Slopes

The final fallacies of clarity, *heaps* and *slippery slopes*, result not from the fact that words can have multiple meanings but from the imprecision of language. They both relate to difficulties in determining when a difference in degree becomes a difference in kind. They may be easier to grasp with examples than with definitions. Here are examples of the fallacy of the heap. A man in his early 20s decides to grow a beard. As it comes in, its color is dark. When the man turns 30, he notices a few white hairs in his beard, but there aren't enough of them to notice much difference in the color of the beard; it is still dark. At 32 there are a few more, at 35 a few more, and so on every year or two. But never do enough hairs change color to change the overall color of the beard. How, then, does it happen that at age 75 the man's beard is solid white? We have just shown that there was no point at which the beard changed color! You probably can see why this fallacy is called the *heap*. It says that since the addition of one grain of sand does not make any appreciable difference to what was there before, we are never able to pile up the sand into a heap. Another example of the fallacy begins with the statement that giving a person a penny will not make that person richer than before (because a penny makes such a trivial difference to the person's wealth). You could say the same about the second penny you give to the person, and the third, and the fourth. By this reasoning there is no number of additional pennies that will make a person rich, even though we know that a person with trillions of pennies would be very rich indeed,

We now can define the fallacy of the heap. It consists in the assumption that because there is no specifiable point when a difference in degree becomes a difference in kind, therefore a difference in degree *never* becomes a difference in kind. This fallacy had serious consequences for the United States during the 1960s. President Lyndon Johnson escalated US involvement in the Vietnam War through a series of relatively small increments to the number of US troops. Each time he did so, the president assured his country that he was neither changing the mission nor widening the war, only making assistance to the South Vietnamese more effective. This claim, to some degree, disarmed critics of his policy. Yet in retrospect it is clear that as the American presence grew from 16,000 military advisers in 1963 to more than 500,000 troops in 1968, the character of the war changed and Vietnam became an American war – even if we cannot say precisely when this happened.

The fallacy of the *slippery slope* is the reverse of that of the heap. It consists of the assumption that *any* difference of degree will become a difference in kind, because once we start on a particular path, events will push us along on a course that we can neither reverse nor change. The fallacious claim is that we should not take a particular action now, because if we do, there will be no opportunity to reverse or change course later. Inevitably we will continue along that path until a difference in degree has become a difference in kind.

One of the most famous examples of the fallacy of the slippery slope was the "domino theory," articulated by President Dwight Eisenhower at the height of the Cold War during the 1950s. He argued that the United States must defend all countries in Asia against communism because if one country were to fall, neighboring nations would topple over like falling dominoes. Soon we would be left without the buffer of protection offered by friendly nations. The argument often was encapsulated as "If we don't fight the communists in Vietnam we will have to fight them in San Francisco." Under the growing threat of international terrorism, the same argument has been recycled into the claim that we must take the fight to terrorists' homelands or else they will bring it to ours.

Fallacies of Relevance

A third category of fallacies in everyday argumentation is fallacies of relevance, those in which an irrelevant element is introduced and appealed to, disrupting the relationship between the evidence and the claim. A simple example is the argument, "Jones clearly established that we could save money on a project if we accepted his bid, but we all know that he is a Demoblican; therefore we cannot believe whatever he says." Whether Jones is a Demoblican or not has nothing to do with whether his bid is the most attractive, yet this irrelevant element – his political party affiliation – becomes the basis for declining his competitive bid. The fallacies in this group often are identified by their Latin names, and many begin with the word *ad*, meaning "to" and referring to the irrelevant element on which the arguer fallaciously is relying. Here are some common examples of fallacies of relevance.

Ad Hominem

Probably most common is the argument against the person (*ad hominem*). This usually is understood as a personal attack that diverts from the substance of the argument, but that is only one type of ad hominem argument, and as we saw earlier is better identified as ad personam. The example about Jones, the alleged Demoblican, illustrates one kind of ad hominem argument, the *abusive* or "bad character" type. It will be fallacious if the alleged character trait has no bearing on the argument. That is particularly likely if it is used just as an epithet, a means of name-calling the other party. Another kind of ad hominem argument is the *bias* type, which alleges that an arguer's claim should not be taken seriously because it is swayed by self-interest or some other form of bias. "Of course she supports the tax cut bill; she will get a huge benefit herself if it passes," is an example referring to self-interest. "He didn't like that book, but then, he never likes anything by authors who are gay," is an example referring to another kind of bias. This form of ad hominem argument is a bit harder to evaluate. A person's argument can be sound even though she or he has a bias, in which case referring to the bias would be an irrelevant diversion. On the other hand, there are situations in which a person's bias can be so strong or so central to the person that it prevents him or her from seeing alternative possibilities or making sound judgments. In such a case the charge of bias would not be fallacious at all. The question is whether the allegation of bias is a substantive response to an argument or whether it is a means to deflect the argument.

There is a third type of ad hominem argument that is almost never fallacious, though sometimes it is treated as if it were. This is the *circumstantial* ad hominem argument, which suggests that a particular person cannot advance a specific claim because it is inconsistent with other commitments that person has made in the argument, or with the person's own behavior. Suppose someone says, "Defense spending should be increased significantly," and another person says, "You can't say that. Only ten minutes ago you were saying that every single area of the budget should be cut significantly." That is an example of a circumstantial ad hominem argument in which an arguer's own previous commitments are used to refute the claim at hand. The suggestion is that the current claim should be rejected because it is inconsistent with those earlier commitments. Making that suggestion does not automatically end the argument – the first arguer can try to work his or her way out of the inconsistency – but making the charge is not a fallacy. As we will see in Chapter 8, charging the opponent with inconsistency can be a powerful means of refutation. This also applies to inconsistencies between claims a person makes and the person's own behavior. A simple example is the adult who urges a teenager not to smoke, only to be told in response, "You can't say that. After all, you smoke two packs a day." The teenager's point is that the adult's own behavior casts doubt on the sincerity of his or her opposition to smoking. Of course, in this example the adult could respond – as many smokers do – that he or she regrets having started smoking and becoming addicted to nicotine, and that his or her own experience is the reason to implore the teenager not to make the same mistake. The point is that the teenager's accusation would require the adult to make this or some similar response if the adult wished to advance the argument. The teenager has not committed a fallacy with the circumstantial ad hominem argument.

The ad hominem argument has been the most thoroughly studied of the fallacies of relevance. Other such fallacies can be described more briefly.

Ad Verecundiam

Appeal to authority (*ad verecundiam*) is a fallacy if the authority being appealed to is unrelated to the argument at hand. For instance, suppose someone were to say, referring to the basketball star, "Michael Jordan says that abortion is immoral; therefore it is." Even if that were Michael Jordan's belief (and this argument is invented, not necessarily an accurate statement of his views), his authority relates to basketball, not the morality of abortion, so appealing to his authority would be irrelevant and therefore fallacious. This is a common occurrence with celebrity endorsements of commercial products unrelated to their expertise. Or suppose an arguer asserts, "John F. Kennedy was a great president. We should do in Afghanistan what he did in Cuba." Here the suggestion is not that Afghanistan presents similar issues to Cuba – that would be an analogy that could be tested as such – but rather that Kennedy's achievements in Cuba should lead us to follow a similar course in Afghanistan. That is an irrelevant appeal to authority because it actually diverts us from examining the strength of the analogy. Finally, consider the stereotypical response of old-timers in response to a suggestion of new ideas: "Yes, but we've always done it that way." This appeal to a generalized "tradition" is fallacious because, even though tradition may create a presumption for continuity (since change is not an inherent good), that presumption has already been countered by the arguments advanced by the newcomer for a different approach. At that point, invoking the authority of tradition actually blocks consideration of whether or not the newcomer's proposal is a good idea. That is why it is fallacious.

Ad Populum

Appeal to popular opinion (*ad populum*) is a fallacy if the argument is not about what public opinion is – in which case it would be directly relevant – but rather about the truth or falsity of some other claim. Consider the statement, "Most people believe that serious crimes have increased in the United States; therefore, they have." The argument is about whether crime rates have gone up or down, not about what people believe, so the appeal to popular opinion is not relevant. (In fact, rates of most serious crimes have declined, even though many people do think they have increased.)

Ad Baculum

Appeal to threat (*ad baculum*) asks someone to support a claim not because of its own strength but because of the threat of harm if he or she does not. "You ought to contribute to my campaign, because if you don't I will ruin your reputation" is a simple example. It is perfectly rational to act in order to avoid threatened harm, but avoiding such a threat is not relevant to the merits of supporting a person's campaign. Like the other *ad* fallacies, though, this one is not always fallacious. For example, avoiding the threat of future environmental disaster may be a very good reason to spend money on cleaning up the environment now, even if we are not confronted by a clear and present danger. There is a difference, however, between discussing a generalized future threat as part of a decision whether to act now or to wait, and taking an action otherwise unwarranted because of the danger of imminent personal harm.

Ad Misericordiam

Appeal to pity (*ad misericordiam*) asks for support for an argument based on sympathy for those who have suffered harm or loss, rather than on the merits of the action itself. A simple though understandable example was the appeal to rebuild the World Trade Center in New York, destroyed in the terrorist attacks of September 11, 2001, in a certain way, not because it was the best policy choice but because doing so would be an expression of sympathy for the families of those who lost their lives. Pity is not always an irrelevant consideration, but the argument at hand was not about creating a memorial but about building for the future. (In contrast, the wishes of the families were appropriately given serious consideration in planning the September 11 memorial itself.)

Ad Ignorantium

Appeals to ignorance (*ad ignorantium*) consist of treating ignorance regarding a claim as if it were positive proof of its falsity. It is a fallacy because it prematurely stops discussion of how we should act in the face of ignorance about the claim's truth. A classic example occurred during the Iraq War of 2003, when the inability to prove that Saddam Hussein, the Iraqi dictator, had eliminated weapons of mass destruction was widely (and, as it turned out, erroneously) taken as proof that he currently had them. As the cliché says about this fallacy, absence of evidence is not evidence of absence.

Fallacies of Vacuity

The last category of fallacies that we will consider are those of vacuity, or emptiness. They are so named because, while they may look like arguments, the arguments really do not go anywhere. There may be no inferences at all or there may be "holes" left in the argument that prevent any determination of whether the inference is warranted.

Circular Reasoning

Circular reasoning is a fallacy in which the claim merely repeats the grounds in slightly different terms. As its name suggests, the argument proceeds in a circle, without advancing. There is no inference at all, which is why the statement is "empty" (vacuous) as an argument. "The reason Smith died is that he stopped breathing" does not really tell us anything about the cause of Smith's death; it merely provides a standard definition of what death is. Or imagine a politician proclaiming that "freedom of speech is for the common good, because the unrestrained opinion is in the best interest of all concerned." What this statement really says is that freedom of speech is for the common good because it is for the common good. As with many other fallacies, this one is easily spotted when the examples are simple and the statements that form the circle appear close to each other. It is less easily located when their repetitive character is less obvious and they are spread through lengthier arguments.

Begging the Question

Begging the question (sometimes called the fallacy of *many questions*) occurs when a claim treats as a settled matter some other claim that itself is controversial and needs to be proved. It assumes to be true something that must be proved to be true. The standard example is "Have you stopped beating your spouse?" The question assumes the answer to another question, "Did you ever beat your spouse?" that has not been established. The abortion controversy reveals this fallacy in a more emotional context. Pro-life advocates often will *assume* that the fetus is a person in the course of arguing that the fetus deserves greater legal protections. Meanwhile, pro-choice advocates will be equally quick to *assume* that the fetus is part of the woman's body in the course of arguing that the woman's privacy should be protected from government regulation. Of course, whether or not the fetus is a person is itself a contested question at the very heart of the abortion dispute. In this example, both parties are bypassing the question by assuming the answer.

Incidentally, the term "begging the question" is often misapplied. Sometimes you will hear a person say, when referring to an obvious question raised by an observation or a story, "That begs the question of such-and-such." What the person really means is that the situation *invites* the question, *raises* the question, or, sometimes, *demands a response* to the question. What the advocate is trying to do is to put the burden on the other party to respond to the question at hand. This move is a legitimate tactic and is not fallacious, but it is not the same thing as begging the question.

Ignoring the Question

Ignoring the question is the result of a digression or a focus on a matter extraneous to the subject at hand. It occurs especially in dialogues in which one party finds a topic uncomfortable and would like to divert the conversation to a different topic. An advocate of tax cuts, confronted before a hostile audience with the claim, "It is simply immoral to give tax cuts to rich people who don't need them when we have serious unmet public needs which ought to be our focus," might instead reply colloquially, "How about them Cubs?" preferring to shift to the less controversial topic of the improbable success of the Chicago baseball team in winning the World Series in 2016 after more than 100 years. The fallacy of ignoring the question is sometimes referred to as a "red herring." This is a metaphor from fox hunting in England, when a red herring would be drawn across the trail to train dogs in the hunt.

Non Sequitur

The fallacy of *non sequitur* ("it does not follow") may sound like a catchall term for all fallacies, because what they have in common is that the claim does not follow from the grounds since the inference is not warranted. But this fallacy has a more specific referent. It occurs when an arguer makes two or more statements, one of which is assumed to be the claim, and the other(s) the grounds, when in fact the statements have nothing to do with each other and there is no basis for connecting them. Consider the argument, "Your candidate would be a really poor public servant. After all, he has a beard and he can't carry a tune." One's facial hair and musical ability are generally thought to have no connection to one's fitness for public office. It may seem farfetched, but even this form of argument can at least be imagined not to be fallacious in some circumstances. The argument, "George W. Bush was a poor president; he couldn't even pronounce the word 'nuclear,'" would usually be considered a non sequitur – unless it was uttered in a conversation among pronunciation experts considering the claim that correct pronunciation is an essential element of presidential performance.

Straw Man

The fallacy of the *straw man* consists of erroneously characterizing another person's position, making it weaker than it really is, and then responding to this weakened characterization. You can see how this fallacy gets its name: instead of responding to a real argument, one defeats an argument made of straw. Early in his presidency, Donald Trump proclaimed that Americans would end the "War on Christmas" by starting to wish each other "Merry Christmas" again. There may be grounds for Christians to believe that the religious holiday of Christmas is under attack (for example, by its rampant commercialization), but the claim that whether people greet one another by saying "Merry Christmas!" or the more generic "Happy Holidays" (which recognizes that not everyone is a Christian) marks a position in a "war" is such a weakened form of the argument as to merit the label "straw man." It is as though Trump, not wanting to take on the enormous economic effects of commercializing Christmas, goes after the choice of an innocuous term of greeting instead.

Self-Sealing Arguments

Finally, a *self-sealing argument* is a fallacy because there is no way one possibly could prove it false. Ironically, this sounds like exactly what we should be looking for – a "perfect argument." Indeed, in formal deduction a self-sealing argument would be valid, because the conclusion follows absolutely from the premise. But this occurs not because the argument is "perfect" but because it is designed to adjust its shape to envelop any challenge. If there is no possible way to prove it false, there is no way to know whether it is really true.

An example of a self-sealing argument is the allegation that there is a conspiracy afoot, a group plotting in secret to bring about some undesirable result. If an advocate can produce documentary evidence of the plot's design, that proves the existence of the conspiracy. But if the advocate cannot produce such evidence, that *also* proves the existence of the conspiracy. After all, wouldn't you expect a true conspirator to deviously disguise his or her intentions so that you could not find them out? No matter what claims you might advance to deny the existence of a conspiracy, the maker of the charge could reinterpret those claims as proof *supporting* the existence of a conspiracy. This does not prove that there really is a conspiracy, but rather that the allegation is self-sealing – it can be morphed into whatever shape is required to respond to a challenge.

Self-sealing arguments are the stock-in-trade of advocates who are committed to totalizing ideologies. They assume that an opposing force is so powerful that it is implicated in every problem. Everything is the fault of late capitalism, or a manifestation of racism, or a weakness of liberalism, or an evil of socialism, or whatever the case may be. A characteristic of totalizing ideologies is that their advocates cannot imagine that they might be wrong. They do not accept the risk of engaging in argumentation that we discovered in Chapter 1. They may rest comfortably in the belief that they are always right, even if others are inclined to regard that belief as delusional. When many people in a society engage in competing self-sealing arguments, reasoned discussion becomes very difficult.

Exercises

1. In the following examples, there is an argumentative statement with a potential fallacy listed in parentheses. Evaluate the argument to show what information or evidence you might need to determine whether the argument is fallacious or not.

a. The use of alcohol by the students building the bonfire was the cause of the collapse that injured one of them. (multiple causes)

b. Anyone who protests against his or her own country cannot be a patriot. (vagueness)

c. Whenever Apple is about to report earnings that exceed expectations, they always invite employees to be in the audience for the announcement. This quarter, no employees have been invited, so we expect the earnings to be disappointing. (sign)

d. Zain knows more about video games than anyone else I know. When he says that drone warfare is going to revolutionize the battlefield of the future, I have to believe him. (ad verecundiam)

e. Once consumers find out how much easier it is to buy groceries online, they will begin to have more food on hand, which means they will be less likely to go out to eat on a whim. This will be devastating for "fast-casual" restaurants, which depend on people with nothing to eat at home. Therefore, I recommend selling stock in any company that owns "fast-casual" restaurants. (slippery slope)

f. Yes, inflation has been creeping up. But a quarter-point rise in interest rates is not something that we should worry about. As long as interest rates are going up slowly, inflation will not be a problem to the average American. (heaps)

g. Dr. Huy has been recommending the use of a new topical anti-inflammatory cream for arthritis pain. I happen to know, however, that she has participated in some of the clinical trials for this treatment and stands to receive a commission based on the amount of the cream that is sold. (ad hominem – bias)

h. I have noticed that the students who are admitted to the most selective colleges do much more community service on average. It seems, therefore, that community service leads to high academic achievement. (confusing sign and cause)

2. The following are examples of fallacies of specific warrants. Identify the potential fallacy and explain what is potentially deficient in the relationship among the statements.

   a. Tilda gets up at 5:30 each morning to exercise before work. She is one of the most successful salespeople in our department. I guess the early bird does get the worm.

   b. As soon as Dr. Belasco became the superintendent of District 114, our test scores rose 25 percent, so we made a great decision in hiring her.

   c.   Grayson is a member of the Portland Chess Club. That club has won the state title in seven of the past ten years. I don't want to have to face Grayson in the first round, if I want to make the finals.

   d.   The last three people who came into the delicatessen bought cheese sandwiches. We really need to have more vegetarian entrees because of the growth in the number of people who don't eat meat these days.

   e.   If Buffalo wins the Monday night game, then they are going to the playoffs. They are going to the playoffs; therefore they won the game.

   f.   All pickles are salty; all seawater is salty; therefore all pickles are seawater.

   g.   Peter works hard all day and is kind to everyone. He just won the lottery, which proves that good things happen to people who work hard and are kind.

   h.   People who drive red cars get more speeding tickets than those who drive any other color car. Red must set off the radar detectors that the police use to catch speeders.

   i.   Today is a holiday, so we can go swimming or hike the nature trail. We did go swimming, so we must not have hiked the nature trail.

3.   The following are examples of fallacies of relevance. Identify the potential fallacy and explain what is potentially deficient in the relationship among the statements.

   a.   Each year more people buy more Vermont cheddar cheese than cheese made in Maine. Therefore, it is clear that the Vermont cheese is of a higher quality.

   b.   Emilia is in favor of allowing nonresidents to use the beach without having to pay a fee. She is the kind of person who doesn't even keep her own property up, however, so of course she doesn't care if our beach is overrun by tourists.

   c.   Yancy told me that this antique table is worth $1,500. However, he also told me that my painting was authentic when it turned out to be a fake. I don't think his opinion is one I can trust.

   d.   The twins want us to go to the fried chicken place for dinner tonight. When I asked them why, they told me that if we go anyplace else they are going to make life miserable for us.

   e.   My neighbor wants me to spray my lawn with pesticides. I have told him that I am concerned that these chemicals could be detrimental to my health. He demanded that I show him one person in the neighborhood who has been sickened by pesticides. When I said I didn't know, he said I had no excuse not to follow his advice.

f. Last night I received a call from an organization that raises money to help families who have children with serious diseases. When I asked the caller about how well the organization used its funds, he told me several stories about the sick children and how much they needed my money.

g. Can you imagine the nerve of my mother? She is always yelling at me for staying out past my curfew, but she never gets home before midnight when she has her bridge club!

4. The following are examples of fallacies of clarity or vacuity. Identify the potential fallacy and explain what is potentially deficient in the relationship among the statements.

a. Kim Kardashian is a celebrity because she is so famous.

b. Do you know Paula, our outgoing vice-president of sales?

c. I don't see what you are so angry about; I simply borrowed your car when I needed to drive to New York. I never meant to steal it.

d. My mother thinks I was lying, but it's her fault! She asked me if I was finished with my homework and I was. She didn't ask if the problem set was complete.

e. Brussels sprouts are better than chocolate because Brussels sprouts are better than nothing, and nothing is better than chocolate.

f. This morning on the way to work, I saw a truck with a sign that said "Slow Down Tree Removal." I'm glad to see that people are finally getting serious about preserving our forests.

g. Time flies like an arrow. Fruit flies like a banana.

Extensions: Toward More Advanced Study

In these pages, fallacies have been considered as arguments in which it is not reasonable to infer the claim from the grounds provided even if the grounds are true. The problem is that there is a flaw in the inference, making it unwarranted. The relationship between the statements making up the grounds and the statement of the claim is not right. On this account, the error is in the argument itself – although, as we have noted frequently, this judgment is also dependent on context. For almost any type of argument, even if generally fallacious, there may be circumstances in which its use would be perfectly reasonable. Besides formal reasoning, in which fallacies are purely errors of form, there are two major alternatives to the view of fallacies articulated here.

Informal Logic: Douglas Walton

One approach is associated with the Canadian philosopher Douglas Walton.[4] Starting from the observation that arguments can be reasonable or fallacious depending on circumstances, Walton concludes that it is therefore a mistake to locate fallacies in arguments themselves. Rather, he finds fallacies in the way arguments are used. Specifically, he regards a fallacy as an argumentation technique that is used wrongly in the context of a dialogue. He is concerned with argumentation in dialogues between people, and he theorizes that there are various types of dialogues: information-seeking dialogue, inquiry, negotiation, deliberation, and persuasion dialogue, for example. Each has its own assumptions, conventions, and procedures, and a move that is appropriate in one type of dialogue may be out of place in another.

For instance, in negotiation it is assumed that parties will open by espousing positions that are more extreme than those for which they are finally willing to settle. They may employ overstated claims, offer testimony from biased authorities, draw hasty generalizations, make ad populum (bandwagon) and ad baculum (threat) arguments, and the like. They do so in order to create space for mutual concessions along the way to a final agreement that neither party may really like but both can live with. Arguing in this fashion is just being a good negotiator. But if one were in a persuasion dialogue, in which the goal is to convince a critical listener of a position, these same moves would be out of place. They would interfere with the dialogue for the very reasons that we called them usually fallacious when discussing them above.

In fact, for Walton the paradigm case of a fallacy is a dialogue-shifting move, one that changes the type of dialogue from the one on which the parties initially embarked. Moreover, Walton assumes that dialogue-shifting moves are not just weaknesses or harmless errors but the result of deception or the attempt to create an illusion. Charging an opponent with a fallacy is a serious matter, therefore, because it suggests bad intent on the opponent's part. Walton's is a more limited conception of fallacies than the one presented earlier. Walton holds that many arguments commonly labeled fallacies really aren't. They are either perfectly acceptable

---

[4] See Douglas Walton, *A Pragmatic Theory of Fallacy* (Tuscaloosa: University of Alabama Press, 1995).

arguments in context or weak arguments that, nevertheless, are not fallacious. Pursuing this idea, Walton has examined most of the fallacies of relevance (*ad* fallacies), concluding that in many cases they are not fallacious at all and that they become fallacious when misused in the context of dialogue.

Pragma-Dialectics: Frans van Eemeren and Rob Grootendorst

The other major alternative approach to fallacies is the work of the Dutch scholars Frans van Eemeren and Rob Grootendorst.[5] Their model case is also dialogue, although their theoretical approach can be adapted to any of the model forms of discourse presented in Chapter 1. They are concerned specifically with argumentation that adopts the standards of *critical discussion*. As they use the term, a critical discussion is one in which the shared goal of the parties is to resolve a disagreement on the merits. A critical discussion is a normative goal that actual arguments approach to greater or lesser degree. As van Eemeren and Grootendorst theorize a critical discussion, they postulate that it would be guided by certain rules. For example, the *freedom rule* holds that parties must not prevent each other from putting claims (they call them "standpoints") forward or casting doubt on them. The *relevance rule* holds that a party may defend his or her standpoint only by offering argumentation that is relevant to it. The most widely known formulation includes ten of these rules (endearingly known as the "ten commandments"). Fallacies are violations of these rules. For instance, the freedom rule is violated by declaring a claim to be either sacrosanct or taboo and hence not arguable. It is also violated by pressuring the other party (ad baculum), playing on the emotions of the other party (ad misericordiam), or discrediting the other party (some of the varieties of the ad hominem). The effect of each of these moves is to interfere with the examination of competing claims on their merits. Similar accounts could be given of how each of the other nine rules might be violated.

For van Eemeren and Grootendorst, then, fallacies are *functional missteps* in an undertaking to resolve a controversy rationally (that is, on the merits). They are features of the interaction between the disputants, not features of the text of the argument. The implication is that *procedural* errors in everyday reasoning are the analogue of *formal* errors in deduction.

---

[5] See, for example, Frans H. van Eemeren, *Strategic Maneuvering in Argumentative Discourse* (Amsterdam: John Benjamins, 2010), esp. chapter 7. Van Eemeren and Grootendorst are joined by other colleagues in some of their publications.

Like Walton, van Eemeren and Grootendorst ground their understanding of fallacies in arguers rather than in the text. Unlike Walton, however, they make no assumptions about the motives of the arguers in committing a fallacy, and they do not focus on dialogue-shifts as the paradigm case of fallacy. Indeed, they are not concerned with dialogue-shifts because they examine only one kind of dialogue: that guided by the standards of critical discussion.

Interestingly, van Eemeren and Grootendorst identify fallacies very similarly to the treatment in this book, although they sometimes offer different explanations for what is "wrong" with the fallacies. For example, they suggest that nothing is wrong with the inference in the argument ad baculum – it is perfectly reasonable to act so as to avoid threats – but the flaw is that the threat substitutes for the critical examination of claims that is needed to resolve controversies on the merits. Likewise, van Eemeren and Grootendorst point out that what we have called circular reasoning is a perfectly valid deduction, as we also noted. But whereas the treatment in this book labels it fallacious because it really contains no inference, van Eemeren and Grootendorst label it fallacious because it contributes little or nothing to the resolution of a difference of opinion on the merits.

On the surface, it might seem that the approach of the Dutch scholars is less dependent on context than are the other approaches we have considered. After all, if one of the rules of critical discussion has been violated, then by definition a fallacy has been committed. But whether or not a rule has been violated is itself not an open-and-shut case. The arguers may disagree about that between themselves, and impartial observers could interpret the situation differently from one another. So it seems fair to say that the major approaches to fallacies in everyday argumentation, as opposed to formal deductive reasoning, do not regard the attribution of fallaciousness as absolute.

CHAPTER 7

Case Construction

In Chapters 4–6, we have considered factors that strengthen or weaken individual arguments, focusing especially on the evidence on which an argument is based and on the patterns of inference that are expressed in various argument schemes. Usually, though, these individual arguments are combined into larger units to advance or defeat a resolution, the main claim in a controversy. The structure of subsidiary claims and evidence to support or oppose a resolution is called a *case*. If the case supports the resolution, it is called an *affirmative* case (because it affirms) and if it opposes the resolution, it is referred to as a *negative* case (because it negates).

While the concepts in this chapter apply to the building of both the affirmative and the negative case, we saw in Chapter 3 that in a controversy in which there is an identifiable resolution, the burden of proof, the initial responsibility for developing a case, commonly rests with the affirmative. Accordingly, in this chapter we shall focus on developing the affirmative case, with the understanding that we could develop a negative case in much the same way. Conversely, since those opposed to the resolution usually have the first opportunity to challenge the adversary's case, in Chapter 8 we shall discuss attack and defense focusing primarily on the activities of the negative. It bears repeating, though, that the construction of one's own case, the attack on the opponent's case, and the defense of the original case are engaged in by both supporters and opponents of the resolution.

The Case and the Issues

The first responsibility of an advocate is to present a prima facie case. The Latin term *prima facie* means "first face" and refers to a case that, on first reading or hearing and in the absence of attack, would be sufficient to convince a reasonable person of the merit of the resolution. This does not mean that the case is "airtight" (it is unlikely that there is any such thing) or even necessarily very strong, but rather that the presentation has no fatal flaw that would doom it even if the opponent said nothing against it. A case based on preposterous evidence, outlandish interpretation of the evidence, a blatant contradiction, dubious relevance to the resolution, or an obvious omission would be an example of a case that might be rejected even if nary a word was said against it; its flaw is almost self-evident. But very few cases are so manifestly flawed. The vast majority of cases hold together well enough that, *at least so long as nothing is said against them*, they would justify the assent of a reasonable audience.

How, then, do you assemble a prima facie case? First, remember our discussion of *issues* in Chapter 3. The issues are the questions that must be answered satisfactorily in order to affirm the resolution. So the place to begin is by determining what the issues are in the specific controversy. There are three basic ways to do this:

1. The issues can be determined by quizzing the terms in the resolution. For example, if the resolution in dispute is "Mixed marriages seldom succeed," you will need to answer the questions, "What is a 'mixed marriage'?" "What counts as 'succeed'?" "What do we mean by 'seldom'?" and "Are these conditions satisfied?" These will be the issues on that particular resolution. Now, not all of these issues will prove controversial. For instance, although in the 1950s "mixed marriages" was used to refer to marriages between Christians of different religious denominations, there may be general agreement that the term currently refers to interracial marriages. If so, then the answer to that question may be stipulated and not controversial. In that case it would be removed from the list of issues that must be answered in order to affirm the resolution. So after quizzing the terms of the resolution, the issues would be those questions that remain contested between the parties.

2. A second way to discover the issues is by examining the contemporary context of the subject matter. For example, one of the recurring controversies of the past forty years has been what the ideological composition of the US Supreme Court should be. If you examine the discourse of this controversy, you will discover that there is fairly widespread agreement that Supreme Court Justices should not "make law from the bench." But what that phrase means is neither clear nor consistently maintained. When the Supreme Court intervened to effectively decide the 2000 presidential election, their ruling was

decried as "judicial activism" by many of the same people who
applauded an activist Court in other contexts, and it was celebrated
by those who often had condemned judicial activism in other rulings.
You will quickly discover that the ideological disposition of the Court
cannot be stated in such broad terms but is related to specific contexts.
So if you wanted to argue that there should be more conservative
Justices on the Court, you will need to examine such things as the
principles of the Federalist Society in order to determine what counts
as conservative in the current context. Again, not every potential issue
will actually be contested – for example, it may be the case that
virtually all jurists calling themselves conservative believe that there
is an individual right to own guns. That could be stipulated as one of
the characteristics of conservative judges. The issues are those contextual questions that are contested, after removing from the list those
that are stipulated or agreed to by the parties to the dispute.

3. A third way to determine the issues is by applying the concept of *topoi*
    that we discussed in Chapter 3. If you can determine, for instance,
    that the resolution that the United States should adopt a single-payer
    system for financing health care is a policy resolution, then you can
    refer to the *topoi* for claims of policy, and you will know that you need
    in some fashion to speak to the questions, "Is there a problem in
    financing health care?" "Will the problem persist in the absence of a
    single-payer system?" "Will a single-payer system solve this problem?"
    and "On balance, will a single-payer system be desirable or undesir-
    able?" Now, once again, although all of those questions are potential
    issues, not all will be contested in any given case. It may be the case
    that virtually everyone agrees that there is a problem in financing
    health care (whether because costs increase at a rate outstripping
    inflation, because significant numbers of people are left without
    insurance, because the health care consumer lacks the incentive to
    try actively to control his or her costs, because people have an incen-
    tive to overconsume, or for whatever reason). If that is so, then
    whether there is a problem is no longer an issue, because it can be
    stipulated that there is. As with the other methods of determining the
    issues, the actual issues in a controversy are what remain after deleting
    the matters agreed to from the list of potential issues.

Who determines what potential issues can be stipulated or agreed to? The
answer is the audience for the argumentation. In a dialogical argument,
the audience is also the other party to the argument. In a public setting, the

audience is the collection of people who come to hear the argument or who are affected by it. And in a mass or cultural context, the audience is the people who will be affected by the outcome of the controversy, whether they are physically present to hear and participate in it or not.

When assembling your list of potential issues, you should have in mind what we described in Chapter 3 as the "universal audience" in the terms proposed by the philosopher Chaim Perelman.[1] That is, you should imagine an audience of all reasonable people, not swayed by the appeals to self-interest or prejudice of any particular audience. But then, when you determine which of the issues are actually relevant and important to your particular audience, you should select from your storehouse of potential issues the ones that are meaningful for that particular audience. This is not pandering to your specific audience, because you are identifying issues selected from a set of issues that you constructed with the universal audience in mind. Yet it recognizes that the issues in any dispute are determined by the audience to that dispute. It will be a waste of the advocate's time to argue potential issues that the specific audience does not believe are important, unsettled, and relevant.

Constraints and Choices

If building a case requires that you address the issues, that is virtually the only constraint you face. You have considerable latitude in how to do it. In this respect, case construction is a creative art. You may choose which arguments to use, how to arrange the arguments, which evidence to draw on to support the claims you advance, and how to arrange the evidence. Each of these choices is subject to strategic considerations. While meeting your obligation to address the contested issues, you naturally will try to make those choices that will increase the odds of prevailing in the argumentation. You not only want the controversy giving rise to the resolution to be resolved, but you want it to be resolved in your favor.

Subsequent sections of this chapter will consider choices related to the selection of claims within the case and to the selection of arguments within the claim. Then, since the arrangement choices are essentially the same for both claims and evidence, we will consider them together. Choices related

---

[1] On the "universal audience," see Chaim Perelman and Lucie Olbrechts-Tyteca, *The New Rhetoric: A Treatise on Argumentation*, trans. John Wilkinson and Purcell Weaver (Notre Dame, IN: University of Notre Dame Press, 1969), esp. 31–35.

to style, language, and other presentational devices will be deferred until Chapter 9, when they will be our principal focus.

Selection of Claims

Suppose you are engaged in an argument about what the international trade policy of the United States should be. From your reading and exploration of the controversy, you know that since the 1930s the basic policy of the United States has been to encourage free trade through the mutual reduction of tariffs and other trade barriers. You also know that since about 2010 this policy has been challenged both by some liberals and by some conservatives, and that President Trump departed from it to some degree. You have decided to advance the resolution that the United States should abandon its commitment to free trade by reimposing protectionist tariffs when it is to American economic advantage.

One way to prepare for this argumentation is to imagine all the arguments that could be used to establish each of the issues. We will not review this entire procedure, but for illustrative purposes will confine ourselves to the issue of "harm." You know that you will have to answer affirmatively the question, "Is there a problem with the present United States policy concerning international trade?"

The process of generating a list of possible arguments is referred to as *preparing a brief*. This is a misnomer because the resulting list usually is not brief at all! On a complex subject such as international trade policy, there are many considerations and thus many possible claims that could be advanced on each of the issues. On the issue of harm, suppose that you came up with the following list of potential claims:

1. Free trade widens the nation's unfavorable balance of trade.
2. Free trade leads manufacturers to make their products in other nations, leading to a loss in American jobs.
3. Free trade encourages competition for low-cost labor, threatening workers' wages and benefits.
4. Free trade enriches the treasuries of other nations at the expense of the United States.
5. Free trade retards the development of new domestic industries.
6. Free trade leaves the United States at the mercy of other nations whose trade policies do not reflect our values.
7. Free trade leaves us vulnerable if we depend on other nations for vital materials or products.

8. Nations enriched by our trade turn out to be our adversaries.
9. Free trade leads to negotiations with nations that we do not trust.
10. We are made to look like chumps when we negotiate with other nations that do not keep their word.

We could develop a much longer list but this should give us enough to work with.

Now, two questions present themselves. First, how many of these claims should we try to develop? And second, which one(s) to pick?

How Many Claims?

Borrowed from physics, the term *amplitude* refers to the number or range of supporting arguments to establish the main claims of a case. The more supporting arguments or the more varied they are, the greater the amplitude. At first glance it might seem that the greater the amplitude, the better; we should try to use as many supporting arguments as we can. But this seldom will turn out to be a strong strategic choice.

For one thing, some of the supporting arguments may be too difficult to prove. Either the evidence to support them may be lacking or weak, or the inferences on which they depend may be tenuous. Even if the argument could be established, the effort may not be worth it. In our example above, the argument that free trade leaves us at the mercy of other nations that do not respect our values might be weaker than some of the other arguments on offer. It requires us to prove that trade – which, after all, is an economic transaction – has anything to do with judgments of mercy, that nations as well as individuals can be said to respect values, and that we are made dependent on nations that do not respect our values. These would be difficult proofs, compared, for example, with the argument that free trade has led to the loss of American jobs, for which there is empirical support (although free trade also has led to the creation of new jobs).

But why not include both the difficult and the easy to prove? There are two main reasons. First, time is limited. Even if there are no formal time limits (in oral discourse) or space limits (in written discourse), there are limits to an audience's attention and patience. Since time and space are scarce resources, better to employ them in the service of arguments that are easier to prove. And second, audience doubt is contagious. An argument that a listener or reader judges to be not credible is likely to impair the credibility of the rest of the arguments as well.

This leads to a second consideration that may lead us to reduce amplitude. Some arguments are simply not credible to most people, even if an arguer could establish that they might be true. Perhaps the most famous example of an argument lacking credibility is that nuclear war is good because it will curtail the excess population of the earth. No matter what expert testimony or historical evidence you might provide, most people simply will not accept that nuclear war is good – thankfully! You will be wasting your breath and listeners' time if you try to establish this claim. Better to spend your time on other arguments you might have a better chance of making more convincing.

Another consideration is that some arguments may be functionally equivalent – they say the same thing, or close enough to the same thing that little is gained by offering both. For example, the statement that free trade leads us to negotiate with countries that we do not trust and the statement that we look like chumps when others break their word, while not exactly the same, amount to the same thing. Why do we not trust other nations? Because they may break their word. Why do we look like chumps? Because we dealt with those we distrusted. Neither argument adds that much to the other. Given scarcity of time and attention, we would be better off developing either one of the supporting arguments in more detail rather than presenting the two arguments as if they were completely distinct.

Yet another factor to consider is whether presenting a supporting argument will do us any good. Suppose we could establish that free trade retards the development of domestic industries. This in fact was widely accepted as true when the economy was young, and this belief justified protective tariffs until well into the twentieth century. But what if free trade also *encourages* the development of domestic industries, in those cases in which our nation enjoys a comparative advantage over others? In that case, we could say that free trade *both* retards and encourages the development of domestic industries. And if it encourages more than it retards, then we have accomplished nothing by establishing that free trade retards domestic industries, even though we have shown it to be true. Examples like this one, which ultimately rest on on-balance considerations, are often not worth advancing unless we are sure that the balance works out in our favor.

Yet another risk is that some of the statements may rest on assumptions that themselves cannot be well supported if challenged. For instance, the statements that free trade leads to loss of American jobs and that free trade widens an unfavorable balance of trade both depend on the assumption that American goods cannot compete successfully in a market governed by free trade. Fail to sustain that assumption and neither one of these statements will hold up. And while anyone could cite some examples of American failure to compete, this has to be an on-balance judgment. If the benefits are greater than the harms, then the case against free trade will not stand up.

Finally, whenever we present a large number of arguments, there is the danger that some of the arguments counteract one another. This can happen in either of two ways. The arguments could be contradictory, meaning that one denies the other so that they cannot both be true. Or they could be contrary, meaning that they work at cross-purposes. Logically they might both be true, yet they are in tension with each other. Consider, for example, the statements that free trade leaves us vulnerable and that free trade retards the development of domestic industries. These are not contradictory effects; they could both be true. But they work at cross-purposes: the very vulnerability cited in the first argument should create an incentive to *encourage* the development of domestic industries, thereby negating the second statement.

For all these reasons, it is not always or necessarily a good idea to try to achieve the greatest possible amplitude. Claims are not decided by counting up the number of supporting arguments for and against, but by making a judgment about whether the supporting arguments, taken together, establish the claim. In light of the dangers of increasing amplitude, then, maybe an advocate should take the opposite approach, offering as *few* supporting arguments as possible, maybe only one. This is sometimes a wise move, but only in the rare case in which there is a "killer" supporting argument that would be sufficient to convince virtually anyone of the main claim being put forward. But this does not happen often either. It is usually the case, especially if the audience is large or heterogeneous, that some people will find one supporting argument more compelling than another, whereas for other people it is just the reverse. Having analyzed the audience, the strategic arguer will include both arguments, in order to have something that will appeal to both segments of the audience – so long as the arguments do not run the risks involved with increasing amplitude, discussed above. For example, one group within the audience might evaluate trade primarily as an economic arrangement, and would be most attuned to an argument that free trade caused the loss of American jobs, while another group might see it mainly as a political matter and be most swayed by the argument that free trade enriches nations who then become our adversaries. Nothing is lost by including both of these arguments.

Furthermore, one supporting argument does not usually establish all the links needed to support the inference the arguer is making to justify the main claim. It may require, for instance, the combination of statistical evidence and expert judgment to establish that free trade threatens wages and benefits in an international "race to the bottom." The statistical evidence would establish a correlation between trade policies and wage growth, while the expert testimony would validate the causal link implicit in the argument.

If neither the greatest nor the smallest possible amplitude is the goal, then what is the middle ground? How many arguments are enough? Unfortunately, there is no way to answer this question in the abstract. While an assignment to write an argumentative essay might state that you need "three pieces of supporting material," this is a pedagogical device and not a statement that three (or any other number) is what will be most convincing. That judgment has to be made case by case, considering the specific audience, the content of the supporting arguments, and your strategic objectives.

Which Claims?

The judgment of how many claims to present is closely related to the judgment of *which* claims to present. The objective is to present the strongest arguments from among those that are available. The strength of an argument is a function of two considerations: How easy will it be for you to establish the claim? And if you establish it, how much will it advance your case by contributing to the main claim (resolution) you are trying to establish?

In considering the first of these questions, it is important to consider *for whom* you are seeking to establish the truth of the supporting argument. Not for yourself, although it usually helps if you believe that the arguments you are putting forth are true. But your goal is not to convince yourself but to convince a third party – an interlocutor, a group of listeners, or an impartial judge. From this standpoint the claims easiest to establish are those that support what the audience believes. Only slightly lower in priority are those that follow from audience beliefs or those that could be shown to be consistent with audience beliefs. For instance, a person known to believe that immigrants are potential terrorists will find it easier to accept an argument that procedures for vetting prospective immigrants are not tight enough, than would a person known to believe that there is little connection between immigration and terrorism.

While there are such things as objective facts, determining the ease with which an argument can be established is not an objective matter. As we saw in Chapters 1 and 2, argument ultimately depends on agreement between arguers, or between arguer and audience, and what we are considering here is how easily that agreement can be reached. This is not a matter of pandering to the audience or saying things that the arguer knows not to be true in order to take advantage of the audience's gullibility. Those things sometimes happen, to be sure, but they are perversions of audience analysis, not positive examples of it. Rather, recognition of the audience's starting point is a way of recognizing what Aristotle observed long ago, that arguments are not persuasive in the abstract; they are persuasive *to a person*.[2]

Another aspect of determining how easy it is to establish a claim is deciding how well it will withstand attack. It will do little good to establish the claim in the first place if it can be easily undermined by a brief attack. But, of course, when you initially present a claim, you don't know whether or how it will be attacked, and yet you need to take that factor into consideration. What you have to do is to imagine a range of likely attacks that the claim might invite, and consider how easily you can repair the claim after these attacks. Some attacks can be easily discredited; others will require much more elaborate repairs of the argument; still others will prevail but not cause great damage to your argument; and yet others could prove fatal.

The initial construction of the case should consider what possible responses it might attract. The advice here is to be your own worst critic. Don't just imagine simple attacks that could be dispatched easily. Ask yourself instead what an opponent might say that would cause your argument the greatest trouble, and then consider how easily you could rebuild the argument in response to this attack. This is what philosopher Ralph Johnson calls *meeting your dialectical obligations* in the construction of your case.[3]

The second component of strength, as noted above, is how much good the supporting argument will do in helping you to advance the main claim that you are trying to establish. Suppose your resolution is that American secondary education is overly dependent on standardized testing. One of

---

[2] Aristotle, *Rhetoric*, 1356b.
[3] Ralph H. Johnson, *Manifest Rationality* (Mahwah, NJ: Lawrence Erlbaum, 2000), discusses the "dialectical tier" as a fundamental component of arguments. Meeting one's dialectical obligations involves addressing this dialectical tier by identifying and responding to likely objections to the argument. His book illustrates this process with reference to his theory.

your possible supporting claims is that standardized tests take time away from classroom instruction. This would be a very easy claim to establish – obviously tests take time away from classroom instruction, since they are given in lieu of class time on test days (unless, of course, the school day is lengthened for tests). But proving this will do you very little good in advancing the resolution. It does nothing to establish that American secondary education is overly dependent on standardized testing; it does not even establish that we are dependent at all; it only states the obvious: that classes are suspended while tests are given.

Applying these criteria to the candidates for supporting arguments that you have identified will enable you to select the strongest from among those available to you, and to make that choice with a clear sense of strategy in mind.

Selection of Supporting Evidence

Once an arguer has decided which claims to advance in order to support the main claim, there will be the further choice among pieces of evidence to establish the supporting claim itself. The considerations here are similar to those for the selection of supporting arguments. If you have many pieces of supporting evidence and present them all, it may seem like overkill. You may run out of time or exhaust the patience or attention span of your audience. Additionally, listeners might conclude that you really do not have much confidence in any of the individual items of evidence and that you are trying to disguise this fact by presenting a barrage. It is unlikely that any individual piece of evidence will stand out or be remembered.

On the other hand, if you present only a single piece of evidence to support a claim, listeners may conclude that no other source supports the claim or that you unjustifiably are "putting all your eggs in one basket." Other advocates may scrutinize your evidence with excessive effort, believing that it is all that you have. In some cases it may be worth these risks because of the potency of that evidence, but in most cases a single piece of evidence will seem too little, just as a barrage of evidence might seem too much. As with selection of arguments, the middle ground will be determined case by case, as a result of your figuring out how completely your evidence can withstand criticism and what good it does for you in establishing the claim that it is used to support.

Supposing that you have more available evidence than you can use, the question becomes how to select the pieces of evidence that you'll choose to include. Doing this means, in the first place, applying the tests for specific kinds of evidence discussed in Chapter 4, to determine whether your evidence is accurate and believable. The following are some additional criteria when you are choosing among different pieces of evidence.

Relevance. Presumably, every piece of evidence you are considering is relevant to the claim you are trying to establish. But there are degrees. For example, if one piece of evidence requires you to extrapolate from given information in order to relate it to your claim, and another is directly on point, the latter generally should be preferred. If one requires you to infer an analogy between the experience of one nation and that of the nation you are discussing, whereas the other is specific to the focus of your claim, the latter generally should be preferred.

Replicability. Empirical evidence should be *replicable*, meaning that others should be able to make the observations or perform the tests mentioned in the evidence and get the same results that your source obtained. One of the signs of scientific fraud is that other researchers, using the same approaches and methods, cannot get the same results as the particular source. This is especially likely if the source's findings fly in the face of common sense or generally accepted beliefs. This doesn't mean that any challenge to common sense should be rejected, of course. It does mean that you should be skeptical of the evidence if no others can get the same results when proceeding in the same way.

With respect to testimony or opinion statements, the analogue to replicability is confirmation by other experts. If your source asserts something that seems to challenge conventional wisdom, and no other expert can be found who will say the same thing, then you should be cautious. A group of experts parroting the same statement is a danger too, because they may just be repeating one another without having analyzed the data or the situation independently. And "maverick" sources sometimes will be proved right even if no one else goes along. Still, it is a good idea to be skeptical of statements offered by a single source when nobody else can be found who agrees.

Underlying reasoning. Suppose that two experts make the same statement, but one indicates how she reasoned to the conclusion, whereas the other offers only the conclusion and, in effect, challenges you to accept the conclusion just on his own say-so. The first is generally to be preferred, because you can assess the thought process that your expert used to reach her conclusion. The latter asks you in effect to agree to the statement on the basis of his expertise alone. That may not be enough, especially when equally qualified experts disagree.

Knowing the underlying reasoning is especially important when the evidence itself is controversial. Suppose, for example, that an expert stated that workers of one race are "better suited" for a certain task than are workers of another race. If that is all you have to go on, you will have no idea how the expert reached that conclusion. He might have been reasoning from a racist assumption that people of one race are inherently better than those of another, a premise that the vast majority of people would reject. Or he might have been reflecting on differences in education and training resulting from discrimination or social policies that are remediable. The latter piece of evidence should carry greater weight than the former – in fact, the former should carry no weight at all. But you won't know which of these scenarios, or others, applies if all you have is the expert's conclusion without any indication of the underlying reasoning.

Source credibility. Another consideration in choosing among pieces of evidence is the credibility of the different sources. Some sources are worthy of more deference than others, by virtue of their training and experience. Doctors who tell you that a certain procedure they wish to perform is perfectly safe will be more credible if they have performed the procedure many times without any adverse results. Those who have been trained in the use of the specific instruments and certified to have been observed while using them will be more credible than those who have "figured them out" through curiosity alone. And those who are talking within their own specialty and expertise will be more worthy of acceptance than those who are talking about a specialty other than their own. In each of these examples, we are appropriately more dubious about one source than the other. When risks to our health or life are at issue, we want every possible advantage of training and expertise.

When we are making assessments not about our own health and survival but about policies affecting the community or nation, we tend to be a bit less rigorous, perhaps because the risk seems more removed from us personally and the process of assessing the sources requires effort. The Internet has been a great means of democratizing knowledge. With few gatekeepers, however, almost anyone can post almost anything, and someone can be found who will believe it. Some of the postings claiming to be factual have been found to be fabricated, and some of the experts offering their judgments have been found not to be experts at all. The fact that some of the least reliable sources have accused some of the most reliable sources of themselves posting "fake news" only clouds the picture further. The tendency to accept any evidence that sounds like it comes from a qualified source can be especially toxic in situations like this. Likewise, the tendency to seek out and accept only evidence that reflects our own ideological point of view leads us to be less careful about checking the credibility of the source than we ought to be.

Track record. Even if sources are well qualified with regard to their training and amount of experience, it is appropriate to ask about their track record of interpreting data or making judgments. A source with a consistent record of getting things wrong will have less credibility than one who has been on the mark in the past. To cite a simple example, most expert pollsters were mistaken in their predictions of the outcome of the 2016 US presidential election. When they subsequently published polls showing that the approval rating of President Donald Trump was very low, the president's supporters could call those poll results into question by noting that these were the same polls that were incorrect in calling the election. The implication was that, being wrong on such a significant matter in 2016, they should not be taken seriously in what they said later. In contrast, the few polls that correctly noted that the Trump campaign would make inroads into the working-class vote in states in the industrial Midwest, possibly enough to pull those states away from their traditional Democratic leaning, sometimes were given additional weight in later polls on other subjects because of their success in election polling, even though they bucked the trend.

Something about this does not seem quite right. After all, anyone can make a mistake. We might wonder why an error in the interpretation of data about the 2016 election should offset the accumulated expertise of the pollsters. But listeners do make precisely these judgments, and the assessment of one's earlier track record does affect their judgment about the evidence at hand. This tendency is even more pronounced if the record of error is cumulative. An otherwise well-qualified economist who consistently underestimates the rate of economic growth or the performance of the stock market, for example, is not likely to be taken seriously when he predicts that economic growth in the next quarter will be disappointing or that the stock market is about to take a nosedive.

In this as in other matters, past performance is no guarantee of future success. Still, in determining the relative strength of different items of evidence, the previous track record of the source is a legitimate factor to take into account.

Timeliness. The dates on different pieces of evidence sometimes make a big difference. A statement that there has been a significant increase in protest demonstrations "in the past year" means one thing if it is dated

1969, something quite different if it is dated 1985, and something different still if it is dated 2018. Knowing the date of a piece of evidence is sometimes crucial even just to understand what the evidence means. It is also important in assessing the truth of empirical statements. The statement that 20 percent of the American population lacks health insurance may have been true in 2008, when health care was a major issue in that year's US presidential campaign, and yet it was completely outdated by 2016, after the Affordable Care Act resulted in the uninsured percentage dropping to 9 percent. Presenting the 2008 evidence to support a claim you advance in 2018 about the number of uninsured is not a wise strategy because you quickly will be exposed as relying on outdated evidence to make your case. In situations like these, having the most recent evidence is of great importance.

It can also be important to have timely evidence so that it reflects current thinking about economic, social, and political matters. One of the most rapid shifts in social attitudes is the transformation of public opinion about gay rights between, say, the 1990s and the 2010s. Gay marriage, about which there was such stigma in 2004 that few responsible politicians would endorse it and many campaigned against it in that year's elections, by 2015 was so widely accepted that politicians regarded their support for it as an asset rather than a liability. This experience is a dramatic example, but attitudes and mores on other topics change too, even if not so quickly.

But not always. Sometimes evidence may concern matters that are timeless, such as beliefs about human nature, the tension between freedom and equality, the balance to be struck between individual liberty and government action, and so on. There are matters of moral philosophy on which the ancients effectively had the last word, just as there are statements about political theory where Aristotle cannot be improved on. On matters like these, there is no virtue in preferring a more recent expression just because of its timeliness. It usually is not difficult to determine, for any given claim, whether or not the supporting evidence will be enhanced because it is recent.

Conciseness. A final factor that should affect the selection of evidence is a stylistic one: how simply and concisely the evidence is stated. This is not just a stylistic matter, however, because it affects how the evidence will be heard and understood by the audience. Especially when listeners do not have a chance to read the evidence themselves, their understanding of the argument and its importance will be influenced by how brief and to the point it is. A short and pithy phrase will be remembered easily; a lengthy and diffuse statement may fade away or be remembered, if at all, as a distraction.

Applying these criteria will make it more likely that the best pieces of evidence, like the best arguments, have been selected: those that most forcefully establish the point they are trying to make and for which establishing that point clearly works to support the claim in whose behalf it is offered. Moreover, they will satisfy the tests for inclusion of arguments (or evidence) by answering affirmatively these four questions: (1) Are they simply stated? (2) Are they discrete rather than repetitive? (3) Are they coherent, making sense in their own right? (4) Are they complete, so that taken together they speak to all the issues?

Arrangement

Besides selecting the arguments and the evidence to be used, the other step in case construction is arranging these materials. Because the principles of arrangement are the same whether we are discussing supporting arguments that contribute to the main claim or pieces of evidence that contribute to the supporting arguments, we will consider both at once.

In Chapter 2 we considered three basic structures of complex arguments: multiple, coordinative, and subordinative. *Multiple* arguments are those in which each supporting claim separately and independently establishes the main claim. The supporting arguments are not dependent on one another. *Coordinative* arguments are those in which the supporting arguments are still not dependent on one another but in which the totality of the supporting arguments is needed to establish the main claim (or to give it force). *Subordinative* arguments are ones in which each of the supporting arguments is dependent on the previous arguments, like links in a chain. The whole set is needed to establish the main claim, even though only the last argument in the chain actually links to the main claim. If any link is broken, the argument will fall. It is also possible that an argument will offer a *combination* of these structures, for example a series of supporting claims that are multiple, with one of those supporting claims arranged in a subordinative structure and another in a coordinative structure.

The first decision to make about arrangement is which of these structures the argument employs. If you have a subordinative structure, your options are quite limited. You can either begin with the first link in the chain, showing how each step leads to the next, and finally to the main claim, or you can begin with the last link in the chain (the one that connects to the main claim) and show, how, in turn, it is the product of each of the previous links. Either way, you will want to keep the links in order. A simple example should show why. Consider the following argument:

(1) Airline travel requires arranging trips with short connections.
(2) Short connections make it likely that connecting flights will be missed.
(3) Missed connections require job applicants to cancel scheduled interviews.
(4) Without timely interviews, job candidates will not be hired.
(5) Airline travel schedules cause job candidates not to be hired.

It is apparent that this is a subordinative argument; each step depends on the preceding ones. If it is not required that travel be arranged with short connections, for example, then the rest of the argument falls away as being moot. It does not matter that short connections lead to missed flights if short connections aren't a necessity in the first place. In this argument, either of these arrangement patterns would make sense:

(1), so (2), so (3), so (4), so (5).
(5), because (4), because (3), because (2), because (1).

On the other hand, a pattern such as (2), (4), (1), (5), (3) would not make any sense. It would not be clear how any argument led to the next step in the chain. So, if you have a subordinative argument, your choices regarding arrangement are limited to either *first step to last step* or *last step to first step*.

You may be wondering why, in light of this constraint, one would ever choose to employ a subordinative argument structure. The answer is that this structure develops a sense of momentum. If you can establish clearly that step (1) leads to step (2), you are showing that step (1) has a certain degree of causal force so that a listener might expect it to lead to steps (3), (4), and (5).

If you have a coordinative or multiple argument structure, however, you have additional decisions about the order in which to present the supporting arguments. Because these arguments are independent of one another, it is logically a matter of indifference in which order they come. This means that considerations other than logical sequence can come into play. These decisions illustrate what van Eemeren and his colleagues call *strategic maneuvering*:[4] increasing the chances that the argument will be resolved in one's favor while still meeting one's dialectical obligations as an arguer (and, it should be added, one's obligation to reason well). The following are some examples of these choices.

Should the strongest argument be presented first or last? As noted above, a strong argument is one that is relatively easy to establish, because the audience either is prepared to accept the conclusion or could be convinced without difficulty to do so, *and* the argument, once established, will go a long way toward establishing the main claim that is in dispute. If you have chosen to present several different arguments, it is unlikely that they will all be of equal strength. So the question arises: What role should argument strength play in determining the order in which to place the arguments? This question has been tested empirically but the results are not conclusive. Some studies support placing the strongest argument first, in order to make a powerful first impression on the listener, which in turn will enhance the perception of the remaining arguments – a sort of "halo effect" in which the glow from the strongest argument will shine on all the others. Other research has suggested just the opposite – that the strongest argument should be presented last, in order to make a strong final impression that will remain with the listener even after the entire presentation is over.[5] The point on which the research seems to agree, however, is that the weakest argument should be placed in the middle – that both the first impression and the final impression are more important than the impression made by the arguments that come in between.

How should listeners' familiarity with different arguments affect the order of presentation? Again, if you have several different arguments that are logically independent of one another, it is not likely that listeners will be equally familiar with them all. Should an arguer begin with what an audience will find familiar and then proceed gradually to less-familiar arguments, or should the arguer do just the reverse, starting with the unfamiliar? Underlying this question is the knowledge that audiences often reason analogically, accepting a main claim because it is similar in some important respect to a claim they already have accepted. The argument for starting with the familiar is that this will make it easier for audiences to sense the resemblance between the new argument and what they already believe; then they

---

[4] Frans H. van Eemeren, *Strategic Maneuvering in Argumentative Discourse* (Amsterdam: John Benjamins, 2010).

[5] The classic research studies on this subject were conducted during and shortly after World War II. See, for example, Carl I. Hovland, ed., *The Order of Presentation in Persuasion* (New Haven, CT: Yale University Press, 1957).

can see the resemblance between this new argument and the next one, and so on until gradually they come to see the resemblance between the main claim the arguer is putting forward and what they already believe. The argument for the opposite approach assumes that audiences must do more work to accommodate an unfamiliar argument and that they will be more likely to exert this mental energy at the beginning of a presentation than at the end. So, the reasoning goes, they will do the work to understand the less familiar argument and then they will be rewarded for doing so by seeing gradually how this new argument resembles what they already believe. The answer to which of these paths you should follow is "It depends." The more complex or counterintuitive the new argument, the more it makes sense to proceed from the familiar to the unfamiliar. On the other hand, if the new argument – though unfamiliar – is easily grasped and can be said to be a matter of common sense, it might be better to do the work of presenting the unfamiliar argument at the start.

In what order should different topics be taken up? One very common organizational pattern is *topical*, in which a subject is taken up according to different categories. For example, Great Britain's plan to withdraw from the European Union might be discussed with reference to its economic aspects, its diplomatic aspects, its military aspects, and its symbolic aspects. In what order should the topics be presented? Suppose that you want to argue that this action (nicknamed "Brexit") is a bad move, with disadvantages falling under each of these categories. Deciding which to present first is often influenced by which aspect is most *salient*, that is, most on the minds of listeners. In the case of Brexit, the most attention has been given to economic aspects of the subject: its effect on trade relationships between Britain and Europe, and its effect on Britain's ability to control its labor market by changing its immigration policies. It probably will make good sense to begin with these topics. Meanwhile, it may be that the symbolic aspects have the greatest long-term significance – what this move could imply about the prospects for a consciousness of European identity that transcends nationalism. So it might be wise either to start or to end with that. In contrast, starting off with aspects of the topic that may not be salient to the audience may lead listeners to think that you are dodging the question or arguing about trivial or inconsequential sidelights.

Should you include anticipatory refutation? Another question that comes up when you have more choices is whether to include any arguments attacking your position (presumably in order to refute them) or whether you should "leave well enough alone" and depend on the opposition to come up with the opposing arguments. Supplying a small dose of the opposing argument is referred to as *inoculation*, using an analogy to medical procedures in which a person receives a small dose of a disease in order to build an immunity against it. This question was tested empirically in the closing months of World War II. Troops that had fought in Europe were hoping and expecting to be demobilized quickly, but before the atomic bomb had been tested, the military leadership believed that another eighteen months might be required in order to subdue Japan and that soldiers could not be demobilized until that was over. So the practical problem was how to convince men hoping and expecting to come home that they would need to spend many more months in uniform. The findings indicated that the "two-sided" message was more effective under either of two conditions: the audience was highly educated or the audience was known to be predisposed against the speaker's view. The reasons were that a highly educated audience would likely be engaged in critical thinking and would likely realize that the subject was complex and that not all of the supporting arguments were on one side. The initially hostile audience would be disarmed by the realization that its views were taken into account and acknowledged by the speaker.[6] The philosopher Ralph Johnson has maintained that arguers are *obligated* to acknowledge and respond to opposing arguments that come to their mind,[7] but for most theorists this is a matter of choice and should be guided by strategic considerations.

Should you employ one of the common organizational patterns? Textbooks on writing and public speaking usually will identify common organizational patterns. Among them are (1) chronological order, moving either from past to present (and possibly to future) or the reverse; (2) spatial order, proceeding from near to far, far to near, or along a directional arrow (east to west, north to south, etc.); (3) topical order, identifying a common pattern of topics such as economic, military, and political; (4) causal order, either proceeding from cause to effect or from effect to cause; (5) problem–solution order, first identifying a problem and then offering and defending the candidate solution; and (6) residues, a pattern that identifies and eliminates all possible options save one, which then becomes the preferred choice almost by default. Although these standard patterns sometimes may be thought to lack originality, their very familiarity presents arguers with an advantage. Audiences will know the patterns, will be able to anticipate

---

[6] The basic studies on this question are reported in Carl I. Hovland, Irving L. Janis, and Harold H. Kelley, *Communication and Persuasion* (New Haven, CT: Yale University Press, 1953).
[7] This is what Johnson holds to be an arguer's dialectical obligation. See *Manifest Rationality* (note 3 above).

correctly what is coming next, will follow along easily, and will feel rewarded for correctly figuring out where the arguer is going. Under these circumstances, form itself can be persuasive, just as we saw in Chapter 5 where we considered arguments from form as a common argument scheme. At the very least, a common organizational pattern will reduce the mental effort required of listeners to understand and follow a complex argument.

These choices often are dismissed as "merely" rhetorical, or as embellishments added to a basic argument. It is true that they come into play when the arrangement of arguments or evidence is a matter of logical indifference. But they are nonetheless important for being rhetorical considerations, and the pattern in which an argument is cast affects perceptions of the argument itself; form and content are intertwined. For these reasons, considerations of strategic maneuvering should be taken seriously when choices are available.

Executing Case Construction Decisions

Two common tools are available to help in executing decisions about selection and arrangement of arguments and evidence: the brief and the case outline.

The brief is a comprehensive outline of all the possible arguments you can imagine for and against the resolution at issue, and all the evidence you are aware of that will support these various arguments. It is an exhaustive catalog of your options. Its advantage is that it forces you to make selection and arrangement choices consciously, because you cannot include everything. Thinking strategically about which arguments and evidence are the strongest, you can make your selections from among the options identified in the brief.

The case outline, as the term suggests, is an arrangement in outline form of the arguments and evidence you have chosen to use, arranged in the order in which you have chosen to present them. If you are speaking extemporaneously, you should be able to present your argument from the case outline. But before doing that, you can test the case outline by asking some key questions. First, does it address the *topoi* on which you must prevail in order to establish the case? If not, you will need to modify the case outline by adding more material until it does. Second, does the case outline display the strongest strategic choices? Compare the selections you have made for the case outline against others on the brief that you rejected. This is a way to double-check that the selections you have made indeed are the best available and that you have arrayed them in the order that you believe will do you the most good. Third, is there too much on the case outline? If so, this is the opportunity to eliminate unnecessary duplication or repetition of arguments or evidence, or to streamline the structure of the case outline, so that you will not bore your audience or exceed whatever time limits you may have. Of course, if you do not have enough material to cover the ground or to fill the available time, this is your opportunity to make additional selections from the brief. But it is far more likely that you will have too much material rather than too little.

Exercises

1. In the following examples, determine whether a prima facie case is made. Why or why not?
    a. We should act militarily to stop the revolt because all of our allies agree that it is the only way to stop harm to the citizens in the affected city. We have the power to end this situation with minimal loss of life on our side.
    b. The chicken from dinner was left on the counter for six hours. Cooked food that has been left at room temperature longer than two hours becomes unsafe, according to the US Department of Agriculture. Therefore we should throw out the chicken.
    c. Most people like chocolate for dessert, so you cannot go wrong serving chocolate cake at the holiday party.
    d. All swans are white, so the swan that Khalid just saw on the pond must be white.
    e. I don't like scary movies, which is why no one will ever go to a scary movie.
    f. I bought three bags of dog food last week. We don't use more than half a bag per week. Therefore, we do not have to buy any dog food for the rest of the month.
    g. The last time I saw Gianna she was wearing a green hat. The woman you pointed out doesn't have a green hat, so she cannot be Gianna.
2. Define each of the following and explain how it is important to case construction.
    a. Case
    b. Prima facie case
    c. Brief
    d. Amplitude

e. Relevance
f. Replicability
g. Underlying reasoning
h. Source credibility
i. Track record
j. Timeliness
k. Conciseness
l. Arrangement
m. Multiple arguments
n. Coordinative arguments
o. Anticipatory refutation

3. Choose a controversy that is important to you. It could be related to politics, entertainment, sports, a hobby, a personal dispute, or an academic issue.

   a. Write a resolution (major claim) that applies to your controversy.
   b. Determine the audience for your resolution – who is going to hear your argument and decide if they are persuaded by your case.
   c. Draft a case brief that lists all of your options for supporting the resolution.
   d. Choose the arguments you think will be most effective in persuading your chosen audience.
   e. Draft a case outline in which you decide the order in which you will present your case and the evidence you would like to use. (For this exercise, you do not need actually to find the evidence.)
   f. Pair up with another student in your class (or find a willing partner). Lay out the argument you have drafted and allow your partner to critique it.

Extensions: Toward More Advanced Study

To improve your understanding of the strategic choices discussed in this chapter, you might want to examine a sample of argumentation to see how the choices are deployed. A good example to work with is the US Declaration of Independence, adopted by the Second Continental Congress in 1776. It was written for the very purpose of making the case for independence to the roughly one-third of the colonial population who remained undecided, and to foreign powers (mainly France) whose help was being sought. Locate a copy that you can consult as you read through the following analysis.

The overall organizational pattern of the Declaration was, first, to establish the existence of a right to revolution if conditions were intolerable and peaceful redress was impossible; second, to enumerate grievances in order to establish that conditions in fact were intolerable; and third, to catalog unsuccessful efforts to gain redress through peaceful means, concluding by residues that the exercise of the right to revolution is justified. Several reasons suggest that this pattern was advantageous. First establishing the right to revolution *in principle* will then make the factual claims of grievances seem less surprising, extreme, or outrageous. This will render them more acceptable to the potential audience than the contrary position that there is no such thing as a right to revolution, no matter how bad conditions are. The examples of grievances were offered in a cumulative pattern. This was done through a coordinative organizational structure. The individual grievances were logically independent of each other, but each of them individually might be claimed to be a trifling matter, hardly justifying such a radical step as independence. But the cumulation establishes significance: taken together, all of these grievances show how intolerable the situation has become. Similarly, cumulating the unsuccessful attempts to obtain redress of grievances supports the perception that the colonists have gone more than halfway to try to resolve matters peaceably; they are reluctant revolutionaries who are left with no other choice. This pattern of residues proved to be more effective than the contrary claim that the revolutionaries were treasonous hotheads. It also suggests a certain inevitability to the colonists' actions since all other possibilities have been foreclosed.

Once this basic structure was established, the arrangement choices were fairly clear. The principal selection choices involved which grievances and which attempts at satisfaction should be included in the respective lists. For example, Thomas Jefferson's original draft of the Declaration included a complaint against the British monarchs for introducing slavery into the American colonies. This was ultimately omitted from the Declaration, partly because some deemed it farfetched to blame the king for a situation in which they themselves had been not only complicit but active participants, and partly because several of the members of the Continental Congress did not believe that slavery was a bad thing and did not want to give the king "credit" for it. Delegates realized that whatever their own beliefs about slavery might be, the inclusion of this provision in the Declaration would threaten the integrity of the document and the consensus that they hoped to develop among themselves. They took it out, leaving the question of slavery to be addressed another day, and still had a strong coordinative argument establishing that the king had perpetrated conditions that, taken together, were so bad as to justify the exercise of the right of revolution.

To strengthen your sensitivity to the choices involved in case construction, take a more careful look at this document and ask whether the Declaration reflects the strongest possible choices of selection and arrangement or whether these choices can be improved on. Then examine other argumentative documents with an eye to the same questions. Newspaper editorials and op-ed columns are good places to look. Becoming more attuned to the creative choices in case construction, you should become more capable of making such choices yourself in the cases you construct.

CHAPTER 8

Attack and Defense

The case represents what its advocate believes are the strongest arguments for the claim (usually an explicit or implicit resolution) that the advocate has undertaken to defend. If the selection and arrangement choices described in Chapter 7 have been made with care, there will be a prima facie case – one that seems persuasive at first glance, before anything is said against it. But a prima facie case will not lead an opponent simply to concede on hearing its first presentation. Rather, the burden of rejoinder discussed in Chapter 3 will come into play. The opponent will try to marshal claims and evidence that will either deny the resolution outright or at least raise sufficient doubt about it that the original advocate will need to strengthen the case beyond its first presentation. The burden of rejoinder will continue to move back and forth between the advocates until one is convinced by the other or, more often, until a neutral third party renders a decision in the dispute.

The progress of the argument described in the preceding paragraph is achieved through the interrelated processes of attack and defense. The goal of attack is to undermine the case; the goal of defense is to revive and strengthen it. Sometimes the term *refutation* is used as a synonym for attack and *rebuttal* is used as a synonym for defense, but in fact both refutation and rebuttal are employed in both attack and defense. Furthermore, these processes themselves are interrelated. Attacking one's opponent's arguments is also a means of defending one's own, and vice versa. This chapter will also explore the interrelation of these key terms.

One concern needs to be addressed at the beginning. Terms such as *attack, defense, opponents*, and *adversaries* have connotations of military combat, of victories and defeats. They can seem to connote all-out, no-holds-barred warfare leading to the emergence of victor and vanquished. With those connotations in mind, some scholars and teachers discredit argumentation, believing that it instills unhealthy competitive personality traits and maintaining that better results can be obtained by purely cooperative methods of decision-making.

But this view seriously misunderstands the terms *attack* and *defense.* First, the competition that takes place is not between people but between ideas and arguments. Second, the adversarial elements of argumentation serve a larger cooperative purpose: rigorously testing arguments so that the strongest will emerge. As discussed in Chapter 1, such a rigorous test is in the interest of all parties because it is most likely to produce beliefs and judgments they can embrace with confidence. So understood, attack and defense are constructive processes benefiting both arguers. In contrast, one might more easily be led astray by too quickly accepting an untested claim in the desire to reach agreement for its own sake.

What *does* ring true about the military connotations of attack and defense, however, is the concern for making strategic choices carefully. Attacks and defenses are more likely to achieve their goals if they are planned than if they are haphazard. As with case construction, attacks involve a series of choices about the selection and arrangement of arguments. Defending a case involves choices too, but there are fewer of them and they are constrained by moves that the attacker has made.

Selection Choices in Attack

Which Arguments to Attack?

A case, as we have seen, will be composed of several arguments. Diagramming the arguments, as discussed in Chapter 2, will help in figuring out which arguments must be attacked and which need not be:

- If the case was composed entirely of arguments within a *subordinative* structure, then only one need be defeated for the entire case to fall. Undermining one of the steps in the claim would defeat the opponent's position on one of the issues, questions that are vital to the opponent's case. The rest of the case might be entirely true and yet the loss of the critical link would demonstrate that the resolution has not been supported.
- If the case was composed entirely of arguments within a *multiple* structure, then it would be necessary to defeat *all* the arguments in order for the case to fall (assuming that the arguments really are different and are not restatements of the same point). This is true because multiple arguments independently establish the resolution. If one of the supporting arguments were to fall, the remaining supports would still provide reason for the resolution. There is a practical

consideration, however. If all the strong arguments in a multiple structure were defeated and only weak ones were to remain, an impartial observer might conclude that the remaining weak arguments are not weighty enough to establish a prima facie case.

- If the case was composed entirely of arguments within a *coordinative* structure, then it is necessary to defeat at least one of the coordinative elements linking to the resolution. Suppose, for instance, that an advocate has argued that a hostile adversary poses a significant military threat because it has the means, motive, and opportunity to develop nuclear weapons. What makes it a threat is the *combination* of means, motive, and opportunity. For instance, if it had the motive but lacked the means to develop nuclear weapons, then presumably it would not pose a threat.

These general guidelines, however, are overly simplistic in two main respects. First, cases almost never will be composed entirely of arguments of one structural type. They will contain combinations of multiple, coordinative, and subordinative structures. As a result, the process of selecting what needs to be attacked will be more complex and intricate. Take another look at Fig. 2.14 in Chapter 2, for example. If you were planning to attack this case, which arguments would you need to defeat?

Second, we have been referring to defeating or undermining arguments as if this was a clear-cut outcome, analogous perhaps to unconditional surrender. This is seldom what happens in actual practice. Usually one cannot tell at the time of making an attack just how strong an impact the attack will have. This is especially true if the decision is to be made by a third party and not announced until the entire argumentation is over. Often an attack, rather than completely undercutting the argument, will cause it to seem less likely or less significant in the eyes of a judge, without eliminating its force altogether. For this reason, advocates usually are advised to attack more arguments than the absolute minimum they need in order to prevail, as a means of hedging one's bets.

Nevertheless, it usually is not necessary to attack *every* argument in the opponent's case, and there may be good reasons not to do so. Several examples suggest circumstances in which attacking an argument may be unwise:

1. Doing so may waste the attacker's time on arguments that are extraneous to the case. Suppose, for example, that the resolution is that the United States should withdraw from military alliances and the case contends that these alliances are obsolete. In an attempt to provide context, the case might include claims about why military alliances

were established in the years after World War II. Especially if advocates are allowed limited time, it may not be worth it to attack these historical claims, as they are probably not directly relevant to whether the alliances are obsolete today. You will have spent valuable time in a dispute that did not matter.

2. Attacking some arguments might do you little good even if you prevail. Remember that the purpose of attacking an argument is to defeat it, not merely to have something to say about it. Suppose an opponent has advanced a case that traveling by airplane is generally unpleasant and one of the supporting arguments is that airports have become too crowded. You might be tempted to reply that *fewer* people will fly because of widely reported cases of airlines' mistreatment of passengers, in one case dragging a passenger off a plane that was full. But this is likely to be a short-term effect since people's memories are short; it is not a response to a general trend. Besides, think about it: if concerns about crowded airports are replaced by concerns about abusive treatment, can we say that flying has become any less unpleasant? You actually will have provided an *additional* reason that travel is unpleasant, strengthening rather than weakening the opponent's case!

3. Attacking every argument might involve you in internal inconsistencies, weakening the credibility of the attack. Suppose the resolution is that colleges should be permitted to disinvite controversial speakers if there is a threat of violence. The case includes the argument that unruly protesters should not be able to exercise a "heckler's veto" over someone else's speech, and also that campus police do not have enough resources to control the dissidents and prevent violence. It might be tempting to attack the first argument by maintaining that some ideas are so repulsive that they do not deserve a hearing, and then to respond to the second argument by suggesting that police resources can be increased as much as necessary to discipline unruly dissidents. But consider the relationship between these two positions. If tougher discipline can silence the protesters, then they will not be in a position to prevent the seemingly repulsive ideas from gaining a hearing. Whatever one thinks of these two attacks individually, presenting both of them in the same argument is probably not a good idea. This is particularly the case when we remember that audiences often respond to inconsistencies psychologically rather than logically: by discrediting *both* parts of the alleged inconsistency, even though logically only one need be cast aside.

These examples illustrate when it might not be a good idea to attack an argument. There also may be cases in which an attack is not necessary for a specific audience because it is known that its members already subscribe to the attack. This can be dangerous, of course, and one is well advised to err on the side of assuming that the audience's views are unknown. But there are situations every now and then – such as when you know you are addressing an audience that shares your partisan or ideological predis-positions – when a simple statement that you reject the argument will be enough and a full-blown attack is not necessary.

If you choose not to attack an argument, you have two other principal options: acknowledging it or ignoring it. The first of these is sometimes referred to as "admitting" the argument, but that has connotations of being caught in a trap. In fact, acknowledging the argument is often accompanied by a statement trivializing the argument or its significance, such as "Everybody knows that," "The argument doesn't matter," or (in an ironic tone) "What a surprise!" The other choice is simply to say nothing about the argument, rather than calling attention to the fact that you are letting it pass.

Decisions about which arguments to attack have the effect of narrowing down the potential issues to the actual issues that will be considered in the dispute. Doing this is a means to focus attention on the questions that will determine the outcome.

Which Step in the Argument to Attack?

When we drill down to the core of an argument, we will find the basic components of *claim*, *evidence*, and *warrant*, as described in Chapter 2. An attack can be focused on one or more of these elements. As was true of case construction, the criterion should be where the strongest attack can be pointed – the one that can most clearly be established and that will contribute most to weakening the case.

The claim. One option is to attack the claim directly, either by denying it outright or by developing a counter-claim. Denial locates the stasis (see Chapter 3) at conjecture, whereas a counter-claim picks one of the other available stases. If, for example, the claim in the case is that airline delays have increased in recent years, denying the claim would involve asserting that such delays have *not* increased. The choice between the competing claims would then depend on how well each has been supported by relevant evidence and inferences. The question the decision-maker would seek to answer is straightforward: Have airline delays increased or not?

On the other hand, one might counter the claim without denying it directly. For example, one might argue that airline delays are only a minor nuisance, not a significant problem. This attack would invoke the stasis of quality and the key question would be: Is the problem of airline delays serious or not? Or, also invoking the stasis of quality, the attacker might mention that airline delays are justified by safety and security considerations, and if delays are increasing, it is because more attention is being paid to these factors. In this case the question for the decision-maker is: Are airline delays warranted or not?

Which of these attacks on the claim would be strongest? If the evidence really establishes that delays have not increased, that is probably the best approach, because it defeats the argument without the need to consider whether the delays are serious or whether they are justified. On the other hand, if delays really have increased (and especially if that fact is well known), nothing is gained by trying to deny what is clearly true. Even though the other attacks implicitly grant that delays have increased, they nevertheless provide means for attacking the argument by countering the claim.

The evidence. Another approach is to attack the evidence on which the claim relies. Undermining evidence does not establish that the claim is clearly false, but rather that it has not been proved to be true. For example, suppose the evidence on airline delays is drawn entirely from the Los Angeles (LAX) and Chicago (ORD) airports, two of the busiest in the nation. That hardly seems like a sufficient or representative sample from which to establish a claim about the nation as a whole. This approach either would require the advocate for the case to defend the selection of LAX and ORD as indeed being representative or would require the advocate to produce additional evidence from a wider or more representative sample of airports. The best time for the attacker to launch this sort of attack is when the attacker is confident that no better evidence actually exists.

If the evidence takes the form of a statement of opinion by a source, the evidence can be attacked by maintaining that the source is unqualified or biased. To sustain the case, its advocate would need either to reestablish the credibility of the original source (by defending its credentials or denying its alleged bias) or to provide similar statements coming from other sources that are clearly qualified and unbiased. In general, it is not a good idea to attack the evidence unless you can clearly establish its deficiency, since audiences often tend to give presumably expert sources the benefit of the doubt. On the other hand, if the evidence can be clearly discredited and it is unlikely that any stronger evidence is available, then this may be a powerful attack indeed.

In Chapter 4, we encountered a variety of tests and critical questions for evidence. These can be used to set up attacks on the evidence if that is where the prospects for a successful attack seem strongest.

The warrant. We saw in Chapter 2 that evidence is connected to claim by an inference and an explicit or implicit warrant licensing that inference. The warrant is a general statement that, on the basis of information like that in the evidence, one is justified in drawing a conclusion like that contained in the claim. There are several ways in which one might focus an attack on the warrant and thereby demonstrate that the argument has not been proved.

1. One approach is to deny the warrant explicitly. Suppose the evidence is that the value of stocks rose in the weeks following the election of Donald Trump as president of the United States, and the claim is that President Trump's election caused the stock market to rise. The implicit warrant is that if one event precedes another, the first can be said to be the cause of the second. Remembering what you read in Chapter 5 about the post hoc fallacy, you could attack this argument by saying that the warrant is false: chronological order does not establish causality. There might in fact be no connection at all between the two events, or the connection might be purely a matter of coincidence. By breaking the link between the evidence and the claim, you have shown that no basis has been established for the claim.

2. A second approach to attacking the warrant is to maintain that the case at hand is an exception to a warrant that may be generally applicable. To understand this, we need to review the discussion from Chapter 2 about warrants. They are *general statements*, identifying relationships that hold ordinarily or as a general rule. But they are not absolute statements that permit no exceptions. That, after all, is what distinguishes them from the premises of formal, deductive logic.

   If one were going to attack the warrant in this way, one would indicate that the warrant, while it might be correct generally, does not apply to the situation at hand because of some atypical or exceptional characteristic. For example, the warrant might be that items alike in most respects will be alike in the respects in question – the basic warrant for an argument of analogy. Suppose this warrant is used to establish that Houston and Atlanta, both major metropolitan areas with diverse populations, healthy economies, rich histories, and sprawling growth, will have similar cultures as well. But suppose culture is affected by other factors: the southern tradition and the significance of race and the civil rights movement in Atlanta's case, contrasted with the "boom town" mentality, frontier tradition, and strong Latino influence in Houston's. Then, even though the cities are generally alike, they would not be alike in culture because culture is a more complex variable that cannot be predicted from similarities in other variables. The general warrant is not discredited, but it is set aside in the particular case because of exceptional circumstances. In response, the maker of the original argument would need to show either that the allegedly exceptional circumstances are not all that unusual or that the general warrant would still apply despite the atypical circumstances.

3. Yet another way to attack the warrant of an argument is to invoke a balance of considerations. This approach suggests that the warrant is fine so far as it goes, but that there is another competing or counteracting warrant that moves the argument in the opposite direction. Therefore, the original warrant – even if correct – cannot license the claim by itself; it must be weighed against the counteracting warrant to determine, on balance, which has the greater force.

Consider a simple example. The basic sign warrant, as presented in Chapter 5, is that the existence of a sign allows us to predict the existence of the thing signified. Suppose that large numbers of students loading luggage into cars is a sign that the school year is coming to an end. We observe cars all over campus being loaded with students' luggage, and without even consulting a calendar, we infer that the school year is about to end, drawing on the sign warrant to license our inference. But suppose that a power outage has cut electricity to the campus for a week, forcing an emergency evacuation requiring that students take with them enough clothing and supplies for a week. Here the causal warrant (an emergency evacuation order causes students to load luggage into cars) counteracts the sign warrant (loading luggage into cars predicts the end of the school year). Which of the competing warrants will dominate can be determined only by a balance of considerations in the particular case. If you think you can demonstrate that the counter-warrant outweighs the original warrant, this may be a potent way to attack the argument at the level of the warrant.

The underlying context. Finally, in addition to the claim, evidence, and warrant, an argument can be attacked at the level of its underlying context and assumptions. All arguments are embedded in such a context, although it usually is left implicit. For example, in the argument about airline delays, there is an underlying assumption that when it comes to travel, speed and efficiency are desirable qualities, so that actions limiting speed and efficiency are taken to be harmful. Likewise, it is assumed implicitly that there is such a thing as a right to travel, so that actions hindering people in their travel provide just cause for complaint. If these assumptions could be successfully challenged, then the arguments about the problem of airline delays would carry little or no weight. Unless the original advocate is caught unaware, challenges to underlying assumptions are not likely to be completely successful. Yet it is tempting at least to consider this approach, because it offers the prospect of undercutting an argument without engaging with its particulars.

Obviously, we have considered more places where an argument could be attacked than an attacker would want to invoke at any one time. Once an argument is defeated, nothing is gained by defeating it again. That is unnecessary overkill and it risks wasting valuable time. As with other strategic choices, the key considerations are which attack you will be able to establish most clearly, and which attack will take you the greatest distance toward defeating the case.

How Many Attacks?

The final choice regarding attacks is how many to present, both how many arguments to attack and how many attacks to launch against a given argument. The considerations are precisely the same as we saw in the discussion of amplitude in Chapter 7. Present too many attacks and many of them may be inadequately developed, casting doubt on the attackers' credibility and risking inconsistency among those arguments. But present too few and your attack may seem thin and uninformed, not up to the considered judgment the subject required.

Types of Attacks

Another choice that should be addressed is what type of attack to develop. Several possibilities suggest themselves.

Asking a Question

Sometimes an argument will seem to be missing essential information, which the attacker might try to elicit by asking a question. For example,

"You've said that 'many' airports are experiencing delays, but just how many is that?" In order to evaluate the claim, the attacker suggests, we need to know whether the proponent of the case is referring, say, to 10 percent of all airports, 50 percent, or 90 percent. How public policy should respond will depend on what the magnitude of the problem is, and a vague term such as "many" does not provide this information.

Of course, it is not enough just to ask the question. It is necessary to explain why the answer matters to the argument, and hence, why the case will be damaged if its advocate cannot present and defend an answer. Otherwise, raising questions will seem like nit-picking. Even when the rationale for the question is provided, moreover, asking questions is usually a weak strategy. The reason, to use a term borrowed from real estate, is that asking questions *builds no equity* in the argument. Once the question has been asked and answered ("You wanted to know how many airports experience delays; currently the figure is 65 percent"), the attacker has nothing left to rely on. For this reason, asking questions should be done sparingly, and probably in combination with some other type of attack.

There is one exception to that generalization: the question that is naturally suggested by the opponent's argument but that is unanswerable. Probably the clearest use of an unanswerable question has to do with things allegedly being done in secret. For example, an attack might proceed thus: "You say that administration officials profited on business deals they secretly negotiated with Russia. How many secret meetings have taken place?" The supporter of the case might be tempted to reply, "Well, we know that the president's advisers have sat down with the Russians on this and this and this occasion." But the attacker could answer, "Wait a minute. Those are meetings that we know about. How many *secret* meetings have taken place?" Of course, by the very nature of secrecy, one doesn't know what one doesn't know, and yet the logic of the case depends on the answer. If it cannot be established that any truly secret meetings have taken place, then the basis for taking action to eliminate secret meetings is seriously weakened.

Identifying Internal Deficiencies

A second kind of attack is to identify internal deficiencies in the argument. The evidence might be outdated or the warrant might commit the post hoc fallacy (the assumption that one thing causes another because the first precedes the second), for example. As with asking questions, it is critical that the attack not only point out a deficiency but also explain how it imperils the case. For example, the post hoc fallacy means that no causal force can be necessarily attributed to the alleged cause, and hence that a remedial action addressed to that supposed cause cannot be assumed to work. Furthermore, identifying internal deficiencies is similar to asking questions in that, if the deficiencies are remedied, the attacker has no equity left in the argument. It is best, therefore, to concentrate this method of attack on deficiencies that the attacker is reasonably sure cannot be remedied.

Pointing Out Inconsistencies

A third approach to attacking an argument or a case is to identify inconsistencies among parts of the argument or among arguments in a case. There are two basic kinds of inconsistencies: logical and pragmatic. Logical inconsistencies are *contradictions*, arguments that cannot both be true. For example, the argument that North Korea is developing missiles that could reach the United States and the argument that North Korea is not developing such missiles are contradictory statements. They cannot both be true. Pragmatic inconsistencies, in contrast, are not literally contradictory but they work at cross-purposes with each other. For example, the argument that the federal budget deficit should be reduced by curtailing spending is at odds with an argument made by the same person that spending on his or her favorite program should be increased, regardless of its effect on the federal budget deficit. Notice that these arguments are not contradictory; they could both be true. One could favor cutting spending as a general rule and also favor increasing it in the case of a particular program that would be treated as an exception. But the arguments work at cross-purposes. We would not expect anyone to take both these positions at the same time and would be inclined to regard anyone who did so as a hypocrite.

Identifying inconsistencies of either the logical or the pragmatic kind has two major psychological benefits as a type of attack. One benefit is that when confronted with inconsistency, audiences often tend to discredit *both* of the inconsistent positions. Logically, there is no reason to do so, since an inconsistency means only that both positions cannot be true, not that both are false. But perhaps unsure which of the positions should be maintained and which jettisoned, audiences often will be dubious about both. The second is that an arguer who presents an inconsistency is likely to find that the audience, in addition to discrediting both positions, will doubt the sincerity or credibility of the arguer too. Western culture places a high value on the law of noncontradiction and an arguer who violates it will suffer a penalty.

Labeling the Opposing Argument's Strategy

Sometimes labeling the strategy of the opposing argument will be sufficient to defeat it. An arguer might say, "You're relying on loaded language when you define capital punishment as murder," "You are making a hasty generalization," or "You're creating a false dilemma." The idea here is that the strategic success of the opponent's argument depends on the strategy being concealed. Unmasking the strategy makes apparent that something is deficient about the argument, and identifying the deficiency will be sufficient for the argument to fall. It may not be necessary to explain the deficiency, as in the example above, because the connotation of a term like "hasty generalization" suggests that something is amiss. On the other hand, it is a mistake to assume that audiences will be familiar with technical terms. Rather than saying merely, "That is a post hoc fallacy," and leaving it at that, it is better to explain what the fallacy is in the case at hand.

Counter-argument

This is a direct confrontation of an argument with a competing argument. It represents a denial of the claim itself and forces an audience to choose between the two conflicting claims. This is the method that would be used in attacking the claim, as discussed above. The attack might be a straight-forward denial of the claim, or it may advance an alternative claim that is incompatible with it. Either way, the evaluator is presented with two discrete claims that cannot both be correct, and he or she will need to decide which is the better reasoned and supported.

Recontextualizing the Argument

The last option among types of attack has been suggested earlier, when we learned that an interlocutor could focus attack on the (often unstated) underlying context of the argument. The attack then casts the argument in a different context in order to challenge its underlying assumptions. During the health care debates of 2016 and 2017, for example, Democrats were proud that the Affordable Care Act ("Obamacare") had insured some 20 million Americans who previously had lacked coverage, and they pointed with alarm to the contention that the proposed alternative would remove more than 23 million from the rolls. Clearly, the Democrats' working assumption was that extending coverage was the principal object-ive of federal health care policy. But Republicans countered that cost control and individuals' economic freedom were the most important goals. They maintained that the prospect of declines in individual coverage meant only that some individuals would be making the free choice that insurance was not worth its cost for them and that, if that was their view, declines in the number of insured are not necessarily harmful. Meanwhile, they cited the potential benefits of lowering average premiums and redu-cing the federal budget deficit as powerful arguments for the Republican alternative. By changing the assumptions, critics of Obamacare could cast the health care controversy in an entirely different light.

Arrangement Choices Involving Attack

Some of the choices attackers face in organizing their attacks are identical to those related to case construction, especially where to put the strongest attacks (first or last) when the attack is structured as multiple argumenta-tion. But there is one choice that uniquely belongs to the attack: Should one follow the same sequence as the original case did, or should one organize the attacks in a different order? There is no universally right answer to this question, but it needs to be answered based on the specifics of the case and the nature of the attack.

On the one hand, using the same structure may make the dispute easier for an audience to follow. If they have outlined the original case, for example, audience members can note whether the attack responds to each of the case arguments. They will be able to keep track of which arguments were answered, which agreed to, and which ignored. (A note-taking system can allow one to follow the internal pattern of the speech in vertical columns and the development of arguments across the controversy in horizontal rows; some call this note-taking "flowing" the arguments.) The drawback of always following the opponent's structure is that it puts the attacker on the proponent's grounds. Arguers presumably organize their cases as they do because they perceive that doing so is a strategic advantage, especially if they can draw their opponents to it.

Consider the example introduced in previous chapters, that of the person alleging that a series of mishaps by airline companies resulted in the loss of his or her job. If you were going to adopt the order of the case in developing your attack, you would take each of the steps in the sequence of the case as developed, and ignore, agree, or refute each step. This should be easy to follow, but it does focus the discussion on the ground chosen by the adversary.

Now suppose instead that you respond to the argument by saying only, "Your termination notice was written before you ever left on the trip you are talking about." This does not deal directly with any of the substructure of the argument, but it does focus attention on the question, "Is it the airline's fault?" Obviously, if the worker had been effectively fired before ever having started on the trip, it could not be the case that airline-caused mishaps were the source of the trouble.

There is no clear rule to guide the choice. Sometimes it makes more sense to follow the structure of the case in developing the attacks, while at other times it makes more sense to proceed out of order or to group several elements of the case and attack them jointly. Factors to consider include whether there is a common attack for multiple elements in the case and whether the case depends significantly on unstated assumptions that render it vulnerable. The possible benefits of diverting an opponent from his or her own case structure need to be weighed against the potential for confusing the audience by having more than one organizational plan on the table at the same time.

A second arrangement choice is how completely to develop the attack. The question is what is needed in order to make clear the clash between the argument and the attack. A fully developed attack has four key parts. First, the argument that is going to be attacked should be stated clearly, and it should be stated in a way that the opponent would recognize and acknowledge. The danger of restating the argument in other terms or of using overly loaded language is that you can commit the fallacy of the straw man – attacking an argument that was not the one your opponent presented. Second, the attack itself should be stated and its importance explained. An example would be to say, "I'm going to show you that airline mishaps are not the cause of your troubles, which means that you are ignoring the real culprit and going after an innocent party." Third, the attack is developed, with whatever supporting evidence and reasoning are appropriate. And fourth, the attacker explains what has been accomplished by the attack. For example, one might say, "Since the case identified the wrong culprit, its basic premise is faulty. And without a sound basic premise, the case really has nothing to stand on."

Argumentation theorists might be pleased if all attacks were developed this fully. Audiences always would understand what was being attacked and why. The problem is that a presentation so complete takes time and effort. Just like presenting arguments, attacking them involves *opportunity costs*: time and effort spent on one task cannot be spent on another. (This is particularly true when one is in a formal setting with time limits.) So it is necessary in each case to decide how much of the complete structure of an attack to use. If the opponent's argument is apparent, it may be possible to refer to it without stating it fully ("the proliferation argument"). If you think the importance of the attack is self-evident, you may choose to omit that step, saving some time. You may be able to abbreviate the statement of what the attack has accomplished. And you should consider carefully how much supporting evidence and reasoning are needed to develop the attack, so that you can omit whatever might be superfluous. Of course, you should not do all these things on the same attack, or you will have little left! But, as with the question of whether or not to follow the structure of the case, there are no clear rules to guide the choice; it must be made in the context of the particular situation. Factors to consider include how obvious the attack is, how clear it is that the attack engages the argument, and how easily the audience will accept that the attack, if successful, will do major damage. And, like all such judgments, these decisions have to be made with incomplete knowledge of the audience and situation. The attacker should rely on whatever information and insight are available but also will need to make judgments that are intuitive.

Options for the Defense

So far, this chapter has been entirely about attacking arguments, and mostly about choices for selecting arguments to attack. In contrast, the options available when defending an argument that has been attacked are quite limited. Here we shall consider the defense's basic strategic options, the key choices involving selection and arrangement, and preemptive moves the defense can make.

Basic Strategic Options

Four basic strategic options are available to the defense, and these involve different ways of contextualizing the attack. First, one can show that the attack is *inapplicable* to the case. Suppose that in a discussion of Social Security, an advocate maintains that the Social Security trust fund will be depleted by 2042, so that full payments cannot be guaranteed beyond that date. Upholding the health of the trust fund, the attacker might observe that it is large now and has been growing since the early 1980s. The defender might note that the attack is inapplicable to the case, which is concerned not with the present but with what will happen in the future after all the baby boomers have retired.

Second, one can show that the attack is *trivial* – that even granting the attack will do little or no damage to the case. For example, if the original argument is that giving the PSAT in the eleventh grade takes valuable time away from the school curriculum, and if the attack is that the argument is mistaken because the PSAT actually is given in the tenth grade, the attack easily can be dismissed as trivial. Which grade the test is administered in is really incidental to the argument; the core is the claim that using school time for the test takes away from coverage of the curriculum (unless, of course, the tenth-grade curriculum was known to include slack time, whereas the eleventh-grade curriculum was packed). Just as not every argument needs to be attacked, not every attack needs to be answered, particularly if it can be dismissed as being of trivial consequence.

Third, the defense can show that the attack has been *inadequately established*. A teenager wishing to stay out past a midnight curfew argues that the enjoyment of an upcoming concert and the teenager's record of conscientious behavior justify the request. Suppose the parent impatiently responds, "You are always trying to test your limits in order to see what you can get away with." Defending the argument, the teenager might observe – respectfully, of course – that the broad generalization in the attack has not been established and that in fact he or she is making a special case for an exception to the rule. As you may have thought, this sequence of attack and defense is quite common in family arguments. Both parents and children can be tempted to respond to specific claims with broad generalizations beginning, "You always ..." or "You never ..." and the original arguer can try to defend the argument by noting that the generalization in the attack has not been established adequately.

Fourth, the defense can show that the attack is in *error*, that the case has been attacked on a faulty basis. During a political campaign, for example, the candidate from the challenging party might allege that the economy is in bad shape – leading to a recession, to rising unemployment, or to inflation, as the case may be. The candidate of the incumbent party might try to attack this argument by saying, as Senator John McCain actually did in 2008, "The fundamentals of the economy are strong." The defense could show this attack to be in error by citing the relevant economic indicators and noting that the fundamentals really were rather weak, thereby defending the original argument. (One could imagine a side discussion about which aspects of the economy are really "fundamental," but that did not occur in this case.)

These basic strategic options are really ways in which to contextualize an attack in order to set up a defense. In executing the defense, the advocate's options are limited.

Selection and Arrangement Choices

In a sense, defenses of an argument are also attacks on the attacks made in response to the original argument. In that sense, the defense has exactly the same range of choices regarding the attacks as the attacker had with respect to the case. Keeping this observation in mind will be especially helpful to the defense on those occasions when the attacker does not directly engage the case but instead presents a largely alternative case.

But to think of matters that way in all cases is to abandon one's own ground for the attacker's. In most situations, the burden of proof will rest with the defender of the case, since he or she was the original proponent. At the end of the dispute, the question is whether the case has been sustained, not just whether specific attacks against it have fallen short. For this reason, the selection of a way to contextualize the attack always must be made with a view to which approach will rebuild and strengthen the original case.

The basic arrangement choice is whether the structure of the original case or the structure of the attack (assuming it to be different) will be the dominant organizational choice for the defense. Each approach has benefits and drawbacks. Returning to the original focus of the case will remind audiences of the way the case proponent wanted to lay out the argument. It can also highlight elements of the case that the attacker has ignored, which the defender can regard as having implicitly been conceded. But in returning to the original case structure, the danger is that you will merely repeat the original argument without extending it to answer the attack that has been made on it. You might be tempted, for example, to repeat that airport congestion leads to delayed flights which cause economic losses, forgetting to answer the opponent's claim that the problem of congestion-caused delays is statistically insignificant.

The alternative to returning to the original case structure is to follow the structure of the attack, responding as you go and defending the case by undermining the attacks. If the attacker followed the structure of your case, this defense structure may be indistinguishable from the first option. But the attacker may have advanced his or her own structure instead. If you follow *that* structure, listeners should be able to match up attacks and responses. But the danger is that you may be drawn completely away from your own case structure, which you presumably had adopted for a reason. Suppose, for instance, that your case argued that stem cell research should be expanded because of its scientific and medical benefits. Suppose further that the attack had not addressed these benefits but focused entirely on religious objections to expanding stem cell research. If you were to organize your defense along the lines of the attack, you would focus on answering the religious objections and, by mistake, you might abandon entirely your focus on scientific and medical benefits.

Neither of these arrangement choices is in principle better than the other, and it may be possible to combine elements of both. What is important is to be aware of the dangers you risk by each approach and do your best to avoid them.

Preemptive Moves

If the same persons who presented the case in the first place are responsible for its defense, there is a wider range of options. They involve incorporating into the original argument the responses to attacks you can anticipate. Suppose you are advocating for subsidies for the creation of jobs focused on new technology, and your case says that subsidies will induce workers to move, if necessary, and to undergo training to qualify them for new jobs to replace jobs lost to automation and new technology. You anticipate that one of the major attacks will be that unemployment is coming down to levels once thought unachievable – below 4 percent by July 2018, for instance. The implication of the attack is that the economy is providing jobs to absorb workers who want them, without the need for any subsidies. Anticipating this attack, you might set up the initial case to preempt it. For example, you might argue as part of the case that even though the overall unemployment rate is dropping, not enough people are being attracted to these new technology jobs or to the training that would enable them to qualify for them. If the opponent makes the attack you anticipated, that the overall unemployment rate is going down, you can respond that you took that into consideration when you presented your case in the first place.

It is easier to make these preemptive moves if the person defending the case is the same person who advanced it initially. But even if different people are involved, the defender often can find in the original case an implicit answer to an attack the interlocutor has made. When this happens, the defender of the case can offset some of the selection advantages that normally accrue to the challenger.

General Means of Refutation

To close this chapter, we shall consider some general methods that can be used in refutation, whether in attacking the case or attacking the attacks. These moves also can be made when one is in a defensive mode, although that happens far less frequently.

Reductio ad absurdum. This phrase means "reduction to absurdity." But it does not refer to making fun of the opposing argument or ridiculing it. Rather, it is a claim that the opposing argument should be rejected because the consequences of adopting it would be unacceptable, even unreasonable. A proposal to track all citizens who had made statements critical of the government, for example, might be reduced to absurdity by calculating the number of people and the cost required to do this, noting that it might consume the entire economy of the nation – to say nothing of the principles of privacy and free expression that the proposal would violate.

Turning the tables. This refutation strategy consists in showing that an argument will have the opposite results from those claimed in its behalf. Something claimed to be a reason to avoid a certain action might be shown actually to be a reason *in favor* of the action. A proposal argued to benefit the attacker of a case might be shown actually to benefit the defender instead. The power of this means of refutation is that the attack or defense retains all of its force and strength, but the benefit of it goes to the opposite party from the one who first introduced the argument.

Dilemmas. A dilemma is a situation in which the opposing arguer is forced to choose between unacceptable alternatives. The possible options are limited, ideally to two, and each possible outcome is shown to be unacceptable. The choice cannot be avoided, so whatever one does, the result will be unacceptable. The arguer claiming the existence of a dilemma does not need to predict which option *will* be chosen, but rather to say that *whatever* is chosen, the results will be unfortunate. A person charged with facing a dilemma will naturally seek to escape it, by arguing that there really are additional options that do not have such dire consequences, by maintaining that one of the possible options is clearly of greater benefit than the others, or by turning the tables and supporting that the alleged harm is really a benefit.

Argument a fortiori. A fortiori arguments are about more and less. Depending on the context, they suggest that what is true (or false) about the greater therefore must be true (or false) of the lesser, or vice versa. For example, if it is a punishable offense to surf the Internet during a classroom lecture, all the more so should it be to do so during an address by the president of the university. This means of refutation is especially helpful when the interlocutor has agreed to the premise of the argument. If he or she accepts that state secrets should not be leaked, for example, it may be difficult for him or her to resist the claim that family secrets should not be shared: what is true of the greater is all the more true of the lesser.

Argument from residues. When one's adversary resists taking a clear and fair position, this may be a way to maneuver him or her into a position by excluding all other possibilities. During the Vietnam War, President Richard Nixon sought to generate approval for his policy by proposing it as the only alternative to either all-out escalation or precipitate withdrawal, both of which were overwhelmingly unpopular. The only way to avoid one of the undesirable choices is to dispute the assumptions made by the arguer, that these are the only choices and that they all are undesirable.

Contradictions and inconsistencies. A powerful means of refutation is to claim that two or more of the opponent's positions are logically contradictory or pragmatically inconsistent. This has been discussed earlier in the chapter. Of course, the best defense against charges of contradiction or uncertainty usually is to show that the allegedly inconsistent positions can coexist.

The interrelated processes of attack and defense help to move a discussion forward beyond the initial presentation of the case. Along the way, a powerful contributor is the style and language in which the arguments are cast. We come to that topic next, in Chapter 9.

Exercises

1. In the following situations, try to make good strategic choices for attacking the arguments presented. You do not need to know any specific details of the argument. Rather, look at the format, topics, audience, and time constraints to choose the strategies of attack that you think would be most effective.

   a. You are a member of the US House of Representatives. Sara Smith, a representative from the opposing party, has introduced legislation that would reduce funding for mental health services by more than 50 percent. This is a proposal you strongly disagree with, and in fact, you have proposed that these services be expanded. You will have thirty minutes to present your response to Rep. Smith's proposal.

b. You are a member of the Rules Committee for the National Football League. A new rule has been proposed that you believe would be very difficult to enforce because the language of the rule is vague. You will be responding at a meeting of the committee.

c. You have read a tweet from a highly influential social media celebrity. The tweet links to a highly controversial and inflammatory journal article and seems to endorse the sentiments of the article. You have good reason to question the legitimacy of the evidence in this article. You believe that this message is potentially dangerous to the interpretation of an issue you feel strongly about. You have many thousands of followers and regularly post on issues similar to this one.

d. You have made a proposal supporting the introduction of an important new product at the electronics company where you work in design. Your immediate supervisor has rejected the proposal for reasons that you feel are misguided. You have been granted a meeting with both your supervisor and the CEO of the company at which you can make the case for your design.

e. Your elderly aunt tells you that she has developed a friendship online with someone who is requesting money to help with medical bills. You try to dissuade her, but the aunt makes a strong case for the need to be charitable with friends.

f. You are riding with a friend to a concert in a city you have never visited. Your friend, the driver, suggests going straight through the city to the concert, although it is nearing rush hour. She argues that it is a much shorter distance, although you believe that it will take longer in traffic. The exit that will allow you to bypass the traffic is coming up in less than 5 minutes.

g. You have to write a five-page paper for a political science class. You are reviewing an essay by a well-known theorist. You have serious disagreements with the thesis of the essay, but you recognize that the author of the essay has much higher credibility in the field than you do.

h. You are seventeen years old and living at home. You miss your curfew by more than an hour. Your parents respond by grounding you for two weeks. You feel that this sanction is excessive and that there were good reasons for coming home so late.

i. Your band is playing a very important gig and the guitarist argues that you should play her original song. You believe that the song is not very good and, more importantly, that it misrepresents the style of music that you, as a group, most want to play.

j. The zoning board in your town is voting to develop a piece of property for a new subdivision. The developer has made a strong case that this subdivision will provide significant revenue to the town in the form of taxes and other benefits from the new residents. You disagree with the proposal because it would disrupt a bird reserve that harbors many endangered species and is a source of both scientific interest and revenue from tourism.

2. Which type of refutation is represented by each of the following arguments?

a. If you try to pursue a career in Hollywood, you either will fail miserably or will become corrupted by the excesses of that culture. In either case you will be sorry.

b. In order to pay our delinquent tax bill, we will have to sell your Porsche, go into debt, or move. No one wants to take on debt or leave this house, so the only choice is to sell your car.

c. There is no way we can beat Central High in football this year. We lost to North by fourteen points and Central beat them by twenty-four points last week.

d. You claimed that we should not eat meat because you are concerned for the welfare of animals, but you wear leather belts and shoes.

e. The student government voted to cut off funding to the social committee because of the vandalism on campus. However, cutting off funding will only raise the likelihood that bored students will destroy school property.

f. My father says I need to finish my chores because hard work never hurt anyone. But if I keep working, eventually I will get so tired that I make a mistake and get hurt, so I don't buy his argument.

Extensions: Toward More Advanced Study

As this chapter suggests, one of the choices in attacking an argument is which step in the argument to attack – the claim, the evidence, or the warrant. There are two different ways to attack the warrant: either dispute its status as a warrant, attacking it frontally, or accept it as a general warrant but maintain that it does not apply to the case at hand. The difference between these two approaches is not always as clear in practice as in theory.

In Chapter 2 we noted that the "evidence/warrant/claim" model of argument was suggested by the British philosopher Stephen Toulmin.[1] In his own layout of argument, Toulmin incorporates possible exceptions to the warrant within his model itself. He calls them *rebuttals*; others have referred to them as *reservations*. Toulmin holds that the warrant licenses the inference from evidence to claim, unless there are rebuttals that override the force of the warrant in the particular case. Because of the possibility of rebuttals, the arguer must qualify the claim with an explicit or implicit modal term such as "probably," "usually," "most of the time," "almost certainly," or some other term indicating the force of the reservations. This book has not incorporated Toulmin's layout in this particular respect, for two reasons. First, the term *rebuttals* is confusing since "rebuttal" also refers to the process of defending one's arguments against attack. Second, it is not common for an arguer, in the course of making a case, to identify the possible rebuttals that might set aside his or her own argument. (The Canadian philosopher Ralph Johnson has maintained that arguers have an obligation to do exactly that, as we mentioned in an earlier chapter,[2] but his is a distinctly minority viewpoint.) It is far more likely that the rebuttals will come up as the argument develops, if the *attacker* invokes them to set aside the force of the warrant. It seems confusing to include them in the layout of the original argument if they are not introduced into the dispute until later.

Besides, the "rebuttal" is not the only way to challenge the warrant. As noted above, it could be disputed outright. That is the circumstance, discussed in Chapter 2, in which an advocate will need to provide backing for the warrant in order to justify its status as a warrant. "Backing" is also a part of the Toulmin layout, but the distinctions between "backing" and "rebuttal" are not made very clear, leading to possible confusion in attempts to apply these aspects of Toulmin's system to actual cases of argument.

---

[1] Stephen Toulmin, *The Uses of Argument* (Cambridge: Cambridge University Press, 1958), esp. chapter 3.
[2] See Chapter 7, note 3.

CHAPTER 9

Language, Style, and Presentation

Except for the realms of symbolic logic and mathematics, where content-free symbols are often employed, argumentation usually is expressed in language. In fact, arguments typically cannot be separated from the language in which they are cast. This means that language is not just "added on" to an argument for ornamentation, but is an intrinsic part of the argument's substance, shaping what the argument "means" to people and how they will respond to it. But language is inexact. Its meanings and uses cannot be fixed with precision, and it does not completely match the thinking of either arguer or audience. Understanding how language works is a critical aspect of knowing how an argument will proceed.

In this chapter we will consider several aspects of language affecting argumentation. We will review linguistic consistency and then explore definitions, dissociation of terms, figures of speech, strategic imprecision, and linguistic intensity. We will conclude by considering how argumentation is affected by the mode of presentation, whether written, oral, or visual.

Linguistic Consistency

One respect in which language is inexact is that many words do not have a single clear meaning. Or if they do, their arrangement in a sentence may leave the overall meaning of the sentence unclear. Yet in most circumstances, arguers wish to be clearly understood. Only rarely, as we will see later in the chapter, is the meaning of an expression deliberately fuzzy or unclear. Errors are usually unintentional.

Arguers cannot remove all sources of confusion, but what they can do is to insist on linguistic consistency. Even if words or phrases have multiple meanings, the same usage and meaning should prevail throughout a given argument. When it is lacking, the fallacies of clarity discussed in Chapter 6 are likely to occur. These include ambiguity, amphiboly, vagueness, and equivocation, among others.

The expectation of linguistic consistency usually is a minimal standard for arguers. Even while meeting this standard, arguers have multiple ways to use language as a strategic resource to their advantage when formulating arguments.

Definitions

We tend to think of definitions as neutral, found by looking up a word in the dictionary to see what it means. But the dictionary is only one source of definitions, and characterizing common usage is only one of their purposes. Sometimes definitions serve to make a vague term more precise, or to give technical terms a meaning that is comprehensible to someone not an expert in a particular subject. Common usage among experts in the area would be the source of such definitions.

At other times, definitions actually codify new usage. Terminology is invented to fill a vacuum; sometimes the terms "stick" and are picked up by others throughout the culture, and they become accepted as authoritative. Examples include a range of terms that have been invented since the advent of the Internet, such as "download" and "upload," "boot up," "surf the net," and "google" (as a verb).

And sometimes definitions are stipulated by the parties to a discussion, not in order to state what is "right" but to assure that the parties are talking about the same thing. Definitions of this type are adopted "for the sake of the argument." In an argument about the "debt ceiling crisis," for example, all parties might stipulate that "debt ceiling crisis" refers to the consequences of the government's inability to borrow additional funds, not to the problems that will result if Congress passes (or fails to pass) a budget with significant deficit spending that raises the overall public debt. Now, there is nothing wrong with adopting the latter definition instead, but the argumentation will not get very far if some arguers use the first definition and others use the second, all in the same discussion.

The types and uses of definitions discussed so far are relatively uncontroversial; their primary objective is to clarify usage or to facilitate discussion. There is another category of definitions, however, that has a much greater argumentative impact. The philosopher Charles L. Stevenson called these *persuasive definitions.*[1] To understand what they are, recall that words have (at least) two dimensions of meaning: denotation and connotation. Denotation identifies what a term refers to. The denotation of "chair," for example,

---

[1] Charles L. Stevenson, *Ethics and Language* (New Haven, CT: Yale University Press, 1944).

would be something like "an object with four legs and a surface on which a person sits." For terms to be widely understood, there must be a very high level of agreement and acceptance of the denotation. Connotation refers to the positive or negative feelings or values that are associated with the term and that are conjured up by people when the term is used. The connotation of "chair" is relatively neutral, unless we are thinking of, say, Grandma's favorite chair or some other particular chair. But suppose we were to refer to the same object as a throne. That might evoke positive connotations of awe or reverence in the context of chairs occupied by a ruling monarch. On the other hand, "throne" would evoke negative connotations of cynicism or ridicule if the chair in question were a beat-up old stool or, as is sometimes meant, a toilet seat. In either case, the connotation would not be neutral! Our interpretation and assessment of the thing referred to would be different depending on the connotation evoked.

A persuasive definition is one that alters the "meaning" of a term by associating it with clearly positive or negative connotations. The denotation is held constant but the connotative meaning is changed. (Alternatively, we could hold the connotation constant but change the denotation to which it applies. A term with positive connotations, such as "win-win," might be argued to belong to one denotation rather than another.)

Several examples should illustrate how persuasive definitions work. In the 2016 US presidential election, Donald Trump received 304 votes in the Electoral College.[2] (A total of 270 is required for victory.) Trump's results could be described as a *landslide* or as a *squeaker*, and the connotations would be quite different. "Landslide" might be used because Trump won almost all of the "toss-up" states. "Squeaker" might be used because his electoral vote margin over his opponent was only the forty-sixth greatest out of fifty-eight presidential elections. But which definition prevails can make a huge difference to the argument.

On seeing an example like this, one might be tempted to say, "Throw out both connotations and just report the fact that Trump received 304 electoral votes." Facts certainly do deserve our respect, especially in an age in which politicians and others invent "alternative facts" that they would prefer to wish into existence. But facts by themselves do not tell us enough. This report of Trump's total by itself might prompt questions such as "So what?" or "What does that mean?" or "Is that good or bad?" An adage is that "facts do not speak; they must be spoken for." The process of

[2] Mr. Trump won states totaling 306 electoral votes, but two of those electors did not actually vote for him in the final tally.

speaking for the facts is what gets us into analysis and interpretation. And persuasive definitions become a potent means of using language to advance one interpretation or another.

Here are a few other examples of persuasive definitions. In the United States, there has been a long-running dispute about the morality of capital punishment. Supporters of the death penalty may define it as "retributive justice," whereas opponents define it as "murder." Another long-running controversy concerns abortion. Opponents of legalized abortion will define their position as "pro-life" and will define the position of their opponents as "murder of the unborn." But those who would retain legalized abortion obviously will not accept these definitions, choosing instead to define their own position as "pro-choice" and often defining their opponents' position as "anti-choice." Finally, during the war on terrorism of the early 2000s, there was a controversy over certain methods of questioning prisoners who were suspected terrorists, such as sleep deprivation, subjection to extreme cold temperatures, and waterboarding. Those who thought these proced-ures were appropriate in the context of a war against terror defined them as "enhanced interrogation techniques." Those who opposed them called them "torture" and accused their supporters of unjustified euphemism.

Simply invoking a persuasive definition will not automatically cause the definition to prevail. Unless other arguers accept it (or ignore it, in which case it can be deemed accepted by default), it will need to be argued for. As the examples above illustrate, persuasive definitions can be developed on both sides of most controversial questions. Advocates will need to present and defend reasons that their choice of definition should prevail. Previous commitments by the interlocutor, consistency with commonly accepted usage, and utility of one or another definition in achieving the purposes of the argumentation are among the strong defenses one can make for a choice of definition.

So far, we have been discussing the definition of individual terms. But definition as a strategy of argumentation can also be applied to an entire discussion, and, for that matter, to the context or situation in which the discourse is found. This activity is called *definition of the situation*, and the same concepts of persuasive definition apply.[3] (*Framing* sometimes is used as a synonym for "defining the situation.")[4] The way in which a situation is defined affects our view of it and our reaction to it.

---

[3] See J. Robert Cox, "Argument and the 'Definition of the Situation,'" *Communication Studies, 32* (Fall, 1981), 197–205.

[4] For a treatment of framing, see Robert M. Entman, "Framing: Toward Clarification of a Fractured Paradigm," *Journal of Communication, 43* (1993), 51–58.

Definitions of the situation can be used in argumentation to widen or narrow the scope of the conflict, the range of persons who are eligible to participate in it. Typically, the would-be loser tries to redefine the conflict so as to enlist the interest of previously uninvolved persons, enlarging the conflict by bringing in new voices and shifting the balance in the would-be loser's favor.[5] The following are a few examples:

- A proposal to raise the student activities fee is redefined as a stealth increase in tuition or as confiscatory taxation. This will arouse the interest of some who previously had been apathetic.
- During the 1840s in the United States, the debate about slavery was redefined as being not really about states' rights but about the country's common interest in the West. Now everyone, not just the slave states, had a stake in the outcome.
- The siting of nuclear power plants has been redefined from a narrow technical issue to a moral question of interest to a much wider audience.
- What was championed as support for freedom of speech on campus gets redefined as support of hate speech. Now it is more controversial, not so clearly a good thing. Some who object to hate speech may become involved.

In each of these examples, redefining the situation brings additional persons into the fray. Sometimes, conversely, definitions can be used as a way to *narrow* the scope of the conflict by excluding some potential participants. For example, taxation policy might be thought to concern everyone because it is about taking people's money and applying it to the public good. But committed advocates might try to redefine the problem as a technical matter, meaning that only those with expertise in finance and accounting would be fit to evaluate the argument.

Dissociation

The process by which arguers attempt to redefine a term this way is called *dissociation*, and it has been explained in depth by the Belgian argumentation theorists Chaim Perelman and Lucie Olbrechts-Tyteca.[6] Let us

---

[5] The theory about widening or narrowing the scope of conflict comes from E. E. Schattschneider, *The Semisovereign People* (New York: Holt, Rinehart and Winston, 1960), 16.

[6] Chaim Perelman and Lucie Olbrechts-Tyteca, *The New Rhetoric: A Treatise on Argumentation* (Notre Dame, IN: University of Notre Dame Press, 1969), 411–459.

examine an example of how it works. Imagine that the topic for discussion is diversity in college enrollment and that a lively discussion is underway. At some point, a participant asserts, "You are looking at only surface kinds of diversity. What's *really* important is diversity of viewpoints, and we need to attract more conservative faculty to our campus." If this participant succeeds, then the term "diversity" will have been redefined as an *ideological* matter rather than a *demographic* one.

Perelman and Olbrechts-Tyteca suggest that dissociation comes about through the application of one or more *philosophical pairs* to the original usage of the term in question. A philosophical pair consists of two contrasting concepts, one of which is commonly preferred over the other and has more favorable connotations. Some common philosophical pairs are appearance/reality, theory/practice, letter/spirit, and ordinary/special. Notice that the pairs can be expressed as fractions and in each case the numerator term is presented as the less-valued term and the denominator term as the more valued.

In the example about diversity, the appearance/reality pair was applied to the term "diversity." The numerator term refers to the apparent or surface characteristic of diversity as a demographic characteristic, while the denominator term refers to the real or core feature of diversity as a matter of ideas. The ground of the argument thereby was shifted from demographics to ideology.

Other philosophical pairs also can be used in this way. One example is letter/spirit. Actions that fulfill a strict legal or other definition yet do not uphold what is claimed to be its underlying purpose are generally less valued than actions that do fulfill the intention of a policy or law even if they do not adhere to every one of the narrow provisions it contains. Another example is accident/essence. Usually the superficial or coincidental features of a thing are valued less than are its inherent or core elements. Temporary/permanent and being/becoming are other examples of philosophical pairs. On the other hand, there are some pairs that could be argued either way because one term is not consistently preferred over the other. In the pair traditional/innovative, for example, it is not clear which term is preferred; that will depend on the specific context. The same could be said of cheap/expensive, gendered/gender-neutral, and many other examples of philosophical pairs.

In short, what a dissociation accomplishes is effectively to redefine a term or idea by recasting a definition that originally was widely accepted so that it is seen as only a part of the term's meaning (captured in the numerator of the philosophical pair), and the less valued part at that.

The denominator term in the philosophical pair points to a different meaning that, if the dissociation is successful, takes over as the new generally accepted meaning of the term.

Obviously, if you are attempting a dissociation, you will recognize what you are doing. But how can you recognize someone else's attempted dissociation when you encounter it in oral or written argumentation? Besides the explicit mention of philosophical pairs, there are several contextual clues. One is an apparent tautology, a statement that seems just to repeat itself. "There is studying, and then there is studying," would be a meaningless statement unless the word "studying" meant something different each time it was used. The first usage is probably devalued – it might refer to sitting in front of a computer while being distracted by e-mail, text messaging, and games – while the latter is probably the preferred term, referring perhaps to uninterrupted concentration on the material in a textbook.

Another contextual clue of a dissociation is an apparent oxymoron – a term or phrase that seems to contradict itself in usage. Unless a speaker is being incoherent when he or she says that a friend is experiencing "joyous agony" or "living death," it must be that what the friend is going through is something other than the generally understood emotional state of agony or death. The common understanding becomes the less valued term in the philosophical pair, and the oxymoronic meaning becomes the preferred term. Dissociation through oxymoron also calls attention to the fact that it is possible for a person to have inconsistent or even contradictory beliefs at the same time.

Prefacing a term with a prefix such as "quasi-," "pseudo-," or "so-called" is an obvious signal that a dissociation is being employed. When a politician refers to "so-called experts," for example, the clear implication is that the persons identified are not really experts, even though they may seem to be. This is the hint of a dissociation between apparent and real experts. Placing quotation marks ("scare quotes") around a term may be a sign that the speaker or writer does not really accept the common understanding of the term, and the point of the quotation marks is to distance this common understanding (the numerator term) from what the arguer actually believes (the denominator term).

Two other contextual clues to a dissociation involve unusual negations. One is a negation between a term and something generally understood as a synonym for it. A student might be describing her summer job to a friend who replies, "That's not work; that is toil!" Although the friend's response appears to use a synonym for "work," the point is to suggest that the ordinary understanding of work does not really capture the undesirability of the friend's summer job. It is too neutral a meaning to account for the tedium, the manual labor, the unpleasant working conditions, or whatever the negative element might be.

Finally, the self-negation of a term is a fairly obvious clue that a dissociation is being invoked. If you were to read the statement, "He never did study; he was too good a student for that," you should know that the meaning of "study" is being changed through dissociation. "Study" might refer to mechanical actions of memorization or underlining of a text. "Student," on the other hand, is one who pursues a given subject or follows in the footsteps of a mentor. The suggestion of the statement is that study of this kind is to be valued more than acts of rote memory that may not result in understanding or insight.

Not all attempts to make dissociations are successful, of course. Some dissociations are so obvious that others see through what is being attempted and reject it out of hand. They might prompt a response such as "Wait a minute; you're trying to change the meaning of that term away from what we all know it to be." At other times, the dissociation may seem farfetched on its face, making a greater shift in meaning than the context would seem to authorize. But there also are ways that the opposing arguer might counter the attempt at dissociation. One is to claim that the dissociation is useless because the two parts are not really distinct, or because the problem that prompted the dissociation will recur anyway. For example, in the dissociation of "student" above, one might maintain that the best student will *both* show an intuitive grasp of the subject and attend to the mechanics of studying, so that it is not reasonable to imagine a distinction between them. Or suppose that in an argument about how to make Social Security financially secure, an arguer would to say, "There are grandiose changes that won't work, and then there are practical solutions that might." One might counter this dissociation by claiming that it is pointless because financial problems with Social Security are imminent whether we make major or minor changes now.

Another way to counter a dissociation is to make an offsetting dissociation. For example, one might claim that the dissociation itself is illusory, applying the appearance/reality pair to another arguer's dissociation. In response to a claim that "equal outcomes" is the real meaning of "equal opportunity," an arguer might state that it is an illusion to think that "opportunity" has multiple dimensions, whereas in reality it refers only to the absence of barriers imposed in advance.

Finally, one might invert the terms of the dissociation by invoking a different philosophical pair. For instance, the original arguer may have used the theory/fact pair in order to suggest that empirical realities are preferable to abstract speculations. But if one were to use the similar pair phenomenon/principle instead, the hierarchy of preferences would be different. Now an enduring principle – another way to describe theory – would be preferred over a transient phenomenon – another way to describe fact. Likewise, one could invert the dissociation particular/universal (suggesting a preference for a more all-encompassing statement over the accidental features of a particular case) by substituting the philosophical pair abstract/concrete (suggesting a preference for the details of the particular over the more general statement that is abstract). Since the number of possible philosophical pairs is limitless, there is no end to the possible dissociations that advocates can invoke, or of the possible ways to contest them. As with persuasive definitions, there are no dissociations that are inherently stronger or weaker than others. They all depend on the quality of the reasoning offered in their support.

Stylistic Devices

In addition to the features of language we have discussed, arguers have a number of presentational choices available to them. These are often grouped under the heading of "style," which for centuries was imagined as mostly separate from argument. The substance of argumentation was thought to lie in the invention and arrangement of arguments, whereas style was seen as ornamentation of an already complete argument. In recent years, however, this distinction has broken down. Scholars recognize that the way an argument is expressed affects both our perception of what the argument says and our attitude toward it. Without modifying arguers' responsibilities, the use of stylistic devices can make their communication more or less effective.

This section, though not comprehensive, will illustrate stylistic devices including figures of speech, types of statements, strategic imprecision, and linguistic intensity.

Figures of Speech

Figures of speech are literary devices that present one word in terms of another, or that alter the expected or conventional order of words in a sentence. Common examples are the *simile*, which describes one thing as being like another; *metaphor*, in which a word or phrase denoting one thing is used in place of another; and *synecdoche*, which describes a part as if it were the whole. Each of these substitutions heightens our awareness of some aspect of the term. For example, if we wish to highlight someone's youth, we might use the synecdoche, "She is a girl of seventeen summers," since "summer" has connotations of youth and freshness, rather than saying more prosaically, "She is seventeen years old." Or if we want to make the point that the administrative structure of an organization is not very strong, we might refer to it not as "administrative structure" but with the metaphor "scaffolding," because that has the connotations of temporariness. And if we wished to emphasize someone's courage, we might use the (admittedly overworked) simile, "He is like a lion," because courage is an attribute regularly attributed to lions. Analogies, which we discussed in Chapter 5 as an argument scheme, can be thought of as extended similes.

Ordinarily, the substitute terms ("summer," "scaffolding," and "lion" in these examples) come from a different category of subjects from the original term, so that the original and substitute terms are not normally found in the same sentence. Also, the substitute term is familiar to the audience and has clear and vivid connotations. These observations suggest what work the figures of speech do. They make the original term more salient – that is, they bring it to the forefront of our attention – and they cause it to assume more prominently the connotations of the substituted term. It is not that the figure of speech *changes* connotations, as with a persuasive definition, but that it makes a normally latent connotation more important. For example, we normally think of the number seventeen as having fairly neutral connotations. But applied to age, it also has the connotation of freshness and youth, and the synecdoche brings out the normally latent connotation. Perelman and Olbrechts-Tyteca, mentioned earlier, used the term *presence* to refer to these twin characteristics of salience and dominance.

To see how figures of speech affect an argument, we can look at a famous example of metaphors. In 1858, Abraham Lincoln gave a speech accepting the Republican nomination for the US Senate seat from Illinois. The speech expressed Lincoln's fear that the entire country would become slave territory through the work of a group of conspirators including Lincoln's opponent, Stephen A. Douglas, who Lincoln thought were plotting to bring about that result. There was no direct evidence of such a plot – no "smoking gun," to use a contemporary metaphor – but the idea was not completely farfetched. In the "House Divided" speech, Lincoln made the threat seem real and urgent, in large part through the careful use of metaphors. (Contrary to widespread belief, the speech did *not* predict the coming of the American Civil War. In fact, it specifically denied that the Union would be dissolved.)

For example, Lincoln referred to the plan of the alleged plotters as a "piece of machinery." The term "machine" connotes a nonhuman object proceeding relentlessly toward its predetermined goal, without the exercise of judgment. There is something almost automatic about it. The alleged leaders of the conspiracy were the "architects" of the machine, suggesting that they had built it by plan or design. As operators of the machine, they were referred to as its "chief bosses." This also invited an allusion to relatively unsavory political figures who were the bosses of organizations referred to as machines. Douglas's platform of "popular sovereignty" was decried with the "scaffolding" metaphor used above, implying that it was designed to serve a very temporary purpose and was then "kicked to the winds." Finally, Douglas, whom Illinois Democrats had touted as best suited to arrest the spread of slavery, was called a "caged and toothless lion" for the purpose, because his popular-sovereignty position required that he didn't care about whether slavery spread or not. Even without being as familiar with the specific context as one might, we can see how Lincoln's adroit use of metaphors made his individual ideas salient and his desired connotations more dominant. And we can see how, by combining these metaphors, Lincoln was able to build a plausible and reasonable argument even though it was based wholly on circumstantial evidence.

Another type of figure of speech consists of altering the order of words in a sentence. The effect is to call attention to something other than the normal meaning. For example, reversing the normal order of words in a sentence, while not changing its denotative meaning, will heighten the significance of what is normally deemphasized. A famous example is President John F. Kennedy's Inaugural Address.[7] To emphasize that he wanted his fellow citizens to contribute to the country rather than to become dependent on it, he implored, "Ask not what your country can do for you . . ." The normal order of words would have been, "Do not ask . . ." with the emphasis on the word "ask." The emphasis of the sentence would have been on making a request. By inverting the normal order, Kennedy puts the emphasis on negation, making clear that he is talking about what we are *not* to do. To check this, try saying the sentence aloud with both normal and inverted word order and see which words get emphasized.

Another alteration at the sentence level is *antithesis* – the pairing and contrast of opposites. This is a figure that emphasizes making a choice,

---

[7] The text may be found in *Public Papers of the Presidents: John F. Kennedy, 1961* (Washington, DC: US Government Printing Office, 1962), 1–3.

rejecting one alternative and embracing another. Several antitheses can be found in Kennedy's Inaugural Address, beginning with the opening line, "We observe today not a victory of party but a celebration of freedom . . ." Frankly, the inauguration could have been imagined as either, and in other ways besides. But the form of the sentence makes the decision: the event will be seen not in one way but in another. Sometimes the antithesis is used to reject both alternatives separately and instead to accept a compound of them. Kennedy illustrates this figure in the same first sentence, immediately after the phrase just quoted, when he characterizes the moment as "symbolizing an end as well as a beginning, signifying renewal as well as change." Here too the figure emphasizes choice, but the choice is neither of the alternatives taken by itself. Rather, we are to understand the inauguration of the president as embracing both end and beginning, both renewal and change.

Chiasmus is another figure of speech at the sentence level. It emphasizes balance or symmetry. It is found usually in a progression from a starting point up to some fulcrum, and then down from the fulcrum to an endpoint that is the natural counter to the starting point. A simple chiasmus can be found in Kennedy's Inaugural Address when the new president urges, "Let us never negotiate out of fear. But let us never fear to negotiate." The progression is clear: negotiate → fear, then fear → negotiate. A more elaborate chiasmus is found in a speech in which Abraham Lincoln said goodbye to his Springfield neighbors as he prepared to board the train that would take him to Washington for his inauguration. The speech is nine sentences long, and the pivotal fifth sentence is "Now I leave, not knowing when or whether ever I may return, with a task before me greater than that which rested on Washington." Lincoln builds to this pivot with four sentences expressing his sadness at parting from his neighbors and the depth to which the major events of his life have been bound up with Springfield. The message of this half of the speech is apprehension, not confidence. But the direction of the speech shifts in the last four lines, which point out how success is possible with divine help. In the concluding sentence, Lincoln asks God to watch over the people of Springfield and hopes that they will ask the same for him; in that spirit, "I bid you an affectionate farewell." The last sentence is the counterpoint of the first. Lincoln begins by expressing sorrow and apprehension; he ends by expressing confidence and affection. The message of the carefully balanced structure is that the moment contains both sorrow and affection, just as he feels both apprehension and confidence. Yet how much more prosaic it would have seemed, and how much less memorable, if he had just said, "This is a tough job, but with God's help I can do it." That would not have had the emotional depth of the chiasmus, with its progression and balance.

The final example of a sentence-level alteration is parallel structure, whether that is achieved by following the same pattern of words or phrases or by repetition of a key word or phrase. The former type is found in various places in Kennedy's Inaugural Address. Early in the speech there is a series of phrases that takes the form [verb] ["any"] [noun]: we will "pay any price, bear any burden, meet any hardship, support any friend, oppose any foe ..." The parallel structure not only makes the phrases easier to remember but also achieves meaning through cumulation. Taken together, the phrases make clear the extent to which the United States is willing to go if necessary to act on its commitments. The explicit repetition of a word or phrase is probably less common but is also found in Kennedy's Inaugural Address, in a series of promises to different groups of nations, all taking the form "... we pledge ..." There are specific pledges to old allies, to newly independent nations, to the United Nations, to countries in Latin America, and so on. In this case, the message of the parallelism is both that the capacity for American action is boundless – there is seemingly no limit to what we are able to pledge – and also that we are not conducting a one-size-fits-all foreign policy but rather are tailoring our pledge to the needs of each distinct group of nations. Just as listeners are getting used to the litany of pledges, Kennedy confounds expectations by saying, "to those who would make themselves our adversary, we offer not a pledge but a request" – another interesting use of antithesis, by the way.

This is not the place to attempt an exhaustive treatment of figures of speech. In earlier centuries, handbooks were published describing and illustrating hundreds of them. The point of discussing a few here is to emphasize that they are not only literary devices but components of argumentation, affecting what an argument means, how urgent it seems, and how listeners are invited to respond to it.

Types of Statements

Philosophers of language distinguish among analytic, contradictory, and synthetic statements. *Analytic* statements are true by definition, such as "Whatever will be, will be." *Contradictory* statements are false by definition, such as "A bachelor is a married male." Neither of these types of statements requires any reference to the external world. Their truth or falsity is a matter of self-evidence. Of course, this also means that the statements are not very interesting. One merely repeats itself and the other merely denies itself.

In contrast, *synthetic* statements are neither true nor false by definition; they require reference to the external world for verification. They might turn out to be either true or false, depending on the match between the statement and our understanding of external realities. A statement such as "The temperature outside is 85 degrees Fahrenheit in January," is not likely to be true if uttered in Chicago and more likely to be true in Miami, but in neither case is it anything about the statement itself that determines its truth or falsity. Advocates generally will prefer to build their cases with synthetic statements because they can be examined in a noncircular fashion.

Two mistakes are quite common: treating a synthetic statement as if it were analytic and treating an analytic statement as if it were synthetic. An example of the former would be uttering the statement, "Women are smarter than men," as if it were self-evident and required no proof. Whether that statement is true or not requires reference to the external world, such as comparing intelligence test results across genders. To act as though the statement were true by definition would be to commit the error of begging the question, assuming to be true what one is obliged to prove to be true. An example of the second mistake would be to treat as synthetic a statement such as "Good teachers are good." Unless this is some sort of dissociation (discussed above), the statement does not say anything substantial. It merely repeats itself; it is what is called a truism. Treating this analytic statement as if it were synthetic would be wrongly to take seriously a statement that is circular.

In addition to characterizing statements as analytic, contradictory, or synthetic, we can classify them as simple, compound, and complex sentences. You probably are familiar with these categories from studies of grammar and composition. The rhetorical theorist and critic Richard Weaver has suggested that they contribute to argumentation as well.[8] Weaver notes that, in general, simple sentences reveal the work of an advocate unburdened by nuance; they reflect a simple mind. But when properly used, they reflect the essence of a thing, its core, which is stated without qualification, in order to emphasize what is the root of the matter. Compound sentences, if used inappropriately, will convey the artlessness of a refusal to prioritize the elements of a hierarchy. But used at the right

---

[8] Richard Weaver, "Some Rhetorical Aspects of Grammatical Categories," *The Ethics of Rhetoric* (Chicago: Henry Regnery, 1953), 115–142.

times, compound sentences convey a message of equilibrium or balance, suggesting that the scales are evenly matched between the two clauses. And complex sentences, especially if truly complex, can convey that the advocate is disordered, unable to sort things out or to be clear. But used at the right time, they reflect the difficulty of the topic and show how the arguer works out coordination and subordination of ideas. Each of the types of sentences, then, can be well or poorly used, and the choices arguers make about how to combine the different types convey their attitudes about the subject matter and about their approach to arguing.

Strategic Imprecision

We began this chapter by discussing linguistic consistency, the notion that in a productive argument, an advocate will be consistent in his or her use of language and that participants in a dispute will have the same meanings and usages in mind. In Chapter 6, we described ambiguity, amphiboly, and vagueness as fallacies of clarity. But there are occasions in which imprecision is desirable and ambiguity can be strategic. For example, sometimes advocates will wish to leave options open for further consideration later, and will therefore employ a very general characterization. Wishing to defer until later a specific policy choice, advocates might agree that they will pursue the "fairest" course of action, while waiting until later to determine the criteria for deciding what is the fairest.

Another reason for strategic ambiguity may be to permit parties with divergent interests and views to agree on an outcome while doing so for widely different reasons. This frequently happens in diplomatic negotiations and in the course of building electoral coalitions. During the years 2010–2016, Republicans in the United States achieved near-unanimity among themselves that the country should "repeal and replace" the Affordable Care Act, which sought among other goals to reduce the number of people without health insurance. Republicans' agreement could mask differences about which health care policy should substitute for it, so long as they remained the opposition party and knew that President Obama, a Democrat, would veto any alternative they might propose. But in 2017, when Republicans controlled both houses of Congress as well as the presidency, their opposition to the Affordable Care Act became more consequential because they would need to pass an alternative proposal (or leave many millions of people without coverage). Then the imprecision of "repeal and replace" became evident as Republicans were unable to muster a majority in the US Senate for any of their proffered alternatives.

So sometimes it is beneficial for language to be as precise as possible; at other times, strategic imprecision is preferred. One way to achieve strategic imprecision is through *euphemisms*. These are imprecise terms that give a more (or less) positive connotation to the topic under discussion. During the period following the American Civil War, there was a strong desire to reconcile the North and South, to fulfill Lincoln's metaphorical charge to "bind up the nation's wounds." As a result, in some sections of the country, euphemisms were used to refer to the war. In much of the South, it was (and still is) referred to as "the War between the States," suggesting that somehow it was a conflict between equally sovereign groups of states, rather than between rebels and the government, as was conveyed by the negative term, "the War of Southern Rebellion," used by northerners who wished to humble the South. Or the Civil War was referred to sometimes as "the late unpleasantness," a term that really minimized the conflict and its significance. The long-standing religious conflict in Northern Ireland sometimes was referred to as "the Troubles" for the same reason.

Another way to make language less precise is through strategic use of ambiguity, equivocation, and vagueness. The key idea here is the term *strategic*. These things are often thought of as errors in the use of language, but not if they serve a strategic purpose. An important example can be found in the early 1970s when President Richard Nixon broke with precedent by traveling to the People's Republic of China. At the time, the United States withheld diplomatic recognition from the PRC because it was Communist, maintaining the fiction that the Nationalist government in Taiwan was the legitimate government of China. At the end of Nixon's visit, the United States and China wanted to issue a communique announcing understandings reached during the visit. What could they say about the sticky question of Taiwan? They acknowledged that everyone agreed that there was only one China and that Taiwan was part of China. This seemingly clear statement actually was strategically ambiguous. It could be understood as saying that mainland China would eventually encompass Taiwan (the position taken by China), or that the Nationalist Chinese on Taiwan eventually would recapture the mainland (the position taken at the time by the United States, which did not reverse its policy until 1979).

Just as there are ways to make language less precise, there are ways to make it more precise. This is desirable in order to avoid disagreements that are merely verbal – that is, those that are only about the use of language and not about the substance of an issue. One way is to agree on functional, stipulative, or operational definitions "for the sake of the argument." This will allow the parties to a dispute to agree on the meaning of a term in order to proceed with their controversy, but without having to take a final position on what the term "really" means. For instance, a person who does not believe that educational quality can be measured by money might nevertheless agree in a specific situation to accept expenditures per pupil as the basis for comparing the quality of educational systems between states. Another approach is to suggest an analogy to other terms that are mutually understood ("That's just like arguing that …"). And another may be to name the argument, so that a commonly accepted term may substitute for a complex argument that might devolve into verbal disputes ("that's the 'vision thing' argument" or "that's the smoking gun"). These analogies will be helpful, of course, only if the comparison argument is understood in the same way by the different parties to the current dispute.

Linguistic Intensity

The last of the stylistic variables we will examine, and only briefly, is linguistic intensity. While it is true that intense language can affect our perception of what an argument is, it also is true that essentially the same content can be cast in language of varying intensity. High intensity can convey the passion of an arguer's commitment to a topic and the degree of seriousness with which the arguer should be taken. But it also can boomerang, suggesting that an arguer is allowing his or her emotions to cloud judgment. Frequent calls to restore civility to public discourse are pleas that we lower the intensity of our language, reflecting the belief that intensity of language is a measure of our readiness to take offense and that, the higher the readiness, the less likely that the disputants will be able to resolve their differences.

How intense to make one's language is an important choice for the advocate. As a general rule, one should be selective with highly intense language. If an arguer is highly involved emotionally in everything he or she may say, the effect is likely to be counterproductive. The arguer risks being dismissed as a hothead, with nothing that he or she says carrying great weight. Another general rule is that the intensity of the arguer's language should not be greatly different from the intensity of feeling attributed to the audience – slightly more intense if the goal is to strengthen the audience's commitment to a position, slightly less intense if the goal is to weaken that commitment or to change audience members' minds.

Argument Presentation

Everything we have studied so far about argument structure and compos-ition, evidence and reasoning, case construction, attack and defense, and language and style reaches its culmination in the actual presentation of arguments to an audience. Sometimes this is almost impromptu, as when friends argue during the course of a conversation. Sometimes it is highly scripted, as when you write an argumentative essay or present an argumen-tative speech. And often it is somewhere in between. While it is not possible to cover all situations, this section of the chapter offers general guidelines for written, oral, and visual modes of presentation.

Writing: The Argumentative Essay

Perhaps without realizing it, you actually were studying argumentation when you were learning about basic composition. The thesis statement of your essay is the main claim, or resolution, that you will advance in the essay. The paragraphs (sometimes but not necessarily three) that develop the main ideas correspond to the supporting arguments, which can be arranged in multiple, convergent, or subordinate patterns. Selection and arrangement of evidence and supporting arguments follow the same principles laid out in this book. A written essay permits paying special attention to the details of language and stylistic choices discussed earlier in this chapter.

Here are some specific suggestions for writing the argumentative essay.

1. Make sure you write on a topic that is important to your audience and that is controversial.
2. Formulate your main claim so that it can be addressed satisfactorily within the space you have available.
3. Identify the key issues in your main claim, indicate what your position is on the issues, and outline how you will develop your case.
4. Produce the strongest evidence you can to support your claims. Then imagine yourself as your own critic and consider how you might challenge them. Ask yourself whether you could defend and rebuild your position in the face of such a challenge.
5. Consider whether to acknowledge and respond in your essay to attacks on your position, or whether to depend on a challenger to raise these criticisms later.
6. When choices are available, plan strategically the order in which to present your arguments and evidence. When the structure of your

argument requires a particular order, then of course you should follow that order.

7. Review a draft of your essay and check to be sure that you have spoken to all the serious issues and that you have presented a prima facie case.

8. After you have outlined the body of the essay, arrange the introduction and conclusion so that audience members understand well where you are going and are positively disposed toward you and your message.

Speaking: The Argumentative Speech

Everyday arguers are probably more likely to engage in spoken than in written argumentation. Arguments arise, seemingly spontaneously, among friends and co-workers. And some more formal situations, such as negotiations, courtroom advocacy, speeches at city council meetings or neighborhood organizations, or public debates, are wholly or largely oral.

Oral argument is different from written argument. You can read written discourse at your own pace, skimming, reading closely, or anything in between. If something seems unclear or you lose track of the author's main line of argument, you always can go back and reread it. You can stop and look up a term or concept that is unfamiliar. And if you get tired, you can put the writing down and come back to it later.

While you theoretically could record an oral argument and play it back later, as it occurs oral argument is ephemeral. There is no "pause button" that will enable you to replay the argument in real time. And if you forget something important, you can't review it. If you get tired, there usually is no opportunity to come back. Knowing these things about your experience as an auditor, there are several things you can do to prepare effectively for oral presentation.

1. Keep the style simple. Use shorter and more common words than you would in writing. As much as you can, use short, simple sentences to convey your idea. You don't need to "dumb down" your argument or to be condescending to your listeners, but you should make your message easy to understand.

2. Use repetition and parallel structure effectively. Repeating your key ideas will add emphasis and will make it less likely that listeners will forget them. It serves the same purpose as italics or boldface type in print. And when all your main or supporting claims have the same

structure, listeners not only will recognize and remember the pattern but may be able to anticipate what is coming next.

3. Use informal expressions when appropriate. People do not speak in complete sentences or observe all the grammar rules of standard English when they talk; indeed, it will sound stilted if you try to do so. Feel free to use contractions, colloquialisms (such as "gonna" for "going to"), and slang when they are appropriate, but be sure to avoid epithets, especially those with racial or sexual overtones.

4. Refer to yourself and the situation when appropriate. Such reflexive references are more common in speech than in writing, where people still may be expected to limit the use of "I" and other personal terms (although this expectation is relaxing). These references are used especially in forecasting speakers' organizational patterns ("I will develop three main ideas") and in summaries ("So let me review what I have shown you").

5. Use signposting to remind the audience where you are in your argument. Identify supporting arguments by number ("my second reason") or by shorthand title ("the proliferation argument"). Do this when introducing the arguments and when summarizing them as well.

6. Use terms indicating the relationship among your claims. Terms such as "therefore" make clear that you are coming to the conclusion of an argument. "Because" or "consequently" suggest a causal relationship. "Furthermore" or "additionally" make clear that you are presenting a multiple argument structure. "For example" indicates that you will be presenting a specific instance of a general claim. "It does not follow" or "there is no link" signals that you are challenging the connection between grounds and a claim. Using argument terms like these helps audiences to understand (and be influenced by) the argumentative moves you are making.

7. Finally, try to eliminate verbal clutter – vocalized pauses (umm, ah, er), pointless repetition (as opposed to repetition for effect), digressions in midsentence, and distracting words ("right," "you know," "okay," "like"). These characterize oral discourse because we are thinking on our feet and our thinking rate and speaking rate can get out of line with each other. To fill the gap, we utter unrelated and unplanned sounds. The problem is that these expressions call attention to themselves, and in an extreme case audiences might find themselves counting the "umms" rather than listening carefully to the argument. Because most people are not aware of their verbal clutter, it may take recording and listening to yourself in order to

see whether it is a problem. If it is, conscious attention may help you to reduce your verbal clutter. Being thoroughly familiar with your main ideas and overall structure of the speech will help to reduce the number of times that thought and speech are out of sync, and remaining silent for a few seconds will be perfectly acceptable when it does happen. Inevitably, the silence will be much shorter than it feels to you.

Seeing: Visual Argumentation

It has long been recognized that "visual aids" – charts, graphs, diagrams, photographs, and videos – lend support to arguments. Recently, some theorists and critics have maintained that visual elements actually can *constitute* arguments.[9] The suggestion is that visuals can express arguments implicitly that speech and writing make explicitly. Visuals enable audiences to grasp arguments intuitively from the associations in and the composition of the visual. (Other theorists and critics counter that intuitions are not arguments, or that visual elements have to be translated into language in order to count as arguments.[10])

Because visual argument does not speak in words, it is important that the images not be ambiguous, unless the point is precisely to display the ambiguity of a concept. Otherwise, it is desirable that the great majority of viewers decode the image in the same way. Images that seem to have a nearly universal meaning are referred to as *iconic* and are particularly valuable as arguments.

The study of visual argument is relatively new, and much remains to be theorized. The following are a few suggestions that may be helpful in interpreting others' visual arguments or composing your own.

1. Examine *representation* in the image. Does it appear to suggest that the image is a sign, or perhaps an example, of what reality is like? Or is its representation ironic, suggesting that things are not really as they seem?

---

[9] Visual argument has been featured in three special issues of *Argumentation and Advocacy*, in 1996, 2007, and 2016. See David S. Birdsell and Leo Groarke, eds., "Special Issue – Visual Argument," *Argumentation and Advocacy, 33* (Summer 1996, Fall 1996); David S. Birdsell and Leo Groarke, eds., "Special Issue on Visual Argument," *Argumentation and Advocacy, 43* (Winter and Spring, 2007); David Godden, Catherine H. Palczewski, and Leo Groarke, eds., "Twenty Years of Visual Argument," *Argumentation and Advocacy, 52* (Spring 2016).

[10] For example, see David Fleming, "Can Pictures Be Arguments?," *Argumentation and Advocacy, 33* (Summer 1996), 11–22.

2. Study the *composition* of the image. Are things proportional as they are in reality, emphasizing the underlying scene? Or does something loom unusually large, conveying the message that it is a dominant element and perhaps a causal force?

3. Pay attention to *characterization* within the image. What affect is conveyed, and how does that cue the emotion a viewer feels for the image? Does anything seem particularly abnormal? If so, is that abnormality a possible cause or effect of something?

4. Consider the uses of *color* and *materials* in the image. Although it sounds stereotypical, colors evoke different connotations, and in the case of sculpture, different materials have connotations of strength, resilience, versatility, and other characteristics. What claims are made by these artistic components? Conversely, what is the message conveyed by an image entirely in black and white? It might suggest a monochromatic or one-dimensional subject, or it might evoke a time period before the use of color photography was commonplace.

5. Examine the *size* of the visual art. Size for a given piece of art can be manipulated, of course, even for the same image. But a different size can advance a different claim. A very large image may seem to be self-evident in meaning and overwhelming in significance, whereas a very small image may indicate that the truth of the matter is not so easily grasped but must be ferreted out with care.

6. Finally, be sensitive to the very choice to use visual argument as the mode of presentation. The adage is that "a picture is worth a thousand words." Why? Because visual elements resonate with emotions that are at the base of appreciation (or condemnation) and action. They enable audience members to identify with elements depicted in the visual element and, in some cases, convince them that they should act in the way the visual element suggests. This may be more powerful than the arguments cast in linguistic form, but not always. If what is pictured is dismissed as "tugging at our heartstrings" and appealing to an irrelevant or inappropriate emotion, its use may backfire. That can also happen if the visual element is overly complex and frustrates rather than aids our understanding.

The widespread use of *memes* as a way to convey arguments, particularly since the advent of social media, suggests that the prominence of visual argument will increase. It is unlikely to displace written and oral argument, but rather to take its place alongside them as an object of study.

Exercises

1. In the following pairs, explain how the connotation of the sentence differs.
    a. Bertram is childish: Bertram is youthful.
    b. Chung is confident: Chung is conceited.
    c. Donna is elated: Donna is manic.
    d. Ekaterina is inquisitive: Ekaterina is nosy.
    e. Felix is frugal: Felix is cheap.

2. In the following arguments, note how the situation is being defined to support the arguer's position.
    a. My opponent raises a good point about the unfairness of the board's recent decisions. However, this is not a result of bad rules. Rather, we must look to change the people we elect to the board if we want to have better results.
    b. You claim that LeBron James is the greatest basketball player of all time. But the only statistic that really counts is championships, and therefore Michael Jordan must be the greatest until LeBron gets six rings.
    c. I admit that I have not been keeping up my share of the apartment chores recently, but that is only because I have been studying for the MCAT exam. If you consider how much of the housework I did when you were so busy at work last year, you will see that I am more than pulling my weight around here.
    d. I understand that cleaning all the brush from the park is going to be a big job, but last year's class was able to clean an even larger park. This exercise is about showing everyone that you are just as good as the class that came before you.
    e. Yes, putting the new factory in your town is going to cause some additional traffic and noise. However, the benefit to our entire region makes this something that no real citizen can resist. It is a small price that some must pay for the greater good.

3. In the following examples, find the arguers' use of dissociation, identify the philosophical pair being used, and show how the dissociation helps to justify an argument.
    a. Although it seems that raising taxes will help to reduce the deficit, in reality the higher taxes will result in lower revenue generation and actually will increase the deficit.
    b. Sure, Tom Brady seems to be a big part of the New England Patriots' recent success, but the essence of that team is Bill

Belichick's genius for creating match-ups and adjusting on the fly. That is the real reason New England has done so well.

c. I know that we were told not to discuss the take-home test, but that rule was to keep us from sharing notes, not from discussing the format of the exam, so I don't think we will get in trouble for discussing the wording of question 1.

d. Of course that watch is less expensive, but over time the value of a fine timepiece will increase while the cheaper item is discarded.

e. I understand that the software package you want to buy will address our needs today, but as we become a larger organization it soon will be unable to be scaled and will become outdated.

f. We have always referred to our new students as "freshmen," but given that this institution has been coed for more than a hundred years, it is time to drop this archaic and sexist label and instead use the term "first-year students."

4. Go to YouTube.com and type "Best argument for." Choose one or more arguments that have been labeled "best" and listen to the argument. Compare this argument with the tips given in this chapter. Which strategies, linguistic devices, and choices do you recognize? How would you counsel the arguer?

5. You learned that the euphemism of calling the American Civil War "the War between the States" was effective in helping to reunite the country by downplaying the role of the Confederacy in causing the war by seceding or the role of the Union Army in violently suppressing the rebellion. The use of the term "War between the States" (or even "Civil War") rather than a more loaded term allowed both sides to speak of the war without reigniting the tensions that caused it in the first place. Was this a good strategy that allowed the country to move forward or an act of linguistic inconsistency that clouded the analysis of the reasons for the war? Can you think of other examples where euphemisms can be both inconsistent and beneficial? How about in domestic disputes, roommate arguments, or even casual encounters?

CHAPTER 10

Where and Why We Argue

Not only is everyday argumentation cast in language, and therefore inexact, but it takes place in specific contexts. At various points throughout the book, it has been necessary to remark that the application of a principle or guideline depends on context. There are few if any rules that are universally applicable.

It is appropriate, therefore, to close the book with a chapter investigating contexts in argumentation. Different scholars have used different terminology to designate what we are calling *contexts*. The British philosopher Stephen Toulmin introduced the term *field* in the 1950s.[1] Though originally vague about what he meant, he eventually came to see the term as analogous to academic disciplines. They ranged from "compact fields" such as atomic physics to "highly diffuse" fields such as art criticism. It should be easy to understand that arguments work quite differently in such diverse fields. The Dutch argumentation scholar Frans van Eemeren uses the term *context* to refer to subject-matter categories and areas of professional practice, such as the legal, medical, political, and academic contexts.[2] The American communication scholar G. Thomas Goodnight has used the term *spheres* to refer to zones of communicative activity in which argument practices vary.[3] Goodnight distinguishes among personal, technical, and public spheres of argumentation. While the differences among these terms are not trivial, they need not detain us here. For ease of organization, this chapter will follow Goodnight's structure, but within the technical sphere it will place subject-matter fields or domains. Following the treatment of contexts, the chapter will conclude with

---

[1] Stephen Toulmin, *The Uses of Argument* (Cambridge: Cambridge University Press, 1958), 14.
[2] Frans H. van Eemeren and Wu Peng, eds., *Contextualizing Pragma-Dialectics* (Amsterdam: John Benjamins, 2017), contains essays grounding argumentation in different specific contexts.
[3] G. Thomas Goodnight, "The Personal, Technical, and Public Spheres of Argument: A Speculative Inquiry into the Art of Public Deliberation," *Argumentation and Advocacy*, 18 (Spring, 1982), 214–227.

reflections on the social functions of argumentation, returning to one of the questions with which we began the book: Why do people argue?

Spheres of Argumentation

Spheres of argumentation differ along a private/public dimension. The *personal* sphere is of concern only to the people engaged in the argumentation – typically friends, family members, or romantic partners. The same people are both the arguers and the evaluators, and the goal of the process is for them to reach agreement.

In the *technical* sphere, argumentation is conditioned by the background knowledge, assumptions, and working practices of the relevant field or domain. Only those schooled in such "field knowledge" will be able to participate effectively or will be able to understand the technical concepts. The goal of the process is to advance field knowledge by testing, confirming, modifying, limiting, or undermining claims that are meaningful to the field. Thus, for example, economists want to know more about how an economy works, and medical researchers discuss their experiments in order to know more about the treatment of disease. Evaluation of arguments is made not just by those who participate directly (although that sometimes happens) but also on the basis of a generalized sense of the field as a whole. This is not a formal vote but an emerging sense of where the weight of expert opinion lies, inferred from such evidence as citation patterns, peer reviews, and professional honors and distinctions.

Finally, the *public* sphere is "public" in two distinct senses of the term. It is concerned with matters that *affect the public*, that are of concern to people generally in their capacity as citizens. And participation is *open to the public*; anyone can become involved because no specialized expertise or training is required. The term "public sphere" was used by the German philosopher Jürgen Habermas to refer to a zone of civil society distinct from both the state and the market.[4] But both the state and the market are implicated in the contemporary public sphere, in which citizens argue about what policies their governments should implement and in which they recognize that markets are not impersonal entities but are influenced by human decisions and choices. In the public sphere, arguers may act in their own behalf, but more importantly, they are representatives for a broader public. Even if they stand to gain personally from a tax cut or a

---

[4] See Jürgen Habermas, *Communication and the Evolution of Society* (Boston: Beacon Press, 1979).

government program, for example, they most likely will argue for the result on the grounds that it will promote the common good. And agreement is sought not among the arguers themselves – they are likely to be committed advocates who are most reluctant to change their minds – but among the larger public or its elected representatives. The argumentation reaches its conclusion not when everything possible has been said but when those decision-makers are ready to decide.

Migration of Arguments among Spheres

Into which sphere of argumentation does any given argument fall? That is not a straightforward matter. Indeed, it often is in itself one of the matters in dispute. Just as we saw in Chapter 3 with presumption and burden of proof, advocates may compete to locate an argument in one sphere or another. They may gain from limiting participation in an argument, as when public figures accused of marital infidelity claim that it is a private matter of concern only to them and to their aggrieved spouse. Or they may gain from enlarging the relevant body of participants, as when citizens contend that nuclear defense policy is not just a technical matter because it potentially affects the fate of everyone in the world.

Consequently, it is not uncommon for arguments to "migrate" from one sphere to another over time. Until recent decades, topics such as child abuse, day care, and sexual harassment were widely regarded as private matters of concern only to those directly involved. More recently, they have been recast as matters of concern to the larger society. The change is the result of a public judgment that it is in society's interest to protect people who may lack the power to protect themselves, because doing so contributes to the development of their potential and supports human values. Another example of a migrating controversy is the conversion of monetary and fiscal policy from a public to a technical issue. Concerned that relatively unsophisticated citizens held beliefs that were harmful to the health of the economy, such as the conviction that government deficits were always immoral, economists and policy-makers from the 1930s to the 1960s maintained that these were technical matters related to the management of a complex modern economy, not ideological questions. This point of view now prevails, and even in a time of economic trouble such as the Great Recession of 2008–2009, the public was more likely to call for experts to fix things than to engage in ideological crusades for principled but simple solutions. The Tea Party in the United States may be the exception that proves the rule. While it began as a populist protest against excessive taxation, it quickly evolved into a more general hostility toward government and no longer was focused specifically on economic policy.

A final example of a migrating controversy involves the dispute over school vouchers. These generally are payments made by some level of government to parents, who may use the funds to support their children's education at whatever public or private school they may choose (sometimes even including home schooling as an option). Traditionally, education policy was seen as a public issue that surfaced in local school board elections, tax and bond issue referenda, and occasional controversies over matters of curriculum. Vouchers privatize the issue, suggesting that what is the best education for any given children is the business only of their parents, and that beyond a generalized commitment to the value of education, this is not an appropriate argument for the public sphere.

In some cases, the very heart of a dispute centers on the choice of sphere in which it should be placed. The abortion controversy offers an excellent example. This is not a dispute between people who think abortion is bad and people who think it is good. Virtually no one defends abortion as a good in itself. Rather, the dispute is between those who believe the topic belongs in the personal sphere, of concern only to the woman and her doctor and others she might choose to consult, and those who believe that the topic belongs in the public sphere because society has an overriding interest in protecting the fetus and balancing that interest against the concerns of the woman. As these examples illustrate, tracing the history of a controversy often involves tracing its migration among the different spheres of argumentation.

Argumentation in the Personal Sphere

Argumentation between friends, spouses, and intimate partners takes place in the personal sphere. The focus is on how people conduct and seek to resolve disagreements that concern themselves. The arguers and decision-makers are the same people, so the goal is to persuade those who disagree to change their minds, while recognizing that one might be persuaded to change one's own mind instead. The primary "text" of arguments in the personal sphere is naturally occurring talk in which overt opposition is present. Even though the participants are close acquaintances, they maintain what they consider to be incompatible claims, or incompatible positions on the same claim, and the difference matters enough to them that they try to resolve it rather than just "agreeing to disagree." The outcome may be the mutual acceptance of one party's claim, the emergence of a compromise position somewhere between the competing claims, the discovery of a new position not previously considered that transcends the original disagreement, or – only if everything else fails – the parties may abandon the argumentation and "agree to disagree." This happens sometimes when otherwise good friends have sharp disagreements about subjects, such as politics or religion, that are central to their personal identity. These disagreements certainly matter to them, but not so much that they seek to resolve them at the price of jeopardizing their personal relationship.

This last comment suggests a special feature of argumentation in the personal sphere. It typically proceeds on two tracks at once. The participants are concerned with both the subject matter of the dispute and with their personal relationship. They seek to prevail on the substance of the dispute, but also to maintain and strengthen their relationship to each other. Often the relationship goals will be stronger than the content goals. Indeed, when a relationship is broken because of an irreparable disagreement, that is widely understood to be a failure of argumentation.

This dual-track nature of personal-sphere argumentation affects how the participants conduct themselves. The dominant mode of discourse is conversational dialogue. Person A makes a claim; person B disputes the claim. Then A disagrees with B, by either supporting the original claim or disputing the counter-claim. Which choice A makes will determine, as a practical matter, whether the focus of the conversation will be on the claim or the counter-claim, and consequently which party enjoys presumption and which shoulders the burden of proof. The dialogue proceeds from there in either a narrowed or an expanded shape. A narrowed dialogue will remain centered on the original claim or counter-claim and will consist of additional support for, or refutation of, that claim or counter-claim. An expanded dialogue will feature the addition of more claims and counter-claims that are offered as support for the main claim. The narrowed dialogue will resemble a simple argument, as discussed in Chapter 2, and the expanded dialogue will resemble a complex argument.

The dialogue, however, is also influenced by the relationship goals. This means, first, that the conversation employs procedural conventions, such as taking turns, that are learned through socialization and applied intuitively. It means, second, that politeness conventions play a strong role. Each party is concerned with saving face and accordingly with preserving face for the other. It means, third, that there is a strong preference for agreement; overt disagreement, while present, is understood as an intrusion into the conversation and the objective is for the parties to overcome this disagreement. It means, fourth, that the dialogue ideally follows – or at least approximates – the rules for critical discussion proposed by the Dutch theorist Frans van Eemeren and described in the "Extensions" feature of Chapter 6. This does not always happen in practice, especially if the conflict should become heated, but it is a normative standard. And it means, fifth, that the argumentation is often coalescent – that is, different objectives are being pursued at the same time. Agreement on some goals can be leveraged sometimes to achieve agreement on others.

The materials of argumentation in the personal sphere – the statements offered as evidence, or supporting claims – consist mainly of propositions that both parties accept, and it is the fact of their mutual acceptance (rather than any specific content) that enables them to function as support. In discussing whether to spend a weekend studying for an upcoming examination, for example, two friends might agree that the professor is likely to ask "trick" questions for which it is impossible to prepare. It does not matter to them that other students might disagree with this view or that a review of the professor's previous exams would indicate that there are few, if any, "trick" questions. These considerations do not matter, that is, unless one of the discussion participants introduces them in order to challenge their own mutually shared belief. Otherwise, that shared belief will function as evidence. One student might use it to support the claim that it is pointless to spend time studying, while the other uses it to support the counter-claim that one should invest serious time in studying in order to become thoroughly familiar with the key concepts that could be drawn on to answer "trick" questions. As we saw in Chapter 1, *all* argumentation depends at some level on agreement, but in the personal sphere the agreement may be idiosyncratic to the particular arguers. It does not matter whether it is shared broadly by a field, society, or culture, since the only relevant decision-makers are the arguers themselves.

Because arguers in the personal sphere are close acquaintances, they have a "history." They already will know, from previous interactions, what each other's beliefs are and what their areas of agreement will be. It may not be necessary to mention them explicitly in the conversation. They function as what some philosophers call "tacit knowledge" or what we have described as *enthymemes* – arguments that seem incomplete because one or more of the claims, without being mentioned explicitly, is drawn implicitly from the values of the audience. Since the arguers in the personal sphere are also the decision-makers, they are their own audience as well.

A basic example, though it is a complicated one, will illustrate some of the features of personal-sphere argumentation that we have been discussing. Suppose that two otherwise good friends differ sharply on the subject of abortion. Person A believes that abortion is immoral per se because it murders the fetus, whom A continually refers to as the "unborn child." Person B believes that abortion is the concern only of the pregnant woman because the question is about her right to control her own body. On the surface, this seems to be an intractable dispute. A is focused on the morality of abortion, whereas B is focused on who has the right to decide, and each ignores the focus of the other. But remember that they are good friends; the strength of their relationship suggests that they are not likely to degenerate into mutual accusations and invective. Suppose that in their ensuing conversation a few things happen. First, B, knowing that A believes strongly in women's rights and privacy rights, gently asks – without needing to develop the argument in full, since it is tacitly assumed – why A holds a belief about abortion seemingly at odds with A's other commitments. In response, A asserts that the woman is not the only person involved; there also is the unborn child. B denies that the unborn child is a person. A asks, "Well, is it just like a tumor, something growing inside your body that you can try to remove at will?" and B replies, "Of course not." "What's the difference?" asks A, and B says, "While I don't agree that the fetus is a person, it is potential life." They are now prepared to agree that potential life deserves some consideration, that it is not *just* a question of the woman's control of her body. Meanwhile, in the same conversation, B has asked whether a woman should be forced to bear a child conceived as a result of rape, and A replies that rape is a horrible crime for which A would make an exception to the belief that abortion should be prohibited. B gently points out to A that if there are exceptions, or mitigating circumstances, it would be very hard to maintain that abortion is murder per se. The arguers could soon agree that the morality or immorality of abortion, at least to some degree, depends on the circumstances. The conversation might proceed until they both agree to the claim that abortion should be rare. They believe this for different reasons – A because there are very few exceptions to the moral judgment that abortion is murder, B because potential life as well as the right of the pregnant woman has value. The conversation has led to agreement on a new claim that transcended the originally intractable dispute. Neither A nor B has completely abandoned the original position taken, but both have qualified it slightly, in order that they could reach agreement and maintain their relationship. Now, this example may seem most atypical of abortion arguments, which often are repetitive and shrill. But those are usually arguments in the public sphere, not in the personal sphere where they are constrained by close personal relationships and the striving for agreement.

Conversational exchanges are private and ephemeral; the arguers preserve them only in memory. Yet it is possible to record and preserve them, either as oral exchanges or as transcribed texts, and subject them to study, just as one might study newspaper editorials, persuasive essays, or other texts. Among argumentation scholars, Sally Jackson and Scott Jacobs are most prominently identified with conversation analysis.[5] They examine how disagreement is understood as an intrusion in conversation and how argumentation regulates disagreement. Their research also bears out several features of the hypothetical example above. They suggest that conversational arguers often produce enthymemes in which a value claim is left unstated but is presumably shared. They note that arguments often are minimally sufficient to gain agreement (such as the claim that abortion should be rare) without abandoning core convictions of the arguers, And they establish that the desire to maintain the interpersonal relationship is a strong constraint on which arguments get produced in the first place.

Underscoring the emphasis on agreement is the work of Dale Hample on common beliefs people hold about argumentation.[6] Hample finds that argument is characteristically seen as irrational, that arguers are seen as closed-minded, that argumentation is associated with violence and zero-sum competition, and that people focus especially on negative consequences of argumentation, such as hurt feelings. These common views, as we noted in Chapter 1, may result from the connotations of the word "argumentation" in the English language. Among speakers of English, however, they certainly reinforce the striving for agreement that characterizes argumentation in the personal sphere.

Argumentation in the Technical Sphere

The technical sphere is where arguments among experts take place. Like the other spheres, it is not a physical place but a metaphorical zone in

---

[5] For an application of conversation analysis to argumentation, see Frans H. van Eemeren, Rob Grootendorst, Sally Jackson, and Scott Jacobs, *Reconstructing Argumentative Discourse* (Tuscaloosa: University of Alabama Press, 1993). See also Sally Jackson and Scott Jacobs, "Structure of Conversational Argument: Pragmatic Bases for the Enthymeme," *Quarterly Journal of Speech*, 66 (1980), 251–265; Scott Jacobs and Sally Jackson, "Conversational Argument: A Discourse-Analytic Approach," in *Advances in Argumentation Theory and Research*, ed. J. Robert Cox and Charles A. Willard (Carbondale: Southern Illinois University Press, 1982), 205–237.

[6] Dale Hample, *Arguing: Exchanging Reasons Face to Face* (Mahwah, NJ: Lawrence Erlbaum, 2005), esp. chapter 2.

which discourse occurs. Unlike the personal sphere, it does not presume that arguers have a close relationship; they may have no personal relationship at all. But they do have knowledge and training in the subject matter of the argument. Also unlike the personal sphere, the argument matters to more people than just those directly involved. At least potentially, it matters and is of interest to others who identify with the same subject-matter area.

These areas of subject matter are referred to (again metaphorically) as *fields*. While there is broad general agreement about what fields are, there is no universally accepted list of fields. And just as arguers sometimes find it in their strategic interest to migrate arguments from one sphere to another, within the technical sphere they may find it to their advantage either to distinguish or to combine fields, as well as to disagree about which field an argument is in. Fields are sometimes defined analogically to academic disciplines, such as the field of history, philosophy, or mathematics. Sometimes they are defined analogously to general orientations to knowledge, such as behaviorism, postmodernism, or Marxism. And sometimes they are defined as communities of professional practice, such as law, science, or journalism. Sometimes the term *discourse communities* is used as a synonym for *fields*.

Whatever classification system one uses, each field will have its own norms and conventions shared by its members, who are socialized into them during their professional training and education. Those outside the field will not share those norms and conventions; indeed, they may be unaware of them or find them inaccessible. Consequently, it makes a difference in which field an argument gets placed. For example, one norm of scientific argument is that when there is a disagreement among sources, the *more recent* source is to be preferred, other things being equal, because the quality of science improves over time. But one norm of religious argument is that in a disagreement among sources, the *older* source is to be preferred, other things being equal, because it is closer to Scripture, the most sacred text, and hence less likely to have been corrupted by human misinterpretation over the centuries. Now, considering this difference, it matters a great deal whether arguments about the theory of evolution are to be considered as scientific or religious. And it is not surprising that one's choice of field for the argument will correspond closely to one's view about the argument's subject. Similarly, it matters a great deal whether arguments about reform of medical malpractice are to be considered as medical or legal argumentation, just as it matters whether arguments about energy sources belong in the field of economics or ecology.

Space does not permit a thorough examination of multiple fields, but a brief description of a few should make clear how a field's norms and conventions affect argumentation within that field and why the need for specialized education and training restricts participation.

Legal Argumentation

At the most basic level, the field of law involves reasoning with rules. One determines the facts in a case, selects the applicable rule from the body of statutory law or judicial decisions, applies the rule to the facts, and derives a conclusion as to what should govern the case at hand. This almost seems like the certainty of formal deductive reasoning. Of course, matters are far more complicated than this. What "the facts" are and which facts are relevant may require interpretation and judgment. There may be multiple relevant rules, some of which may conflict, and it may be unclear which is most applicable to the case. And what the rule "means" may be open to dispute, as when the spirit of the law seems to be in conflict with the letter. Nevertheless, the basic nature of legal argumentation is that it is about the relationship between facts and rules.

If one were to examine a number of legal arguments, one would find several of the relevant norms and conventions. For instance, there usually are clearly defined standards for what can count as evidence. A witness's own direct observation is generally considered strong evidence, whereas hearsay (repeating another's statement about something about which one lacks direct knowledge) is often inadmissible as evidence. Literal analogies are a frequently used type of inference; they help to establish similarities between the case at hand and the terms of the rule. Situations contemplated by the rule are argued to be fundamentally like those in the case at hand. The value of precedent is reinforced by the legal principle of *stare decisis* (meaning "the decision stands"), which functions as a strong presumption against reversing previous decisions. Causal inferences are used to structure "the facts" into stories relating what happened and to establish responsibility for events. When inferences or warrants are questioned, authority (such as the text of laws or court decisions) is used frequently to back them up. And stasis in place considers whether a controversy properly belongs in the legal system and, if so, at what level. This stasis is at the heart of such controversies as whether drawing congressional district boundaries is a legal or a political exercise, whether or not states have the right to enact laws that are at variance with federal law, and whether a would-be plaintiff in a civil case has suffered harm and therefore has standing to sue. How these various norms work, and how they have been developed and challenged, is generally known to lawyers. The average person, however, may be completely ignorant of them and may regard the working of the legal system as esoteric if not completely mysterious. This difference illustrates how access to the technical sphere depends on training and experience.

Business Argumentation

For another example of an argument field, we can consider business. In this field, claims are typically policy proposals ("our company should do X") of a strategic nature – that is, proposals for action that it is claimed will improve the company's visibility, image, profitability, or other strategic consideration. They rely heavily on causal inferences, especially the pragmatic argument. This pattern, as you recall, is "If we want to achieve goal X, we should take action Y; we want to achieve goal X; therefore we should take action Y." The implicit warrant is that taking action Y is a means to achieving goal X. The goals themselves are dictated by the organization's values and culture, and are seldom subjected to critical analysis except in such activities as the formulation and review of mission statements. Evidence for arguments in the field of business is heavily data-oriented, with data relating to the company's performance (often comparing one time period to another or the particular company to the industry average). Given a choice between factual evidence and opinion testimony, factual evidence generally will be preferred. The unstated but implicit warrants often involve which value should be preferred when choice is required. They include norms such as "favor the efficient," "favor that which is innovative," "favor that which maximizes profit," and, most generally, "favor that which contributes most to the goals of the organization." In cases of conflict, argumentation often focuses on finding the lowest common denominator that all participants can accept, rather than taking more time to search for the hypothetically optimal solution. This process is called *satisficing*. It is used because business operates in a competitive environment and there is a time value to reaching a decision. While one company continues to deliberate in search of additional possible solutions, a competitor may reap the benefits of introducing a new product, service, or marketing strategy first.

Scientific Argumentation

Another argument field is scientific argument. Here the goal is to describe, explain, and predict important aspects of experience. It seeks both to account for individual phenomena and to develop theories that have predictive value. Stereotypically, science was seen as accounting for facts that are unchanging and undeniable. But this view has been severely challenged. Scientific generalizations are inductive, not deductive, as we saw when we examined inferences from form in Chapter 5. They are based on probability and hence can be wrong. Moreover, reports about the "facts" are cast in language, so they are already influenced by theory and perspective.

Thomas Kuhn, a prominent philosopher of science, distinguished between *normal* and *revolutionary* science.[7] Normal science applies and extends theory. It takes an established theory as its warrant to infer what will happen to a dependent variable (the object of one's interest) if an independent variable is manipulated in a certain way. "Water freezes at 32 degrees Fahrenheit" is a simple example of a theory. "Placing this tray of water into the freezer" describes the independent variable, and "turning into ice" the dependent variable. We can state the relationship between independent and dependent variables as a hypothesis: "If we place this tray of water in the freezer, it will turn into ice." We then test the hypothesis and see what happens. If the results are consistent with the prediction, scientists count them as support for the hypothesis. If not, the results are taken as weakening the hypothesis. Now, strictly speaking, this is the fallacy of affirming the consequent, as we saw in Chapter 6. We might get the results we obtained for reasons other than the theory in question. It is a convention of scientific argument to maintain the structure of reasoning from hypothesis but to reduce the risk of fallacy by controlling for as many possible alternate causes as possible. If one has reason to think, for example, that the design of the freezer might make a difference, then one would conduct all tests with freezers of the same design (or possibly even with the same freezer, if the number of tests is small). If the hypothesis is not supported, scientists often look for a possible error in the procedure that might have set things awry. Only when such anomalies accumulate and there is no plausible explanation for them do we begin to question the theory itself. When its explanatory and predictive power are

---

[7] Thomas S. Kuhn, *The Structure of Scientific Revolutions*, 2nd ed. (Chicago: University of Chicago Press, 1970).

in dispute, we have entered the framework of revolutionary science. The accumulation of doubts and unsolved puzzles gradually erodes confidence in the theory itself. It no longer can serve as a warrant and instead becomes the claim that must be established. Specifically, the claim is that one theory should replace another. The evidence is a demonstration that the proposed theory can account for the phenomenon being explained better than the current one can. In this case, the warrant would be the values of theory itself, such as the importance of explanatory power, the importance of predictive strength, and the importance of simplicity. In the social realm, probably the clearest example in modern times of revolutionary science is changes in our thinking about race. For a long time, race was seen as a biological variable that determined personality and experience. Anomalous cases began to pile up, and eventually they brought that whole way of thinking into question, and ultimately race came to be regarded as primarily a cultural phenomenon rather than a biological one. In Kuhn's terms, we can say that a new *paradigm* of race became dominant because it resolved many of the puzzles that the older paradigm could not.

It should be apparent from this discussion that specialized knowledge and training are necessary in order to participate in scientific argument. One must be familiar with the relevant theories and the status of testing them, understand the design of experiments and the nature of hypotheses, identify the plausible alternate hypotheses, and be able to articulate the assumptions of one's own paradigm as well as those of possible competitors. Although scientific argumentation produces claims that are important to nonscientists as well, they may be reluctant to participate in the give and take of the scientific argument. On a topic such as climate change, for example, they may discuss the scientific claims without engaging the technical argumentation that established them.

Ethical and Religious Argumentation

Our final example of an argument field is very different: ethics and religion. Here the underlying assumption is that that which is right should be done, and the controversy focuses on what is right. Often this will not be a yes-or-no question but a comparative one. For example, should one tell the truth at the price of destroying a friendship, or should one promote the self-worth of the other at the price of misleading him or her about what is true? Should one's religious life be guided by the observance of rituals even if they seem irrelevant to modern life, or by the pursuit of social justice even if one's religious motivation is indistinguishable from a secular one? In arguments such as these, evidence can be found in a variety of sources – in analogy, in common observation, or in example, to name a few – but the strongest form of argument is argument from authority. And unlike in some fields where recency of authoritative evidence is preferred, in argumentation about ethics or religion the oldest authority usually carries most weight because it is closest to the ultimate authority, the sacred text (such as the Hebrew Bible, the New Testament, or the Quran) and hence less likely to have been corrupted through centuries of interpretation. And unlike argument in business and management, which often takes place in urgent situations, in arguments about ethics and religion the time horizon is eternity. It is a sign of strength, not weakness, that arguments are perpetual, as subsequent generations take up enduring questions.

More cases could be cited, but these four examples of argument fields should illustrate the nature of argumentation in the technical sphere. It is specialized, influenced by field-specific norms and conventions, and usually unwelcome to participation by those who lack the relevant training and experience in the field.

Argumentation in the Public Sphere

Argumentation in the public sphere has two key characteristics. First, it is addressed to, and offered in behalf of, the general public. Therefore, at least in theory, it is accessible to everyone. Unlike the technical sphere, specialized training or expertise are not required in order to participate. Second, the outcome of the argument may affect the community at large, not just the individuals who are deliberating. The arguments concern people in their capacity as citizens or members of the community.

In ancient times, the public sphere was composed of large public gatherings where citizens would come together to deliberate about the issues of the day. Today, however, we think of the public sphere not as an actual, physical space, but as an imagined gathering place bringing together people who have the freedom to exchange ideas in a context in which a decision is required; addressing the problem requires collective action, and the choice cannot wait until all relevant information has been gathered. Some important information may be unavailable, and information by itself usually is not enough; analysis and judgment are also required.

Traditionally, public-sphere argumentation is concerned with large civic and political issues, such as war and peace, taxes and fiscal policy, health care and social welfare, labor and immigration, but these can manifest themselves very close to home. People may involve themselves in arguments on these subjects because the company for which they work has received a tax cut that it did not share with the workers, because a friend or relative in the military is about to be deployed to a danger spot, because impending changes in the insurance marketplace threaten their own health care financing, or because they know someone who is an undocumented immigrant. These examples also illustrate that the boundary between large public issues and small-scale private or personal issues frequently is in flux, Furthermore, the venues for public-sphere argumentation include not only the obvious venues, such as legislative bodies and political campaign rallies, but also such locations as parent–teacher association meetings, city council meetings, television talk shows, Internet discussion groups, and letters to the editor. Televised or downloaded programs that blur traditional distinctions between news and entertainment also can invite participation in the public sphere.

In public-sphere argumentation, the warrants typically come from the audience's store of social and political beliefs. They may be maxims, such as "If you want a job done right, do it yourself" or "A penny saved is a penny earned." They may be commonplaces, widely held beliefs that audiences will regard as facts, such as that people have responsibilities to one another or that governments cannot be trusted. Maxims and commonplaces often are not stated explicitly in the argument because they are generally assumed. Naïve theories, which are general propositions ordinary people believe about the way the world works, also function as warrants in public-sphere argumentation. For example, people tend to attribute success to their own efforts but to regard failure as owing to causes beyond their control. Most people also strive for coherence in their beliefs, so they may be more likely to assume the existence of a pattern, plot, or storyline than to regard events as unconnected or random. Everyday arguers may accept warrants that arguers in the technical sphere might deny, and vice versa. Experts can try to influence public opinion by arguing against warrants they think erroneous, of course, but they are not likely to succeed if they act as though the warrants did not exist.

Even when there are commonly accepted warrants, though, the public sphere usually is heterogeneous. It will be made up of people with different ways of thinking about the world, and any individual is not likely to be completely consistent ideologically. A person might be very open to change in public policy but nostalgically conservative when change affects him or her personally. Or someone might regard other persons as altruistic and yet be likely to engage in criminal conduct. Or a person may be generally honest and yet cheat on his or her taxes. For this reason, successful public-sphere arguments will often seek to appeal to competing values and presumptions. For instance, innovation may be portrayed as return to tradition. Limited or moderate actions might be characterized in extreme rhetoric, and vice versa. And although people may hold strongly ideological beliefs, undisguised appeals to ideology often will not succeed in gaining the adherence of a public-sphere audience that transcends ideological boundaries.

For this reason, arguers in the public sphere often make strategic choices about how they will present their arguments. Sometimes they will make use of *condensation symbols.*[8] These are generalized symbols, whether physical symbols such as the flag or phrases such as "comprehensive immigration reform," that embrace a host of different meanings. The symbols "condense" the divergent meanings that would emerge if we tried to "unpack" the symbol or to give it a definite and specific referent. For example, "comprehensive immigration reform" could encompass a pathway to citizenship for undocumented workers already in the United States as well as heightened efforts to secure the country's borders to prevent illegal immigration. One person might favor "comprehensive immigration reform" because he favors the first of these and, in order to get it, will swallow hard and accept the second; while another might favor it because she reasons in just the opposite fashion – she will swallow hard and accept "a path to citizenship" for some people in order to get what she really wants, stepped-up enforcement of immigration restrictions at the border. Yet they both can be drawn together to support "comprehensive immigration reform."

Like condensation symbols, persuasive definitions (discussed in Chapter 9) frequently will be found in public-sphere argumentation. One person refers to a health insurance proposal as "single-payer health care"; another calls it "socialized medicine." One person's "estate tax" is another person's "death tax." Each of these definitions presumes the outcome of an argument that needs to be made but is skipped over. The persuasive definition is an attempt to gain an advantage in the argument by appealing to an assumed sympathy from the audience for the connotations of one or another term. It can help lead to an outcome, but the outcome may be spurious, and hence the use of this device warrants careful scrutiny. These

---

[8] The phrase comes from Edward Sapir, "Symbolism," in *Encyclopaedia of the Social Sciences*, ed. Edwin R. A. Seligman (New York: Macmillan, 1934), 492. See also Murray Edelman, *The Symbolic Uses of Politics* (Urbana: University of Illinois Press, 1964).

are but two examples of how arguers adapt to the special conditions of the public sphere.

A robust public sphere is vital to democratic life. It encourages people to participate, to deliberate, and to make discerning judgments about issues of general importance. In the absence of a vigorous public sphere, some issues will be taken over by the technical sphere and others will fall to the influence of would-be authoritarians who will exploit their access to the public sphere in order to bend it to nondemocratic ends. As long ago as the time of the American founders, men argued that in the absence of strong commitments to public life, would-be tyrants would use democratic means to come to power, thereafter to undermine democracy.

With this danger in mind, there are strong reasons for concern about the state of the contemporary public sphere. Surveys show that increasing numbers of people claim little interest in public affairs and deny the efficacy of their own participation. Some are put off by the complexity of the issues; others find satisfaction with simplistic slogans. Legislative bodies are seen as dysfunctional. And polls reveal that since the 1960s there has been growing distrust of politicians and other public figures.

But the picture is not completely bleak. Some of the same people who express disdain for traditional politics are involved actively in their own communities, in public or private organizations, on issues that affect the public good. Since the 2016 election campaign, far more people have participated in rallies and protest movements of various kinds than in the recent past. New forms of discussion are emerging, and the Internet, while it can weaken the public sphere, can also strengthen it by encouraging dialogue and deliberation. Examples like these suggest that the public sphere may not be eroding, just changing. There are signs of hope for revitalizing the public sphere as a place for active democratic civic life.

Reexamining Why We Argue

These reflections on the state of the public sphere lead naturally to one of the questions with which the book began: Why do people choose to argue? In Chapter 1, we answered that question by reference to arguers themselves. Desiring to convince others of the rightness of their own view, yet forgoing the use of coercive or manipulative means out of respect for the personhood of the other, they use methods of argumentation, effective reasoning in communication. In so doing, arguers run the risk that they will be convinced by the other arguer instead. But they run the risk because they respect the personhood of the other and thereby gain similar respect for themselves.

But argumentation is not only a means for individual self-fulfillment. It also serves important social functions, one of which is to improve the quality of public decision-making. It was Aristotle who recognized that the careful examination of opposing claims is the best way to determine what is true. Especially with regard to claims that cannot be verified empirically, argumentation is the closest we have to an analogue to the scientific method. It permits replication of its methods; it is critical in its interpretation of findings; and it emphasizes the ability of human beings to act.

Beyond that, argumentation's key social function is to sustain democratic freedom. That may sound like an overly lofty goal, but what it emphasizes is that freedom of expression does not necessarily lead to sounder choices and a better functioning citizenry, although those are among its key goals. As suggested in the previous section, though, it can just as well give rise to demagogues and authoritarians as thwart them. In the absence of an active public willing to take arguments seriously, scrutinize them carefully, and advance them responsibly, that is what is likely to happen.

A century ago, the public intellectual Walter Lippmann, surveying the history of the nineteenth and early twentieth centuries, wrote that at the crucial moments, public opinion had been disastrously wrong.[9] (He was writing in a time of widespread disillusionment following World War I, when many thought that the war had been caused needlessly by propagandists who played on the emotions of the people.) Moreover, he lamented, the public could not be made competent, because individuals could not be adequately trained to deal with highly complex issues. The only alternative to relying on demagogues and authoritarians, he wrote, was to trust the judgment of experts. Lippmann believed we should assign problems of governance to the technical sphere. A century after Lippmann, some of the same doubt and despair are voiced, and some find in the politics of the early twenty-first century the unfortunate evidence of erosion.

But Lippmann had a prominent antagonist in the philosopher John Dewey.[10] Without denying all the problems of the public, Dewey maintained that an approach to education that focused on active learning and critical thinking, rather than on rote submission to authority, could cultivate the mindset in which people would see themselves as part of a larger community that made collective decisions with public wisdom.

[9] Walter Lippmann, *Public Opinion* (1922; rpt. New York: Free Press, 1965).
[10] John Dewey, *The Public and Its Problems* (New York: Henry Holt, 1927).

Respect for and facility with argumentation are important parts of that mindset.

And Lippmann himself moderated his skepticism as he aged. In a book of essays published in the 1950s, he called for the deliberate cultivation of what he called the "public philosophy" – the inclination to speak on behalf of the public and the common good rather than for one's private or self-interest alone.[11] Speaking for the public involves making claims grounded in public knowledge and supported through effective reasoning in communication with others. Doing that involves argumentation. So, in addition to conferring individual benefits, argumentation also permits a free society to function and flourish by imbuing citizens with the sort of "public philosophy" for which Lippmann called. By studying argumentation – and we hope that this book will not be the end of your studies – you are helping to strengthen the public sphere in which you will live.

Exercises

1. Write one sentence to explain each of the following terms and how it relates to the classification of argumentation contexts.
    a. Argument fields (Toulmin)
    b. Argument spheres (Goodnight)
    c. Business field of argumentation
    d. Condensation symbols
    e. Contexts (van Eemeren)
    f. Conversation analysis (Jackson and Jacobs)
    g. Conversational dialogue
    h. Discourse communities
    i. Enthymemes
    j. Ethical/religious field of argumentation
    k. Legal field of argumentation
    l. Normal and revolutionary science (Kuhn)
    m. Personal sphere of argumentation (Goodnight)
    n. Persuasive definitions
    o. Public philosophy (Lippmann)
    p. Public sphere of argumentation (Habermas, Goodnight)
    q. Scientific field of argumentation
    r. Stasis
    s. Technical sphere of argumentation (Goodnight)

[11] Walter Lippmann, *Essays in the Public Philosophy* (Boston: Little, Brown, 1955).

2. In each of the following examples, identify whether the claim would lead to an argument in the personal, technical, or public sphere. Some of the examples may have "migrated" from one sphere to another or may occur in multiple spheres with different procedures.

   a. Rising summer temperatures due to global climate change will result in significant hardship for the homeless unless we improve our social safety net.

   b. I don't care if you played football in college, I will not let our son expose himself to the possibility of a concussion, so he cannot try out for the high school team.

   c. The patterns of erosion on the surface of Mars demonstrate that life-sustaining water was present on that planet at one time.

   d. If we don't roll out the next generation of our brushless power tools by the next quarter, we stand to lose a big chunk of market share.

   e. I refuse to watch any movie with Kevin Spacey in it after the revelations about the accusations of sexual harassment. It's not enough to condemn the behavior; we need to exert our power as consumers.

   f. We have announced that our university will no longer require that the SAT or the ACT scores be submitted as part of our admission requirements.

   g. If you go out dressed like that, you will attract unwanted attention and perhaps be harassed.

   h. The European Union needs to devote significant funds to resettling refugees throughout the Continent.

   i. So-called three-parent babies where a fetus is created in the lab using DNA from three different people is an exciting development for people who are suffering from infertility, but it raises very difficult ethical issues.

3. What is the effect of the Internet on the status of argumentation? Do you think it helps argumentation because it allows everyone a forum to express opinions, or do you think that benefit is outweighed by the fact that people tend either to stick to arguments that confirm their own opinions or to use it simply to vent their spleen?

4. How can the study of argumentation improve debates in the personal, technical, and public spheres? Could education help to improve the level of discourse in each sphere?

5. Do you belong to a "discourse community"? This could be an interest group such as a video game forum, a political organization, fans of a

team or entertainer, educational specialty, housemates, religious organization, or the like. List some of the norms and practices that your discourse community follows. Are the norms observed? Is the community able to resolve disputes successfully? If you could write a set of rules that would govern argumentation in this community, what would you include?

Learning Argumentation through Debate

We saw in Chapter 1 that debate is one of the genres of argumentation, in which competing arguers present their cases for the judgment of an impartial third party. Debate is also an organized activity that is presented in classrooms, public forums, and interscholastic and intercollegiate competition. One popular way that students learn about argumentation is through participation in debate. This appendix offers basic information about debate. The format and procedures of debate are somewhat artificial, but they operate to enhance learning about argumentation.

The Debate Resolution

The resolution is the central claim in a dispute. In academic debate, it is determined well before the debate begins. At both the high school and college levels, there are elaborate procedures by which participating schools select the resolution for an entire academic year. The resolution is worded broadly so that debates can examine varying aspects of it. For example, on the resolution that the powers of the US president should be significantly curtailed, one debate might concern the war powers, another the power of appointment, another the power to issue executive orders, and another the pardon power. Each of these would offer a discrete set of arguments for supporting or opposing the resolution. Although in theory the resolution could be a claim of any type – fact, definition, value, or policy – in practice, resolutions tend to be either policy claims or value claims with policy implications. These categories permit debaters to address the practical question of "what shall we do?"

Resolutions are worded so that they do not give an advantage to either side. For instance, a resolution should not state, "Resolved: That Congress should usurp the powers of the president," nor should it state, "Resolved: That presidential tyranny should be stopped." Either of these formulations would favor one side or the other. The outcome of the debate should depend on the relative skill of the debaters, not loaded language in the resolution.

Sides and Duties

A debate has two sides, affirmative and negative. There may be many different viewpoints, but they boil down to support for or opposition to the resolution. The task of the affirmative is to present and defend a case for the resolution, while the task of the negative is to present a case that will cast significant doubt on the resolution. The affirmative shoulders the burden of proof on the resolution as a whole. This means that the negative does not have to prove that the resolution is false (although it will often try to do so for strategic reasons) but rather to raise enough doubt that the judge is not prepared to endorse the resolution. Each side has significant latitude in selecting and arranging the components of the case, so long as the affirmative case speaks successfully to all the issues in the resolution and the negative case undermines at least one issue. The understanding of issues, presumption and burden of proof, and case construction follows the principles explained in Chapters 3 and 7.

Although there are some exceptions, it is customary for students to debate on both the affirmative and the negative side, often in successive debates. As a result, they must be familiar with the strongest arguments on each side. If they have a personal belief about the resolution, they may strengthen their conviction by testing it against strong opposing arguments; if they do not, the experience of debating both sides may help them to decide what they believe. Debating both sides also makes clear that it is in the nature of controversial questions that there is no final answer. That recognition, in turn, should induce tolerance for arguments on both sides of the resolution – an antidote to the often sharply polarized state of the public sphere.

Frequently students will participate in public debates, before a general audience, and without the identification of a winner and loser. Competitive debates, however, usually take place in tournaments. Participating teams debate in four, six, or eight preliminary rounds of competition, an equal number on each side of the question. On the basis of the results of the preliminary rounds, the top teams are placed in a single-elimination bracket like that of the NCAA basketball competition. Depending on the size of the tournament, the elimination bracket may include eight, sixteen, or thirty-two teams. On losing a debate in the elimination rounds, the team is removed, and competition continues until a tournament champion is identified. Some tournaments are invitational, meaning that any school and usually any number of teams may be invited, whereas others (such as the national championship tournaments) require prior qualification.

The Debate Format

Academic debates employ a variety of formats, ranging from stump speaking to parliamentary debate and from academic conference to courtroom advocacy. These formats share certain common features. First, there are predetermined time limits – generally between sixty and ninety minutes. Second, time is allocated equally to each side. Since the affirmative shoulders the burden of proof, it usually gets the benefit of speaking first and last; the negative typically will have two back-to-back speeches in the middle of the debate. Third, each participant gives speeches of different types – usually a constructive speech, a rebuttal speech, and (often) a cross-examination period. Time limits are established for each of these speech types as well as for the debate as a whole. All arguments in a debate are initiated during the constructive speeches so as to permit maximum development and testing of the arguments. Each side takes the other's arguments into account in developing its own position. The rebuttal speeches develop, extend, and compare the arguments from the constructive speeches, answer the arguments advanced by the opposition, and summarize the reasons for a favorable decision. Cross-examination permits the debater who has just spoken to be questioned by one of the debaters on the opposite side. This process can be used to clarify ambiguous points, to put the respondent on the record, or to elicit information that may be used in subsequent speeches. It is rare, however, that a respondent will make major concessions under cross-examination.

The most common debate format features two-person teams, with each member giving one constructive and one rebuttal speech and conducting one cross-examination period as well as responding to questions in one period. There is wide variation, however. Some debates have more than two people on a side and some are one-on-one. Some have only one cross-examination period, after all the constructive speeches have concluded. Some have only one rebuttal per side.

It is expected that the first affirmative constructive speech will lay out the basic arguments of the affirmative case, addressing all of the issues, and that the first negative constructive will explicate the basic position of the negative. The second affirmative constructive will extend and further develop the affirmative case, responding to challenges advanced by the first negative speaker. It is sometimes customary that the negative speakers will divide their labor, with one addressing what the affirmative has put forward as the problem to be solved and the other focusing on the affirmative's proposed solution, if one has been offered. The rebuttals crystallize attacks and defenses, and the two final rebuttals summarize the reasons that each side believes it merits a favorable verdict from the judge. This paragraph summarizes common practice, but there are no hard-and-fast rules prescribing the responsibilities of the different speakers. There is considerable room for creativity.

Preparing to Debate

Getting ready to debate involves many of the practices explored in this book. Analysis of the resolution to determine the issues follows the approach of Chapter 3. Conducting research to support arguments for or against the resolution is guided by the framework of Chapter 4. Organizing the case follows the steps of Chapter 7, and anticipating attacks and defenses channels the ideas in Chapter 8. Arguments are arranged in schemes as illustrated in Chapter 5, checked to avoid fallacies discussed in Chapter 6, and structured in multiple, coordinative, or subordinative patterns as presented in Chapter 2. The final step is to refine language and style for presentation, as examined in Chapter 9. Of course, the entire process is guided by the philosophical and theoretical frameworks offered in Chapters 1 and .10. In short, debate is a laboratory for learning and applying principles of argumentation developed throughout this book.

Judging Debate

Just as the debaters play the role of committed advocates for their position, the judge also plays a role – that of arbiter. But the judge is not asked what he or she believes about the resolution. Rather, the judge is asked to determine which side exhibited greater argumentation skills. Some judges will determine this by evaluating specific skills, such as analysis, reasoning, and refutation. Other judges will attempt to decide whether they would endorse the resolution *based only on the arguments presented* in the debate and not considering their own predispositions. Judges frequently will find that they vote for positions they do not personally support. In fact, if the resolution is fairly worded, experienced judges are likely to find themselves voting for it about half the time, and voting against the very same resolution about half the time. This norm of judging, at least in theory, assures any argument a fair hearing from any judge.

Who serves as judges for academic debate? Sometimes they are debate coaches from schools not involved in the particular debate, sometimes recent graduates who are former debaters, sometimes lawyers or people in other fields that rely on argumentation skills, sometimes intelligent citizens without special professional training. Well-prepared debaters will adapt to differences in judging. With expert judges, for example, the debate will resemble argumentation in the technical sphere, whereas citizen-judges are more likely to inspire argumentation like that of the public sphere.

More specialized textbooks are available that focus specifically on learning and applying theories of debate.

Bibliography

The reference book identified in the Preface is Frans H. van Eemeren et al., eds., *Handbook of Argumentation Theory* (Dordrecht: Springer, 2014). It is the most comprehensive overview of argumentation studies from various approaches around the world.

The following are the principal works associated with argumentation theorists and other scholars mentioned in this book.

Booth, Wayne. *Modern Dogma and the Rhetoric of Assent*. Notre Dame, IN: University of Notre Dame Press, 1974.

Dewey, John. *The Public and Its Problems*. New York: Henry Holt, 1927.

Eemeren, Frans H. van. *Strategic Maneuvering in Argumentative Discourse: Extending the Pragma-Dialectical Theory of Argumentation*. Amsterdam: John Benjamins, 2010.

Eemeren, Frans H. van, and Rob Grootendorst. *A Systematic Theory of Argumentation: The Pragma-Dialectical Approach*. Cambridge: Cambridge University Press, 2004.

Eemeren, Frans H. van, Rob Grootendorst, and Francisca Snoeck Henkemans. *Argumentation: Analysis, Evaluation, Presentation*. Mahwah, NJ: Lawrence Erlbaum, 2002.

Eemeren, Frans H. van, Rob Grootendorst, Sally Jackson, and Scott Jacobs. *Reconstructing Argumentative Discourse*. Tuscaloosa: University of Alabama Press, 1993.

Goodnight, G. Thomas. "The Personal, Technical, and Public Spheres of Argument: A Speculative Inquiry into the Art of Public Deliberation." *Argumentation and Advocacy*, **18** (Spring, 1982), 214–227.

Habermas, Jürgen. *Communication and the Evolution of Society*. Boston: Beacon Press, 1979.

Hamblin, C. L. *Fallacies*. London: Methuen, 1970.

Hample, Dale. *Arguing: Exchanging Reasons Face to Face*. Mahwah, NJ: Lawrence Erlbaum, 2005.

Herrick, James A. *Argumentation: Understanding and Shaping Arguments*, 3rd ed. State College, PA: Strata Publishers, 2007.

Hultzén, Lee S. "Status in Deliberative Analysis." In *The Rhetorical Idiom*, ed. Donald C. Bryant. 1958; rpt. New York: Russell and Russell, 1966, pp. 97–123.

Johnson, Ralph H. *Manifest Rationality: A Pragmatic Theory of Argument*. Mahwah, NJ: Lawrence Erlbaum, 2000.

Kahneman, Daniel S. *Thinking, Fast and Slow*. New York: Farrar, Straus and Giroux, 2011.

Kuhn, Thomas S. *The Structure of Scientific Revolutions*, 2nd ed. Chicago: University of Chicago Press, 1970.

Lippmann, Walter. *Essays in the Public Philosophy*. Boston: Little, Brown, 1955.

Mill, John Stuart. *Utilitarianism*. Auckland: Floating Press, 1879.

Perelman, Chaim, and Lucie Olbrechts-Tyteca. *The New Rhetoric: A Treatise on Argumentation*, trans. James Wilkinson and Purcell Weaver. Notre Dame, IN: University of Notre Dame Press, 1969.

Stevenson, Charles L. *Ethics and Language*. New Haven, CT: Yale University Press, 1944.

Tindale, Christopher W. *Fallacies and Argument Appraisal*. Cambridge: Cambridge University Press, 2007.

Toulmin, Stephen. *The Uses of Argument*. Cambridge: Cambridge University Press, 1958.

Walton, Douglas N. *A Pragmatic Theory of Fallacy*. Tuscaloosa: University of Alabama Press, 1995.

  Argumentation Schemes for Presumptive Reasoning. Mahwah, NJ: Lawrence Erlbaum, 1996.

  Fundamentals of Critical Argumentation. Cambridge: Cambridge University Press, 2006.

Weaver, Richard M. *The Ethics of Rhetoric*. Chicago: Henry Regnery, 1953.

Index